T0293948

A Strange Beautiful Excitement

*Redmer Yska describes a New Zealand haunted by Katherine Mansfield –
a landscape to be viewed forever through her eyes. It is the best account I have ever
read of Wellington and Karori as they were in Mansfield's day. This book gives
us a profound understanding of the landscape and the colonial social issues that
shaped Mansfield both as a woman and a writer. It also provides a fascinating
context for her childhood, with new information on the historical events that
affected the family. Vivid and vigorous, it is a pleasure to read.*

– Kathleen Jones, UK biographer and author of
Katherine Mansfield: The Storyteller

⅋

*Just when you think there is nothing more to be said, or discovered, about
Katherine Mansfield, along comes Redmer Yska's account of the writer's childhood
that shatters our previous perceptions of her early life. No other work that I'm
aware of comes so close to Mansfield's childhood Wellington and the profound
influences that shaped her social consciousness. In the process Yska uncovers
previously unseen stories by the writer, childhood sketches that are
kernels of future stories.
Having grown up in Karori, where Mansfield spent so much of her childhood,
Yska sees Mansfield's world from the inside out. Part dreamlike memoir, with
tantalising glimpses of the author's own life, part shocking and forgotten history
of Wellington, this account of Mansfield's childhood is a ravishing, immersing
read, one of those page-turning books that is difficult to put down. It's not enough
to say I immensely enjoyed* A Strange Beautiful Excitement. *It was a wild ride
through previously uncharted territory; it's simply splendid.*

– Dame Fiona Kidman

A
Strange
Beautiful
Excitement

Katherine Mansfield's
Wellington
1888–1903

Redmer Yska

OTAGO

Published by Otago University Press
Level 1, 398 Cumberland Street
Dunedin, New Zealand
university.press@otago.ac.nz
www.otago.ac.nz/press

First published 2017
Copyright © Redmer Yska

The moral rights of the author have been asserted.

ISBN 978-0-947522-54-4

A catalogue record for this book is available from the National Library of New Zealand.
This book is copyright. Except for the purpose of fair review, no part may be stored or
transmitted in any form or by any means, electronic or mechanical, including recording
or storage in any information retrieval system, without permission in writing from the
publishers. No reproduction may be made, whether by photocopying or by any other
means, unless a licence has been obtained from the publisher.

Editor: Jane Parkin
Designer: Fiona Moffat
Index: Robin Briggs

Cover: James M. Nairn, *Wellington Harbour, 1894*, Te Papa Tongarewa Museum of New Zealand, 1939 0009 2

Printed in China by Asia Pacific Offset

[I] have answered all the questions that my grandmother used to ask my father when she came from Picton to gay, wild, evil Wellington.

– Katherine Mansfield, letter to John Middleton Murry,
Paris, 19 March 1918

❧

Million d'oiseaux d'or, ô future Vigueur?

– Arthur Rimbaud,
'Le Bateau ivre', Collected Poems, 1871

❧

*Suspended by the blast which blew amain,
Shouldering the naked crag, oh at that time,
While on the perilous ridge I hung alone,
With what strange utterance did the loud dry wind
Blow through my ears! The sky seemed not a sky
Of earth, and with what motion moved the clouds!*

– William Wordsworth, The Two-Part Prelude, 1799

Contents

Foreword by Vincent O'Sullivan 9
Prologue: Down by the birdbath 13

Part One

1   Parakeets of Pa-kuao 20
2   Mr Beauchamp's doll's house 34
3   The little girl in the picture 44
4   Something rotten 54

Part Two

5   The wind! The wind! 70
6   The inventor 80
7   Labour of sorrow 90

Part Three

8   Little brown owl 102
9   The washerwoman's children 116
10 Their heads in the buttercups: Karori trail 132
11 The bride wore black 146

Part Four

12 Moon at the top of the stairs 158
13 Fly on the wall 172
14 A place in the sun 184
15 Ablutions: Thorndon trail 196
16 Picked out in primroses 210

Epilogue: End of the beginning 237
Notes 243
Select Bibliography 259
Acknowledgements 263
Index 265

Foreword

⤶

Vincent O'Sullivan

There is a handful of writers – Emily Dickinson is one, Emily Brontë another – who at times seem to hold their admirers almost as much by the enigma of personality, or the curious weave of their lives, as they do by their first and sustained impact as writers. Katherine Mansfield is one of that rare band. By now, dozens of writers, scholars, editors, commentators have brought an extraordinary breadth of attention to a writer whose creative *oeuvre,* after all, is modest enough in extent, whose correspondence and notebooks far outweigh her collected fiction. Yet the lure to her biographical unravelling is constant, the hope that the play of fresh light may show her that touch more clearly. Each time we go back to a favourite story as a straightforward reader, or come across a lesser-known one, there is that teasing urge to know more of what came *before* the story, to catch something of what Mansfield herself so vividly described as going into the making of one of them – 'I always remember that feeling that this little island had dipped back into the dark blue sea only to rise again at gleam of day' – fact bathed in memory, the unconscious, the re-emergence into something sparkling and unseen. Making it new is also bringing it home, over again.

The admirable patience of scholars often takes us by surprise. We may have thought a lode was worked out, the traces depleted, when there is a stunning new strike. You see it here in the form of a 'new' story, one of the earliest the young Mansfield wrote and the first to be published nationally, and in the letters, the oldest to survive, that Redmer Yska tracked down, and now passes on to us. And what *frisson* they carry with them, how they tilt the angle we may see her from, this *almost* ordinary girl first breaking out towards something quite new.

Yska's astute persistence draws on so much more than that, as he depicts the city she grew up in, its history and politics and social contours, and writes of these with the authority and affection of a fellow Wellingtonian. So much depends on his discerning eye for what needs to be told, on his instinct for what is essential in the telling of it. And how much he has taken on board, as historian and writer, from his realising that another's biography is to some extent one's own; that contemporary biography, like certain modes of contemporary fiction, is enlivened by *not* accepting the boundaries that traditionally ring-fence it. As James Shapiro's recent approaches to Shakespeare have established, the traditional linear narrative of a life can be so fruitfully crossed by attending to the excavations of even one specific year. Yska has faith in his conviction that to look with far more attention than any other scholar has yet done, at Mansfield's first 15 years, will sharpen our perspective on those later and far more documented parts of her life.

Without the least beating of civic drums, Yska establishes Mansfield as a Wellingtonian before all else. Through his running together so inextricably the place and the girl who lived there, the experiences and memories of a past that more than a century forgets but that Mansfield could not but retain, this becomes a work of a particularly vivid kind. How the reality of what that small city was – wild, exploitative, imperialist, racist, geograpically tough – stands as ground and background to those other fractures, those other delights she found in thinking about her family, her school, her suburbs, her city's busy and productive efforts to establish class in the mimic culture it so aspired to.

And yet how beautiful, too, that world she looked out on, the only one she knew: the unforgettable harbour, its walks and hills, its winds, indeed its winds. And beyond the ranges across the eastern bays, and the Tararuas to the north, variously diaphanous and glittering, that other New Zealand she would later see so briefly as a late teenager, yet took in as masterfully as any writer we have had – 'the savage spirit' out there, as much as the 'strange beautiful excitement' of where she felt at home. Yska's is the story of the pudgy girl in wire-framed glasses who so sized up what she attended to, and the people who surrounded her, the parents whose secret life she was pertly wise to, the relatives she measured with an implacable accuracy, yet gifting them too with the magical ambience that defined her real and imagined world, when both became the same.

Redmer Yska's Kathleen Beauchamp is firmly set there in her raw, vibrant, energetic town, in 'the singular charm and barrenness of that place', as she described it, and that his reading and research and sympathy have made his as well. And now ours. We read her differently because of it. We see her so much closer to home, and for the first time, as a child attempting to tell her stories about it.

The river-stone birdbath, Karori School, inscribed: 'To the Memory of Kathleen Mansfield Beauchamp (Katherine Mansfield) who commenced her education at this school (1895–1898) and later achieved a worldwide reputation as a writer of short stories. Born Wellington 14 October 1888. Died Fontainbleau France 9 January 1923.'

Prologue: Down by the birdbath

ℒ

In 1921 Katherine Mansfield, the writer formerly known as Kathleen Beauchamp, finished 'The Doll's House'. The story's working title was 'At Karori', after the pastoral settlement outside Wellington City where she lived for five years and attended primary school. She'd be fed up with Karori and other childhood surrounds by the time she first departed for England in 1903, returning home once, grumpily, before leaving for good. From Europe, her memories of these landscapes softened, ripened. In time, improbably, she'll even come to compare warm Menton in the south of France to mist-swathed Karori: 'My heart beats for it, like it beats for Karori.'[1]

I grew up in the same valley in the 1950s, around half a century after Katherine Mansfield did. My family lived behind the Mobil service station on Karori Road, across from where the mall is now, in a rickety villa with a pear tree, and a culverted tributary of the Karori Stream beneath. Toadstools grew on our damp wallpaper. Where the tributary joined the headwaters buried under Karori Road, the little stream made a sharp left, surfacing in back gardens, heading west towards Chesney Wold, the house where the writer once lived.

We kids went to Karori School 200 metres up the road, the same school fictionalised in 'The Doll's House'. We got to know the same 'huge pine trees at the side of the playground'[2] where Isabel Burnell boasts of her doll's house painted spinach green and yellow, inviting some classmates – but not all – to inspect it.

Katherine Mansfield was buffed into schoolyard myth by the time I got to Karori School. Yet we pupils knew little about her, other than that she was remembered with a birdbath, an unlikely tribute, by the tennis court above Karori Road. Next to the wire fence: a cairn of dark river stones. A birdbath so very alone, I noted at nine years, keeping well clear.

And there you were: Cold Katherine. Solitary Katherine. *Triste* Katherine. No one to warm your plaque: no birds sang here, let alone bathed. And the company you kept: old wheezing pines with carbuncular roots, trees whose dead needles flew in drifts. You reclined beneath their cracked canopy, visited by the odd sour magpie.

Today I know more about you. It is here at Karori that you found an inkpot, learned to spell. Where you dreamed of a writing prize. I'm back here, investigating the places where you *quickened*, starting out here in our old school. You later scribbled a rough manifesto, proclaimed it in 'The Garden Party': 'one must go everywhere; one must see everything'.[3] Your work started here as you took up a mental camera, making slow-exposure photos, developing them over decades, slicing them into story. Using your words as maps, I'm drawing up an intimate atlas, almost certainly sketchy, of the pathways, the rambles of your formative years – hearth by hearth, avenue by avenue, upland by scrubby upland. We'll retrace a few of your old ways. So much of Wellington is threaded through your writing. Graeme Greene once called childhood the fiction writer's credit balance, and in your case, as a millionaire businessman's daughter, you would leverage your stock to the maximum.

And so much of what you remembered and wrote about – the things that shaped, even flayed you – happened here, making this crown of the North Island, the place Māori called Te-Upoko-o-te-Ika ('the head of the fish'), the seedbed, the blood and bone fertiliser of everything that came later.

So I'm asking: how did this ridgy, clasped terrain, its mobile weather, what you called its 'singular charm and barrenness',[4] form you? How did it make a writer? And what was it like to sniff the air of the frontier city of your birth: an unsavoury, festering place, half capital, half cesspool? I'm picking through the ashes, chasing dusty phantoms, distant laughter, fading reeks of the world you knew. You'd recall 'that strange indefinable scent'[5] of early childhood, writing of coastal Thorndon: 'All around it lay the lovely laughing sea, and there were tall green, "smelly" woods, the like of which you have never seen, down to the water's edge.'[6] Northwards, the stench of abattoir lingered: 'It must be a long time ago but I remember Johnsonville very well, even to the smell of it. Like Chummie [brother Leslie Beauchamp], I always remembered by smells.'[7]

I'm out in the open, retracing the pent wind-corrugated streets of the Wellington you walked as a child and young adult, one day sublime, the next uninhabitable, its gales tearing away certainties, pomposities, much as you did in your deadliest stories. You departed soon enough but the city beneath the writer's skin continued to pulse.

I'm late, I know: you're dead at 34 of the consumption that left you coughing 'bright red blood'.[8] That was in 1923, the year the world's first portable radio crackled to life. Within a decade, Karori was broadcasting your literary glory; the Burnell family, named after your mother Annie Burnell Dyer, was known around the world. In 1933 they 'unveiled' your birdbath here at the school, as your father Harold Beauchamp, your cousin Lulu Dyer and a gaggle of dignitaries looked on: 'To the Memory of Katherine Mansfield Beauchamp who commenced her education at this school (1895–1898) and later achieved a worldwide reputation as a writer of short stories.' Down in Thorndon, by another old family home under the pines, they built an oversized waiting shelter in brick with your name on it.

Karori's Cargill Street is home to Gladys Rainbow, 92, who attended that 1933 unveiling as a schoolgirl. Over ginger cake from Penny's on the main road (by the fish and chip shop) we talk about you, Karori School's hallowed 'old girl'. Gladys finds herself calling your birdbath a *font* (her blue eyes swim with mirth). Another local, Beverley Randell, then in Flers Street, arrived at the school in 1937. She fastened onto the birdbath, enlisted it, her school diary says, to race boats made from leaves. Her school memoir recalled how she and her friends 'pierce the centre of a sturdy leaf with the stalk of a second leaf, create a mast with a sail'.[9] Their harbour was dry when I enrolled as a 'Tiny Tot' a generation later. By then, the birdbath sat, unloved, by the school boundary, where we climbed, making kingdoms with sticks and Matchbox tractors.

Has anyone written so well about children and the treacherous shoals of childhood as you do in 'The Doll's House'? There you set out the order of an eight-year-old's universe, a system inked on a wooden ruler: the poised, cut-glass Burnell cohort at one end; the untouchable Kelveys, Lil and Else, at the other. You'd observed those girls and their hearty laundress mother for years, taken notes; another working title for 'The Doll's House' was 'The Washerwoman's Children'.[10]

I'm running a theory as to why your Burnells shun the Kelveys: in real life, your parents, Annie and Harold, were mourning their dead child, your baby sister Gwendoline. Their own siblings were dying around them. Gwendoline's death from cholera sent them from dirty, contagious Thorndon to rural Karori. They feared what you children might catch from the poor, the possibly infectious: the Kelveys of this world. You make this explicit in 'The Garden Party' when the children are told to stay away from slums 'because of … what they might catch'.[11] Your parents' anxieties lurk above much of your fiction: shapes of things muttered over fried chops, caught by Kathleen with the troubling eyes, who is able to rip a decades-old drawing-room remark, even a passing parental frown, from a canister of imaginary film.

The Karori School pecking order still stood in 1933 as your birdbath, Gladys's font, rose in river stones. The lines still ran in pencil across these playgrounds and glowed red as new divisions, political rather than class ones, emerged after World War II. European refugees became the out-siders, the new group to be looked down upon. Karori hosted the Russian Legation on Messines Road, a menacing construction of the Cold War. In 1953, a new generation of top-dog 'Burnells' rounded on pupils with foreign names, calling them 'dirty Russians'. Children of a White Russian scientist were forced to transfer to nearby Kelburn School, where bullying was not tolerated.[12]

A European name made me, too, a target. My Dutch father, I was informed, was a traitor who 'goes up to the Russian Embassy'. So playtimes were alive with threat. Enemies proliferated. Life at nine was war. I flung a stone up at the eye of a stalking Burnell from the sunken tennis court. Threw it as hard as I could. Watched him reel. I slipped off to cadge chips in the concrete 'shelter sheds' beneath the main school block. No teacher arrived to collar me, belt me. My father took care of that.

I'm sure I caught a glimpse of you as I flicked through our old school's centennial history. A classmate recalled seeing Kathleen Beauchamp skulking on Karori Road in a mud-smeared pinafore, a 'chain' behind her sisters. And though I know a 'chain' here denotes an old-fashioned unit of length – 20 metres – I couldn't help picturing you, linking you, to the metallic livery of punk: the studded choker, caked-on kohl, a thoroughgoing sneer. As an adolescent you'd scour the streets of Thorndon with the same attitude.

At dusk on a blustery Friday, I'm back at Karori School, visiting. The school grounds are deserted. Tennis is over: the sunken playground hosts basketball courts. Your birdbath floats on asphalt by the courtside. Gorse, well poisoned, sprouts at its feet. The same macrocarpa towers over the southern end, 10 metres wide at its base, its tips sheltering your memorial. But for how much longer? The board of trustees is set to fell the old school tree, its great heart bubbling out of the ground, to make space for new classrooms. Protesting pupils have draped long red ribbons high on its branches; they flutter here in the breeze.

Part One

Kākāriki, New Zealand parakeet: 'She looked at me intently and in a low almost tense voice said, "Do you have parrots in Canada?"' (Marion Ruddick on meeting Katherine Mansfield in 1898). Watercolour by Charles Heaphy. Ref: C-025-007. ATL.

One: Parakeets of Pa-kuao

U nder Ahumairangi hill, where Grant Road meets Park Street, is the old Thorndon spring. Locals with jugs, flagons and billies once came here for the soft water. I'm here on a September's day, filling a plastic bottle from the drippy pipe that's tiled in pale green with a red-brick finish like a fireplace. The water was famous for its healing properties. A local bottler announced in 1905: 'If they are sick, give them Phoenix Pure Soda, made from Grant Road Spring Water.'[1] But the stuff I've collected is nothing special. When, in the early 1960s, the city council found the spring was polluted, they connected up the town supply. No one comes here to collect water any more.

Kathleen Beauchamp haunted this place. Back from London, itching to return, she'd meet her painter friend Edie Bendall for twilight walks. One night she vented: 'I'll be dead if I stay in New Zealand. I'll just die under a manuka tree!'[2]

I look up, imagining the pair striding up the windy hill through sloping Queen's Park. She wrote of this spot: 'The pine trees roared like waves in their topmost branches, their stems creaked like the timber of ships; in the windy air flew the white manuka flower.'[3] She and Bendall convened here: when one of them couldn't make it, they'd leave a note in a hiding place.

I head down Park Street towards Tinakori Road, past Burnell Avenue (named after Annie Burnell Dyer, Mansfield's mother). The writer occupied two houses on Tinakori: one of them, her birthplace, now a museum and tourist pit stop; the other long torn down for a motorway. Her uncle Frank

Dyer lived here at 5 Park Street. In 1926, he proposed that water from the nearby spring be piped to drinking fountains across the city.[4]

I cross the motorway bridge where Tinakori Road meets Molesworth Street, towards the city centre. I'm heading for quiet, shady Fitzherbert Terrace. At the age of 10, Kathleen attended school nearby. The Beauchamps later shifted to a grand house at number 23. It was from there that she ventured out for her daily walks with Bendall. It became an outpost of the New Zealand Forest Service where my father worked, scene of childhood Christmas parties. Midway through the twentieth century, the place was demolished to make way for the United States Embassy.

Guzzling my faux spring water, I pass the embassy compound: it is a vast blast-proof concrete bunker crouched behind tall gates. Inside the guardhouse, security guards look heated, animated. As I reach the memorial, 20 metres from the gates, it strikes me that today is September 11, anniversary of the 2001 bombings in New York. And here I am, sauntering along in a zipped-up bomber jacket, khaki rucksack over one shoulder, shaking up a plastic bottle. A man in dark clothes and a beanie is already loping across the lawn in front. He makes a beeline for a seat by a shiny karaka tree; perches there, half turned away. Behind me, a shaven-headed African American is dancing past, unlocking a sleek black vehicle. Deciding this isn't the most restful spot for contemplation, I hoist my Mansfield Molotov and retreat, along Fitzherbert Terrace, past eponymous Katherine Street to my left, beneath the spreading boughs.

⅋

Māori knew the clear spring on the windy hill, pointing it out to the incomers of 1840, at a time when this was thick wet podocarp forest licking the gently sloping, white-sand beaches below. Katherine Mansfield caught those long-ago tangy scents in 'At the Bay': 'The breeze of morning lifted in the bush and the smell of leaves and wet black earth mingled with the sharp smell of the sea. Myriads of birds were singing.'[5]

Her story, set on the eastern side of the harbour, features a cameo by a raffish goldfinch, a new chum, shipped ashore in a cage. Yet there's a whiff of the sombre, primeval forest, heavy with coiled climbers and lumbering native birdlife that had fringed this coast for millennia. Whatonga, a Māori ancestral figure and navigator, named the lake-like harbour Whanga-nui-a-Tara after his son Tara when he ventured south into the head of the fish. The boy was said to have loved this place 'at the nostrils of the island'.[6]

Well, when the air paused, that is. The inhospitable, relentlessly ventilated air of the place British colonists called Lambton Harbour always frustrated attempts by humans – Māori and European alike – to set down roots. By the time Kathleen Beauchamp was born in 1888, on its western shores, the European settlement there was half a century old, Māori long pushed out. But Wellington, by then the colony's seat of government, stiff and haughty on the surface, was a shuddering, vacillating thing beneath: easy for a writer like her to skewer.

Today the names of colonial swells – Hobson, Fitzherbert, Molesworth, Murphy – cling to the streets of Thorndon, itself named after the Essex estate of an English founder. Below the colonial veneer, however, sits a Māori cartography as deep and layered as one of the shell middens once common in these bays. The darkened stack room of Wellington Public Library holds the works of ethnographer Elsdon Best, who wrote down and recorded the original names of the villages, fishing nooks, 'demon rocks' and other fabled corners of Tara's harbour.[7] These were the markers of an unearthly landscape: tribal traditions recall a place of buried powers, where early Māori explorers battled with fanged water-dwelling taniwha (supernatural creatures).

European arrivals, however, struggled with 'the entangled and impervious forest' along its shores.[8] So thick, so knotted in parts was the wet vegetation that lanterns were required during the day. Around what Katherine Mansfield called 'the deep, brimming harbour, shaped like a crater, in a curving brim of hills, just broken in the jagged place to let the big ships through',[9] ancient ferny bush dropped to a shoreline of marshy ground, five-metre flaxes, golden sands and a profusion of tame, booming birds. One arrival, fresh from India, noted:

some of the tree ferns must have been not less than forty or fifty feet high, shooting their slender stems through the dense underwood, and spreading

their wide and delicate fronds to the upper air like so many Hindostanee
umbrellas … innumerable parasites and climbing plants, vegetable boa
constrictors in appearance flung their huge coils from tree to tree, from branch
to branch – dropping to the earth, taking root again, running for a space along
the surface, swarming up and stifling in their strict embrace some young and
tender sapling anon, as if in pure fickleness, grappling and adopting some
withered and decayed stump, arraying and disguising its superannuated
form in all the splendour of their own bright leaves, and blossoms and fruits;
and having reached the top, casting their light festoons to the wind, until they
caught the next chance object.[10]

Wellington City librarian and Te Āti Awa scholar Ann Rewiti guides
me through the written records of pre-European Whanga-nui-a-Tara,
accounts that deepen our understanding of Katherine Mansfield territory.
Here in the dunelands, close to the zigzag path we know from 'The Wind
Blows', lay the small kāinga (village) of Pa-kuao, built on terraces above
the end of Tinakori Road. The village was a stone's throw from where the
birthplace house now stands. Historian James Cowan wrote in 1912:

The people of [Pa-kuao] obtained their water from the little stream which
flowed down through what is now the Queen's Park, and also probably from
the beautiful little spring still running in Grant Road, where the path goes
up in the direction of Wadestown, a spring still esteemed by the pakeha
residents of today above all the water which comes from the City Council's
taps.[11]

Above Pa-kuao, the village in the sandhills, soared the thickly wooded
range of hills known as Ahumairangi, variously translated as 'sloping
down from the sky' or, more appropriately, a lethal species of whirlwind.
The old name for this blowy spot on the northeast tip of Thorndon was
Haukawakawa ('bitter wind in the kawakawa'), mingling hau, wind in
Māori, with kawakawa, a small peppery medicinal shrub still plentiful
here.

Early Māori favoured other parts of the wide harbour. For centuries,
small numbers successfully occupied the rocky southern coasts. But
Tara's descendants, Ngāi Tara, struggled to make a permanent home in
this boisterous latitude, a zone of perpetual transience and contingency.

People kept passing through, never held these exacting landscapes as a prize. Kathleen Beauchamp was no different. Until later.

⅋

The arrival of Europeans upended Māori society. Whanga-nui-a-Tara, too, followed this pattern. Migrations from the north, especially from Taranaki and Kāwhia, gradually pushed out Ngāi Tara who, through intermarriage, became known as Ngāti Ira. These migrants, especially Te Āti Awa and Ngāti Tama people, settled on the western coastline of the harbour. Such was the constant churn – driven by conquest, occupation and resources – that the Taranaki tribe that sold land to British settlers in 1839 and was later recognised in law as the original inhabitants was resident for barely 15 years.

Despite the human turnover and the Ahumairangi whirlwinds, Haukawakawa was a flat, desirable location, with clear streams dropping from the hills and clouds of birds, especially kākāriki. German visitor Friedrich August Krull described them as 'a small green parrot with a long tail, a red topknot and blue feathers in its wings ... the commonest bird here. There were thousands of them hopping about and swarming around us ...'[12]

Another new arrival wrote of the 'giant crimson rata trees, ngaios, tall tree ferns and the star-like trails of clematis that grew thickly on the steep slopes'.[13] Incoming Māori were quick to identify the potential for cultivation. They cleared the area below Ahumairangi of ferns and other vegetation, planting out wide beds – below what is now Grant Road, and beyond – as potato grounds.

And it was these gardeners and their families who occupied Pa-kuao and neighbouring Tiakiwai. High along the Pa-kuao cliffs, kākāriki raised their chicks in crevices above an expanse of white sand shrouded in rātā and pōhutukawa. A European settler noted: 'the indigenous birds had been entirely unmolested, save when the Maori snared them in their furtive and noiseless manner'.[14] Raurimu, another Ngāti Tama kāinga, grew up near what is now the intersection of Hobson Street and Fitzherbert Terrace. Tiakiwai, affiliated with Te Āti Awa, lay beside the beach, enclosed by a two-mouthed stream of the same name. In keeping with the rapid human turnover in this location, these villages existed for barely a generation.

Clear water falling down the Ahumairangi slopes fed the Tiakiwai Stream, over time cutting a channel through the Haukawakawa clay as it headed out to the harbour. Tribal histories relate that the stream forked by what is today the corner of Molesworth Street and Tinakori Road. One of its arms, the Whakahikuwai tributary, carved the gully behind the house where Kathleen Beauchamp was born. Today the area is a deep motorway trench.

℘

Haukawakawa then changed forever. In 1839, local Māori sold 110,000 acres of land to the New Zealand Company for a township initially to be named Britannia. The company's raggle-taggle mob of utopians, propelled by salesmanship and spin, had a property developer's edge of ruthlessness. Katherine Mansfield's great-great aunt Jane Beauchamp was one of the company's British-based investors. The Wellington sections she owned later enticed her London-born nephews Cradock and Arthur Beauchamp to the colony, creating the local dynasty. There are still a dozen Beauchamps in the local phonebook.

In 1840, the New Zealand Company's first ship anchored off the Petone foreshore at the top of the harbour, where a town was to be laid out. Sections had already been bought by many on board. The first thousand settlers then endured earthquake, flooding and fire on an almost biblical scale. A decision was made to relocate south to the more stable locale of Haukawakawa, renamed Thorndon Flat.

Settlers first looked to Māori for food, especially the Haukawakawa spuds. One recalled:

> *Cockles in plenty we found on the beach, fish we bought from the Maoris, and pork, as well as potatoes; we gave a shilling a kit for potatoes, and a kit would weigh sometimes sixty or seventy pounds … Yes, it was a Robinson Crusoe life – but we were spinning our wool. The first watercress was found growing at the waterfall near Grant-road, where the spring is now. That was our water supply. The first cress was carried in triumph to my mother, and she shed tears at the sight of it.*[15]

Midway through 1840, the New Zealand Company unveiled its town plan for the settlement renamed Wellington. It set out 1100 one-acre residential sections (each with 100 country acres), with Thorndon designated the 'official' precinct. Eviction of the Māori inhabitants then began. Part of the compound of the principal Te Āti Awa pā (fortified settlement) at Pipitea was seized for a police office, courts and a gaol. Cultivation areas below Ahumairangi became military and native reserves (Māori were promised one-tenth, but many breaches occurred). At Pa-kuao, known to Europeans as Cliff Pa, hotelier William Couper opened a grog shop, the Caledonian, beneath the pōhutukawa trees where Tinakori Road today joins Thorndon Quay. The village at Tiakiwai dispersed after nearby land was commandeered as an army barracks, where the soldiers were on alert for possible confrontation with local Māori.

By the time she was a teenager, Kathleen Beauchamp had absorbed some of the painful history swirling around Thorndon, connecting unconsciously to what Māori call ūkaipō, the home ground where an infant was breastfed by night. She knew Moturoa Street, along which she'd walked to school daily. It was named for Te Ropiha Moturoa, a local rangatira (chief) and signatory to the Treaty of Waitangi, remembered locally for his tidy weatherboard house and potato crop. Her local school, Wellington Girls' High, bounded by Moturoa Street and Pipitea Street (the name of the former pā), was built on appropriated Te Āti Awa cultivation reserves. By the time the old chief died in 1874, nine Māori occupied the pā. She'd commemorate Moturoa in 'A True Tale', written in 1903. The spelling of his name might have been fumbled, but at 14 Kathleen made her first attempt to write of her birthplace and, importantly, she was imagining pre-European Haukawakawa:

> There were no white people living there, but tall, stately, copper coloured men and women, who sailed all round their country in great, carved canoes, and hunted in the woods for game … They were always having wars among themselves and it is about one of these wars that I am going to tell you. Let us come closer to the fire, dear children, and be glad that you did not live in the time that Motorua did.[16]

There's plenty of evidence that traditional Māori communities were cleaner than many European towns, with wharepaku (latrines) kept well away from living and food-preparation areas. Jerningham Wakefield, a New Zealand Company mouthpiece, however, wrote of 'filthy villages, subject to disease from the accumulation of dirt, and their [Māori] residents in ill ventilated and closely crowded dunghills ...'[17] It was a well-worn and ugly path – setting up a minority for persecution by vilifying them as dirty and sub-human. Relations between the races worsened as a settler authority taxed Māori dwellings. It was a shameless pretext to force Haukawakawa's original inhabitants out of their residential town-based pā, locations a local paper called 'filthy kennels [with] noxious vapours'.[18] A legacy of bitterness remained.

❧

Meanwhile the township veered from misfortune to calamity, and struggled economically as many of the more enterprising left. In 1848 a violent earthquake, equal to magnitude 7.7 on the modern Richter scale, struck. Over nine days of constant shaking, brick buildings and most of the town's chimneys disintegrated. The sky was streaked with red. Churchmen, convinced it was God's judgement, urged the populace to begin communal fasting and prayer as part of what was termed 'humiliation'. A colonial experiment appeared to be unravelling. The quakes were the final straw for many.

But once these prolonged, terrifying shakes had stopped, new vistas opened for those with an eye for opportunity. A local optimist wrote: '[T]he town is vastly improved as a consequence.'[19] A later diarist recorded:

> *After the earthquake of 1848, [William] Fitzherbert and other now 'big bugs' were frightened beyond measure and resolved on abandoning the place. They chartered a vessel which, however, in trying to leave the harbour, got aground, when they returned, stayed and are now – many of them – rich men.*[20]

As settlers took up their allocated sections, the primeval forest progressively vanished. What was called 'bringing the land in' involved hauling up great tree stumps using a team of bullocks and chains. Progress was slow. According to one account, 'Axemen found that it sometimes took an entire day to clear a patch that was big enough to pitch a tent.'[21] The podocarp forest covering Ahumairangi was stripped and milled. A settler wrote of 'trees a 100 feet or more high, some most magnificent, some covered with the gorgeous flowers of our crimson myrtle ... some trees six men could not span – they are more than 10 ft in diameter'.[22] Like Te Ranga a Hiwi (Mt Victoria), on the other side of the township, Thorndon's encircling hillsides remained open and denuded for another half century. Water poured unchecked down steep muddy hills in such volumes that Thorndon Flat flooded incessantly in heavy rain. The municipality tried to tame the wild streams, forcing them into deep culverts of milled tōtara, with varying success.

Re-creation of a little England began. Residents of Thorndon Flat used imported seed to sow pasture for growing or grazing. Nostalgic for home, they also planted out gorse, broom, watercress, blackberry and thistles. Grain and fruit-crop cultivation attracted birds, especially the flocks of red-headed kākāriki from the Pa-kuao cliffs. Farmers and orchardists destroyed the pesky foragers in such quantities that they were all but exterminated by the time Kathleen Beauchamp was born. Their feathers were commonly used to stuff mattresses. William Allan, a pupil at Thorndon School, remembered erecting scarecrows near what is now Murphy Street in the 1850s to protect the corn seed from the wheeling clouds of parakeets.[23]

℘

The streets of Katherine Mansfield's city were set down. Tinakori Road, the long, unsealed way that looms over her childhood, was formed in 1852 of lime and brick. Molesworth Street was cut at the same time. These twin transport arteries appeared after publicans Baron Charles Ernest von Alzdorf and William Couper plotted a direct route between their grog shops: the Wellington at Parliament Hill and Couper's Caledonian at Cliff Pa. I find Alzdorf's 1852 letter to the Colonial Secretary, seeking additional reimbursement for 'making Molesworth Street and Tinakore', using 20 buckets of lime. He received £2 2s, or about $250 in today's money.[24]

There are old, irresistible tales about the source of the name Tinakore. The abiding legend is that on one occasion the Māori roadmakers employed by Alzdorf and Couper were compelled to work on without a break for lunch. The men are said to have exclaimed, 'O Tina a kore.' That meant either dinnerless or unsatisfied, argues Louis Ward in his book *Early Wellington*.[25]

Wellington's inhospitability was again confirmed in January 1855 as an earthquake with a force equal to 8.2 on the Richter scale struck. Alzdorf was one of the few fatalities, killed as he crouched beneath his tavern's toppling chimney. But the quake held a miracle: prized flat land emerged, creating shore platforms that for the first time allowed road travel around the harbour. The sandy eastern shoreline was raised by two metres, with a metre-and-a-half uplift in the western harbour.

From the first days of settlement, Wellington's founders lobbied for the township to become the seat of government. Auckland meanwhile fulfilled this role. In 1858, the superintendent of Wellington province, Isaac Featherston, set aside funding for urgent public works in favour of a sprawling Gothic structure on Thorndon Hill to house the provincial government. With chambers large enough to accommodate the Legislative Council and House of Representatives, the building served as a costly enticement for a General Assembly divided on where to settle. Featherston's cunning plan paid off. When Wellington successfully wrested capital-city status from Auckland in 1865, locals celebrated, and a Wellington paper described the move as 'the tide that leads to fortune'.[26]

A fickle tide at first. Rather than flourish, the city's economy faltered as wars between Māori and settlers backed by British troops erupted in the central North Island. In 1868, Jessica Rankin, the wife of prominent politician Charles Pharazyn, wrote of the city: 'Everything seems sadly depressed. There seems no money in the place; they must borrow again to keep going.'[27] The end of the wars, the break-up of the provincial 'kingdoms' in 1878 and the creation of a centralised civil service finally ushered in prosperity.

The benefits of hosting the parliament in its grand surrounds on Thorndon Hill showed as Premier Julius Vogel borrowed millions to fund railways and other public works, including the construction of opulent public buildings such as the four-storey Government Buildings at the end of Lambton Quay, where many of the capital's 2000 civil servants were housed. Vogel became Tinakori Road's best-known resident, occupying a ministerial residence known as 'The Casino', complete with 'sprung' ballroom. He hosted balls there, frequented by dancers 'with trains 50 feet from their heels – and humps on their behinds exceeding all bounds'.[28] So-called 'society' had come to town.

City fathers worked hard to please this parliamentary cuckoo in the nest. But the amenities on offer fell well short of what might be expected of a capital city. Wellington was soon damned as 'the muddiest, dirtiest, most dusty, worst drained, and worst lighted town in the colony'.[29] Cooped up in the so-called parliamentary quarter on Thorndon Hill, the colony's elected representatives were dismayed by the city's rudimentary infrastructure. When the drains flooded, raw sewage was caked underfoot. The water supply was found to be thick with excrement. In response, the municipality built a new reservoir and erected street lanterns.

As the capital consolidated itself as a commercial hub, the population grew, and the first of Katherine Mansfield's forebears arrived. In 1871, Joseph Dyer crossed the Tasman to open an insurance company head office, renting a house on Poplar Grove by Tinakori Road. Ten minutes from Lambton Quay, it was a desirable address. Intense subdivision, seen in right-angled private roads like Poplar Grove, transformed the old Haukawakawa even further.

֍

As Wellington neared its first half century of European settlement, fresh evidence of polluted waterways came to light. The clear streams criss-crossing Thorndon turned out to be running in filth. Locals already feared local creeks for the way they flooded when it rained, turning into wild, muddy torrents from the water roaring down the slopes of Ahumairangi.

Swingbridge, Hobson Street, Thorndon, circa 1920s: '… a strong stench of fennel and decayed refuse streamed from the gully'. ('A Birthday')

Photograph by William Hall Raine. Ref: 1/2-042034-G. ATL.

Then, as Katherine Mansfield's parents came here to live in 1887, it emerged that there was a more dangerous aspect to the water. The gully formed by the riverbed behind Harold and Annie Beauchamp's new house, spanned with an iron suspension bridge at Hobson Street, served as the local rubbish and manure dump.

The municipality had long condemned this festering spot, calling it 'extremely dangerous to the health of the neighbourhood'.[30] A city councillor described the gully as 'a reeking mass of corruption, and a sort of fetid abomination. The wonder was not that the residents had typhoid fever, but that they did not have it.'[31] Mansfield's story 'A Birthday' shows the old backyard tip still in use at the turn of the century:

> The fence of these gardens was built along the edge of a gully, spanned by an iron suspension bridge, and the people had a wretched habit of throwing their empty tins over the fence into the gully.[32]

This was a city already notorious for shoddy infrastructure. Rather than build proper sewers, the council charged residents to have their excrement, politely known as 'nightsoil', collected. Many Thorndon householders preferred, however, to dump it themselves into local streams and gullies. Springs, like the one we began with at Grant Road, became increasingly precious to local people as a source of water until these, too, succumbed to pollution. To paraphrase one of its European founders, within half a century the Wellington settlement had become a closely crowded dunghill. As we will see, this was to have a lethal impact on the Beauchamps.

Portrait of Mrs Amelia Nathan, Thorndon neighbour and mother of 11,
photographed in 1913: '... like a huge warm black silk tea cosy'. ('Prelude')

Photograph by S.P. Andrew Ltd. Ref: 1/1-014477-G. ATL.

Two: Mr Beauchamp's doll's house

It's hard to imagine today – thanks to acres of harbour reclamation and a motorway nipping at its ankles – but the house where Kathleen Beauchamp was born once soared above the Thorndon beachfront. Now 750 metres from the sea, it abides: the same squat wooden dwelling with salted panes whose 'dining room looked over the breakwater of the harbour'.[1] Katherine Mansfield recalled 'whispery waves'[2] but more often saw, through misted windows, 'a huge pale sky and a cloud like a torn shirt',[3] the sea 'rising in green mountains'.[4] So how would a toddler have absorbed her dress-circle view, eastwards above Thorndon Quay, out to Petone and the Hutt, up to the jagged Rimutaka ridgeline? She'd later frame the setting as 'planted at the edge of a fine deep harbour like a lake'.[5]

The view directly below their east-facing windows was less attractive: a ragged, fennel-covered strip of reclaimed land a hundred dusty metres of clay wide. This valuable ground, formed by a million buckets of soil hacked from hills behind Lambton Quay and dumped into the sea, was cut with railway tracks. On its seaward edge lay Thorndon Esplanade, a fashionable promenade on a good day, with iron seating.

Out to sea, a fleet lay at anchor. Katherine Mansfield would write of the 'green lights fore and aft of the old black coal hulks that lived in the harbour',[6] a dozen moored to buoys off Thorndon Quay, then known as 'Rotten Row'. Entire families lived on board these retired sailing ships that supplied coal to passing steamers. Children were rowed to Thorndon School daily. Around the turn of the century, Wellington was the major bunkering (supply) port for British steamers making the long journey home after rounding Cape Horn. Vessels queued alongside the floating 'black barges', and mountains of coal in great cane baskets were winched over to fill their bunkers. The hulks are glimpsed out in the blustery dark along the Esplanade in 'The Wind Blows': 'In the harbour the coal hulks show two lights – one high on a mast and one from the stern.'[7] This lucrative trade vanished early in the new century with the opening of the Panama Canal.

༂

In 1887, Sir Charles Clifford of Staffordshire, settler and parliamentarian turned absentee landlord, leased Harold Beauchamp a section of 567 square metres at 25 Tinakori Road (then number 11). The Clifford Estate, including the section next door, stretched across the city. Much of this salty periphery of Thorndon Flat, however, remained fallow, scrubby acres on which cattle and horses grazed. The following year, Beauchamp built the modest two-storey town house we know today as Katherine Mansfield's birthplace. His lease called for 'a good and substantial house to the value of £400 [$80,000 in today's money] … with materials of the best description used in the erection thereof'.[8]

First, however, the sloping terrain had to be flattened. The location amidst sand dunes brought problems. A 1992 archaeological report finally revealed the extent of filling required: the original subsoil of yellow sand and clay, topped up with 'relatively unconsolidated' deposits of road fill and household rubbish sourced from the adjacent rubbish and manure tip.[9] The history of the house is not an easy read. The land proved as soft and mushy as the neighbouring reclamations, and the tōtara piles started to sink. Worse, as the deposits of rubbishy fill settled, the house began tilting to the south.[10] By 1900, facilities, including the sewage system, needed replacement.

Harold and Annie Beauchamp were always partial to Thorndon. After their marriage in 1884 the newlyweds initially lived in Hawkestone Street. They then shifted to Hill Street where, in 1885, their first daughter, Vera, was born. Then came Charlotte (Chaddie). Harold recalled:

*From Hill Street we migrated to Wadestown, then a very sparsely settled
suburb, where I purchased land and built a house. Here Chaddie was born.
Finding the wind at Wadestown intolerable I acquired the lease of a section,
No 11 Tinakori Road ...*[11]

Still in his twenties, Harold Beauchamp was taking to the role of both
family breadwinner and *paterfamilias*. At the time of the move, he was
the only male in a house of seven that spanned three generations. There
was Annie, his wife, and their baby daughters. Then three Dyer relatives:
Annie's widowed mother Margaret and Annie's youngest sisters, Kitty
and Belle, both unmarried. Half a century later, in a memoir, Beauchamp
recalled his menagerie. I locate a copy in Wellington Public Library, where
Harold explained life at home:

*Some of my friends thought it was a risky experiment, and often such arrange-
ments are; but I can assure you that in this case it turned out a great success,
and I can look back on our association with feelings of infinite pleasure.*[12]

℀

Architectural plans at Wellington City Archives feature a sketch of the
original house. The eight rooms included four upstairs bedrooms, two
of them doubles, an upstairs night nursery (for infants) and a downstairs
day nursery directly below. Facing Tinakori Road on the ground floor was
a large dining room with bay window, opening onto a drawing room
enclosed by a long veranda. A coal range dominated the kitchen at the
rear, with adjoining scullery and pantry. A century later, archaeologists
uncovered traces of

*roasts of mutton, soups made from beef bones, and the occasional meal of
rock oysters. Meat dishes and perhaps meat pies were served with a generous
dressing of spicy sauces such as Lea & Perrins. Rather large cups of tea were
taken and beer, wine and spirits drunk in moderate quantities.*[13]

On 14 October 1888, a Sunday, Kathleen Beauchamp was born upstairs
as seasonal gales battered the city. Monday's *Evening Post* recorded the event
in the public notices. She'd later fictionalise her grandmother's memory of
the delivery in her parents' bedroom:

*She had come forth squealing out of a reluctant mother in the teeth of a
'Southerly Buster.' The Grandmother, shaking her before the window, had seen
the sea rise in green mountains and sweep the esplanade – The little house
was like a shell to its loud booming. Down in the gully the wild trees lashed
together and big gulls wheeling and crying skimmed past the misty window.*[14]

From this time onwards, grandmother Margaret Dyer deputised for
a mother for whom marriage to virile Harold Beauchamp felt like one
long pregnancy. 'Granny' Dyer spent much of her widowed life as a kind
of executive servant: a firm but warm intermediary between her daughter
and her children, eating with the young and ministering to their needs,
especially the young Kathleen. The poem 'The Candle' celebrates the bond:
'By my bed, on a little round table/ The Grandmother placed a candle.'[15]
The child stood at her window below safe night skies. She 'peeped through
a slit of the blind/ There was nothing at all to be seen/ But hundreds of
friendly candles all over the sky.'[16]

The arrival in 1890 of a fourth and sickly child, Gwendoline, increased pressure for space. Heritage New Zealand files portray a functional dwelling,
with few embellishments: 'the decoration [was] confined to the projecting
eaves and pedimented upper window frames. The effect produced a plain
geometric building, rather reminiscent of a doll's house.'[17]

Survey maps show the house 10 metres from the road, encircled by
spacious gardens. A carriageway ran down the northern side. Out the front
was a patch of lawn where Kathleen and her elder sisters played. It was a
sunny oasis, like the one she described in 'The Aloe':

*Burnell's yard was small and square with flowerbeds on either side. All down
one side big clumps of arum lilies aired their rich beauty, on the other side
there was nothing but a straggle of what the children called 'Grandmother's
pin cushions', a dull pinkish flower, but so strong it would push its way and
grow through a crack of concrete.*[18]

As Kathleen took her first steps, the children next door became an
important if not altogether welcome presence. The Nathans with their 11

Birthplace of Katherine Mansfield, 25 Tinakori Road, circa 1920s: '... very square, very ugly, much too heavy for a heart like Katherine's'. (Robin Hyde)

Photographer unknown. Ref: 1/2-002581-F. ATL

children were Jewish. One daughter, Zaidee, remained a friend, her name recurring in stories, often for a servant. Anti-Semitism was prevalent in colonial society, but Harold Beauchamp befriended merchant Walter Nathan and in time they became business partners.

Katherine Mansfield parodied Nathan's ebullient wife Amelia or 'Amy' as the lisping Mrs Josephs in 'Prelude', 'like a huge warm black silk tea cosy'.[19] She was the eldest daughter of businessman Jacob Joseph, called 'the wealthiest Jew in Wellington'.[20] Joseph, who was totally blind, battled prejudice head on: when a relative was refused admission to the exclusive Wellington Club, he erected a five-storey building on Lambton Quay, forever blocking club members' harbour view.[21] Katherine Mansfield fictionalised the boisterous Nathans as the 'Samuel Josephs', caricaturing them 'not as a family. They were a swarm.'[22] She featured them in 'Prelude' and in 'At the Bay' as children 'who leap like savages on their lawn'.[23]

These portraits scandalised the Nathans. Sybil (born 1880) was still grumbling to a nephew about Kathleen Beauchamp in the 1960s, calling her a 'nasty, vindictive person who brought shame on her family'.[24] Vera Beauchamp tactfully recalled the neighbours as 'absolutely normal and (they) remained life friends of ours, which I think is greatly to their credit because they were rather ridiculed by her [Katherine Mansfield's] stories'.[25]

Was she settling an old, painful score in her writing, a practice she was known for? Then, as now, it is easy to imagine banter, even teasing, among small children. Kathleen Beauchamp, however, appears to have been wounded by it. Biographer Ruth Mantz claims a Nathan 'used to shout over the fence at Kathleen from no. 13, '"Fatty! Fatty! Fatty!"'.[26] In 'Prelude', Kezia is mocked when she falls for a trick offer of 'strawberries and cream'.[27] There's even conflict over home appliances. '"You've only got one WC at your place," said Miriam scornfully. "We've got two at ours."'[28]

The elaborate clothing foisted onto the Beauchamp children further opened them to ridicule. Charlotte Beauchamp later recalled the matching outfits worn at Tinakori Road:

I remember some perfectly hideous dresses the three of us had when we lived here. Navy blue serge … imagine … falling from the most awful beige yokes trimmed with rickrack braid. Can you imagine such ghastly fashions for little girls?[29]

At Easter 1893, when Kathleen was four and a half, the Beauchamps departed for Karori, a move fictionalised in 'Prelude', with 'tables and chairs standing on their heads on the front lawn'.[30] In the story, Lottie and Kezia wait behind with the Josephs. After tea of bread and dripping, Kezia heads next door for a final inspection.

> *Slowly she walked up the back steps, and through the scullery into the kitchen. Nothing was left in it but a lump of gritty yellow soap in one corner of the kitchen window sill and a piece of flannel stained with a blue bag in another. The fireplace was choked up with rubbish. She poked among it but found nothing except a hair-tidy with a heart painted on it ...*[31]

The Tinakori Road house was rented to a succession of tenants, including health reformer Sir Truby King. As the house began to show a pronounced lean in the early 1900s, it was refurbished with extra bathrooms, toilets, a new kitchen. Harold Beauchamp retained the lease but never lived there again. Company director Edward Pearce later bought the house and rented it out.

By 1933, as Katherine Mansfield's reputation grew, a memorial was built at nearby Fitzherbert Terrace, below what writer Robin Hyde called 'huge dark pines ... in an untidy, fatherly-looking row'.[32] She noted the trees 'have been tidied up in order that the street should be laid down in garden plots, with a massive red brick waiting room sort of place (it looks like a "Ladies Only") as a memorial to her. Poor Katherine ...'[33]

The birthplace house received less attention. By mid-century it was divided into a pair of rundown flats. Wellington writer and Mansfield aficionado Pat Lawlor was the first to lament its state, writing in 1958:

> *It was a plain enough house in the first place but in recent years its congruity has been affected by additions so that it now has two entrances ... The bridge has gone, as we know, and portion of the gully has been filled in, and this man-made interference has left the end of Hobson Street blocked with an ugly*

Katherine Mansfield Memorial, Fitzherbert Terrace, Thorndon, 1960s: 'a massive red brick waiting room sort of place (it looks like a "Ladies Only") as a memorial to her. Poor Katherine.' (Robin Hyde)

Photograph by Chris Black. Ref: PAColl-7472-22. ATL.

irregular pallisade of timbering ... there is now a ruthless wire-wove fence,
reminiscent of the wire walls of a prison camp.[34]

Lawlor's remarks helped ensure the house was preserved, as support came from a fledgling Historic Places Trust. The call to arms gathered pace in the 1960s when plans were announced for a motorway through the area, a 'great wounding gash'.[35] The Ministry of Works then said the house would be 'spared the demolition bulldozer by a few feet, though the motorway will cut into part of the back section'.[36]

The house remained a two-flat rental property, fast approaching dereliction. As the 1988 centenary of Katherine Mansfield's birth approached, the Historic Places Trust issued a classification of permanent preservation. Heritage champion Oroya Day then learned that the house's British-based owner might sell. She engineered a Katherine Mansfield Birthplace Society, a charitable trust, and propelled a fundraising effort. Backed by public and private donors, the society acquired the house in 1987, and restored it to a single dwelling. Many in the city celebrated. Others echoed Robin Hyde's view that the house would always be 'very square, very ugly, much too heavy for a heart like Katherine's'.[37]

A series of archaeological digs followed the acquisition. Like a layer cake, four distinct seams appeared. An assortment of memorabilia emerged from the rubble, as the diggers reported: 'The Beauchamp children must have played a lot on the old clinker driveway, the sunniest place in the garden. We found slate and slate pencils, fragments of porcelain dolls, marbles and some tiny blue-and-white china cups. There's also an intriguing white china mouse.'[38]

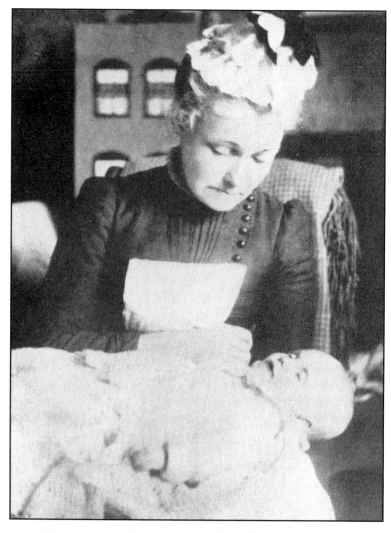

Margaret Dyer cradles her recently dead granddaughter, 11-week-old
Gwendoline Beauchamp, 25 Tinakori Road, January 1891.

Photographer unknown. Ref: PAColl-5124-1-01. ATL.

Three: The little girl in the picture

Here lies Gwendoline Burnell Beauchamp, high on a ridge, beneath dark creaking macrocarpa. The tomb of Katherine Mansfield's little sister looks out onto Bowen Street in central Wellington. A stream of cars hum across a motorway bridge 50 metres away. I'm on the northern heights of the Bolton Street Cemetery, imagining a three-month-old skeleton tucked into the corner of an adult-sized concrete grave. It's as if Harold and Annie intended their daughter would one day grow into it. Gwendoline has managed a posthumous fame of sorts. Her grave is designated number 16 on the Memorial Trail through the old graveyard: she's a neighbour of Samuel Parnell, creator of the eight-hour working day.

She was interred here on 10 January 1891, among the last wave to be buried at the city's overcrowded cemetery. The first European dead were buried in the hills near her parents' house on Tinakori Road. A new town cemetery was then marked out, with Glenbervie Terrace to the north and Bolton Street along its southern boundary. The site was described as 'an irregular shaped piece of ground, having a surface very undulating and broken, and containing eighteen acres or thereabouts'.[1] It remained an overgrown precinct, matted with mānuka trees, two metres tall, within which, one settler recalled, 'were to be found numberless specimens of that curious creature, the Praying Mantis'.[2] Once the vegetation was cleared, cows and goats roamed its bare ridges bisected by the Tutaenui Stream, necessitating the fencing of early graves.

Half a century after settlement, the cemetery found itself encircled by a growing, bustling city. More than 8500 people were already buried here, across the road from the parliamentary precinct, minutes from the Lambton Quay shopping quarter, then known as 'the Beach'. Many deaths, especially those of children, were the result of infectious disease, common on the colonial frontier. One headstone records how in the autumn of 1861, local printer Nathaniel Sutherland and his wife Marion lost five of their children to diphtheria. Their ages ranged from 13 months to 16 years.[3] An outbreak of scarlet fever killed four sons and two daughters of the Wallace family during 1865, including five deaths in a single, sorrowful month. Over the following decades, the infants kept falling ill and dying. In 1876, Thomas Macdonald lost three sons – Thomas, Allan and Rowland – to scarlet fever within days of one another. Harold Beauchamp interred only one daughter here; that was enough. He lost six of his nine siblings, mostly from infectious disease.

Over time, the cemetery at Bolton Street fell into disrepute. Locals saw it as disagreeable, even dangerous: a place where disintegrating corpses were piled on bare hillsides of stiff, damp soil, a stream undermining its gullies and hollows. Slippage was common, with predictably ghoulish results. Attempts to plant conifers from California, wild roses, and the odd holly and yew proved a mixed success; gorse found a natural home here.

Newspapers, egged on by grumpy parliamentarians, urged the place be shut up. The *Evening Post* agreed:

> … lying in the bed of the stream, a child's coffin has been exposed to the public gaze for weeks past, having been apparently dug up and thrown out in the process of making a grave in a spot already far too crowded … six or seven graves have been crowded together until the whole of the soil seems one mass of corruption … We understand that the Inspector of Nuisances has taken the matter under his cognizance …[4]

A display board in the cemetery information centre records a colonial discussion about 'gherms' seen whizzing above tombstones: "'What are they like?" "O, very much like a bumble bee and about the same size."'[5] There were even rumours that the governor's son's typhoid originated in the cemetery.

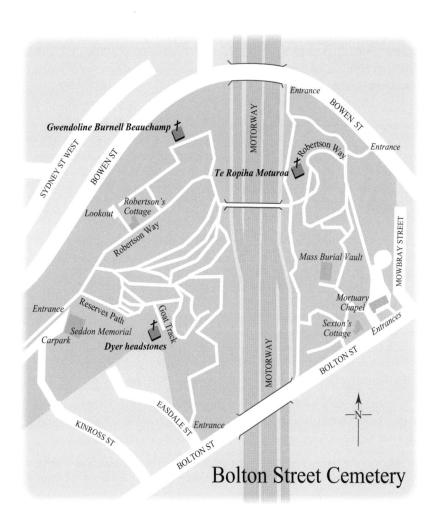

Gwendoline Burnell Beauchamp ✝

SYDNEY ST WEST

BOWEN ST

Te Ropiha Moturoa ✝

MOTORWAY

Entrance

BOWEN ST

Robertson Way

Entrance

Lookout

Robertson's Cottage

Robertson Way

MOWBRAY STREET

Mass Burial Vault

Entrance

Reserves Path

Carpark

Seddon Memorial

Dyer headstones ✝

Goat Track

Mortuary Chapel

Sexton's Cottage

Entrances

BOLTON ST

MOTORWAY

KINROSS ST

EASDALE ST

Entrance

BOLTON ST

N

Bolton Street Cemetery

By 1892, the cemetery was closed. The dead were henceforth shipped over the winding hills to spacious Karori. But the Beauchamps, by then Karori residents, would be regulars at Gwendoline's tomb. They, like other colonial families, observed the great Victorian Sunday custom of visiting and tending the graves of loved ones.

〆

Gwendoline was born at Tinakori Road as Kathleen turned two. The toddler was preoccupied with the new arrival, impatient to see and play with her. But the sickly baby was a disappointment. Mother, too, was unavailable, still recovering from a difficult labour.

During Kathleen's first year, her parents had voyaged to England. Annie Beauchamp returned alone and in poor health a few months before Gwendoline's birth. She was still not well when the baby was born, leaving most of the care to her mother. Her elder sister meanwhile strained for a glimpse, later capturing the scene:

> *They let me go into my mother's room … there lay my mother in bed with her arms along the sheet, and there sat my grandmother before the fire with a baby in a flannel across her knees … [she] nodded & said in a voice scarcely above a whisper 'Come & see your new little sister.' I tiptoed to her voice across the room & she parted the flannel and I saw a little round head with a tuft of goldy hair on it and a tiny face with eyes shut – white as snow.*[6]

From the start, something was wrong. In a notebook dating from 1917, Katherine Mansfield recalled feelings of being left alone, all but ignored. It was not only her sister who was unresponsive. So was her mother.

> *Her name is Gwen, said the grandmother. Kiss her. I bent down & kissed the little goldy tuft – but she took no notice. She lay quite still with her eyes shut.*
>
> *Now go & kiss Mother said the grandmother. But Mother did not want to kiss me. Very languid, leaning against the pillows she was eating some sago. The sun shone through the windows & winked on the brass knobs of the big bed.*[7]

By Christmas, Gwen had displaced Kathleen in her grandmother's lap, and she began to resent the new arrival. The ashen-faced baby had also become a rather frightening presence:

All day & all night grandmother's arms were full. I had no lap to climb into, no pillow to rest against – they belonged to Gwen ... Late one evening I sat by the fire on my little carpet hassock and Grandmother rocked, singing the song she used to sing me, but more gently. Suddenly she stopped & I looked up. Gwen opened her eyes & turned her little round head to the fire & looked & looked at, & then – turned her eyes up to the face bending over her. I saw her tiny body stretch out & her hands flew up, and Ah! Ah! Ah! called the grandmother.[8]

⚘

Gwendoline, even now, was gravely ill. She'd caught cholera – the blue death – the most notorious and feared contagion of the nineteenth century. It killed tens of thousands in England alone but was virtually unknown in New Zealand. The Beauchamp women, caring for the baby upstairs at Tinakori Road, were forced to watch, helplessly, as she became more and more ill.

A London doctor described his sequence of chilling visits to cholera victim Ellen Green, a poor, 11-year-old Irish girl:

Little Ellen was attacked with her first fit of vomiting and purging on 26 October; then with cramps in her legs and thighs. Within days her features had shrunk; her eyes sunk deep into their orbits, the conjunctiva had become effused, the lips were blue, the tongue was white. These were the sure signs of cholera, which killed her about a day later.[9]

At Tinakori Road, Gwendoline was cared for in comfortable, hygienic surroundings. Yet she, too, shrivelled as vomit and milky-white stool poured out as her system battled to flush out the lethal bacteria. Her stomach rejected everything; she dozed fitfully, eyelids frighteningly wide open. Yet she was probably safer with her family than at the public hospital. Wellington's sick were mostly cared for at home, with doctors making house calls. Colonial hospitals were dilapidated places where the poor went to die.

So what was the source of Gwendoline's contagion? Was it polluted water from a kitchen tap? Or a sip of infected milk? A medical officer reported on the alarming conditions at the time in a dairy at Kaiwharawhara, a kilometre from Tinakori Road:

> *At the harbour end there is a piggery and at the other end is a closet, and adjoining this is a shanty dignified by the title of 'dairy' in which the milk is stored. The closet consists of an old pail which the dairyman informs me he empties himself every night. The stalls to my mind contained the droppings and mire of a fortnight's collection, while the yard was a slough of mire.*[10]

Gwendoline had a bacterial disease for which health officials had long been braced. An earlier epidemic in Britain had killed 32,000 in 1832, and there and throughout Europe further outbreaks occurred. Sourced in the Asian continent, the infection entered crowded working-class districts and the mansions of the wealthy alike. They called it 'King' Cholera. Though feared, the other killer contagion, typhoid fever, had a certain respectability in Victorian Britain: the Queen's husband died of it. Cholera had a more sinister reputation: 'Though it had spread slowly westwards from India and had by 1830 reached European Russia, cholera was thought of as an Asiatic disease incapable of attacking a decent Englishman ...'[11]

Fears of a local contagion triggered the first colonial quarantine protocols, with arriving vessels inspected and a yellow flag hoisted should the infection be detected. Arrivals to Wellington were ushered through the quarantine station on Somes Island, identified in 'Prelude' as Quarantine Island. Carriers of less virulent infectious diseases were automatically detained, often for months. Those coming ashore were deloused in the island smoke house before departure, forced to sit in a cloud of chlorine, potassium nitrate and sulphur. Non-compliance could be fatal. Police on the Petone foreshore received orders to shoot should any infected newcomer attempt to escape.

When cholera reached the Southern Hemisphere in the 1880s, Queensland and Fiji recorded a few deaths. The *Evening Post* chimed in with an article: 'What We Know of Cholera'. The local medical officer noted that the capital's chilly weather was its best protection:

> *Discharges [from victims] must decompose before attaining virulent properties and very warm weather is essential to this process. Such discharges either*

contaminate drinking water or clothing; and wet weather followed by great heat is the general forerunner of cholera.[12]

The epidemic stayed away, but the authorities remained vigilant in the face of isolated cases. The Government Printer published information for doctors and the public in 'Cholera and Mode of Treating It'. The document, tabled in parliament, noted the sole antidote was a 'mustard poultice ... mixed with a heaped teaspoonful of powered red pepper, to be placed on the small of the back so as to be over each kidney'.[13] The remedy prescribed for a newborn like Gwendoline was set down as a teaspoonful of brandy, drops of peppermint oil and three drops of opium tincture. The dose for adults was two wineglasses of rum or brandy and 40 drops of opium.

᪥

Gwendoline was 11 weeks old when she died on 10 January 1891. And although her sister was barely two, the emotional impact of the death appears to have registered. Some of Katherine Mansfield's earliest fiction addresses themes of illness and death. In 'She', a stylised Gothic story written when she was 14, the narrator glimpses Death as a tall figure in a long white robe:

> *He was but a child when he first saw Her. Such a wee child and ah, so ill, so very ill!!! It was night. The room was dark. Out of the window he saw the night, the stars, and the tall dark trees ... And he was lying there, hot and fevered, when She came to him ... Her name was Death.*[14]

I pay $26.50 to obtain Gwendoline Beauchamp's death certificate from the Births, Deaths and Marriages section of Internal Affairs. The cholera diagnosis is confirmed, with additional information that the bacteria took hold at 14 days. Dr Martin is named as her doctor. Katherine Mansfield remembered his visits to Tinakori Road: 'The doctor's carriage was waiting at the door, and the doctor's little dog, Jackie, rushed at me and snapped at my bare legs.'[15] Yet there was no mention of the case in the newspapers at a time when the panic over cholera was at its height. The death of Mr Beauchamp's daughter is likely to have been quietly suppressed.

Within 24 hours, the Beauchamps had Gwendoline buried. In a thick shell of concrete. I wonder whether, as was often the practice with contagious bodies, her casket was deliberately encased in cement as a health measure. I imagine the funeral party led by Harold Beauchamp and his male relatives dressed in the glum regalia of British funerals: morning suits with hatbands and scarves of black crepe. They'd have strode behind the horse-drawn hearse decked out in black ostrich feathers, the vehicle making its solemn progress along Hill Street, Molesworth Street and Sydney Street. They'd probably have paused at the foot of the tall, scrubby ridge above Bowen Street before entering through wrought-iron gates – the big gates reserved for hearses, with a side gate for pedestrians.

The Beauchamp girls, along with Gwendoline's anguished mother and grandmother, would also have dressed in black that day. But after the funeral they'd have gone straight home and remained indoors. Women and children were absent from burials during the nineteenth century, a custom that lasted into the early twentieth century. But their period of mourning, especially Annie's, is likely to have gone on for months.

Katherine Mansfield would come to know Bolton Street Cemetery well, though graveyards will hereafter be places to shun in her fiction. The instinct was evident in 'Weak Heart', as the narrator races out of the cemetery gates, down wet Thorndon streets:

> Roddie … stood at the graveside, his legs apart, his hands loosely clasped, and watched Edie being lowered into the grave … he gave a violent start, turned, muttered something to his father and dashed away, so fast that people looked positively frightened, through the cemetery, down the avenue of dripping clay banks into Tarana Road, and started pelting for home. His suit was very tight and hot. It was like a dream.[16]

Undertakers Parsons and Clark on Pipitea Street, a business catering for the city's more select clientele, were recorded as making arrangements for the funeral that day. The Beauchamps were unlikely to have needed mourning 'extras', known as 'mutes', to walk the hearse, dressed in black and carrying wands trailing black ribbons. But they did agree to a 'mort' or mourning portrait, popular in Victorian times. Gwendoline was photographed in her gown. Her grandmother, in high-collar bodice buttoned to the neck and lace cap tinged with black, has laid the baby along her knees. Her right hand, softened into a fist, caresses Gwendoline's jaw. The child's mouth is open, as if dozing. It was the family's sole image of their loved one.

Katherine Mansfield recalled the photographer's visit:

Grandmother sat in her chair to one side with Gwen in her lap, & a funny little man with his head in a black bag was standing behind a box of china eggs. 'Now' he said and I saw my grandmother's face change as she bent over little Gwen. Thank you said the man coming out of the bag. The picture was hung over the nursery fire. I thought it looked very nice. The doll's house was in it too – verandah & balcony and all. Gran held me up to kiss my little sister.[17]

She kept a copy of the photo, the doll's house visible in the background, in a frame on her bedside table for the rest of her life.

Children paddling in Wellington Harbour, circa 1880s: They 'congregated about the mouths of the main sewers of the city, just where the contents empty into the bay'. (Wellington City Council)

Photographer unknown. Ref: Wellington City Archives, 00138:0:2867.

Four: Something rotten

Gwendoline's death had occurred against a backdrop of a city increasingly panicked by wave upon wave of death from other, equally virulent, contagions. The Beauchamps now faced the question of whether this rickety, nauseating outpost was safe enough to raise a family in.

For a glimpse of the beginnings of this crisis of confidence, we'll cast back to the mid-1880s, to another leafy corner of central Wellington, a grand and gleaming mansion on Upper Willis Street with Chippendale furniture, Parian marble vases and an upright grand piano with a black and gold stool. Frederick and Miriam Frankland were in their thirties, old for Victorian parents, busy raising a four-year-old daughter. Since migrating to New Zealand for health reasons, Frankland had climbed the civil service ladder to become Government Actuary. He was a self-proclaimed socialist and friend of Premier Sir Harry Atkinson, with whom he'd masterminded an unsuccessful national insurance scheme.

On a blowy Friday in 1886, the Franklands took daughter Octavia to watch a game of rugby at Newtown Park. In her diary, Miriam recalled her child as 'well and bright' that day.[1] Later, back home, 'Ava' wilted. By Monday, a fretful Miriam placed her fur cloak over her daughter and called a doctor. Eleven hours later, Dr Hutchinson appeared and diagnosed measles.

I'm examining Miriam's diary, a small hard book, brittle with age, at the National Library. Here is her account of five terrible days in September. Hutchinson prescribed medicine, which Miriam shovelled into Ava. But nothing helped. 'She got very restless and feverish and hot. At half past two in the morning, she began to groan and get delirious. Thinking this was unusual in measles, I took her in my arms and nursed her until half past six in the morning.'[2]

Hutchinson was again summoned:

> [W]hen he examined Ava's chest again, he seemed much alarmed and said there was much mischief there and he ordered a linseed meal and mustard poultice which I made at once. [Ava] sat up in bed and looked around the room for me and called out 'Mama, well goodbye, Mama'. And throwing her arms up, fell back and was quite overcome. I rushed to her and knelt by the bed, kissing her very much and calling her my sweet darling. She seemed to know me too and this was the last time she knew me properly.[3]

A second doctor appeared. The pair suggested sponging the child's body with tepid water every two hours. As Miriam prepared Ava's bath for the second time, she heard the rattle in her daughter's throat:

> I called to darling Fred to come quickly and I sat by the fire with her in my arms just then doctor came in just in time to see my sweet darling child die peacefully on my lap. Oh, I shall never forget that dreadful day.[4]

Little Octavia was an outrider, an early casualty of a public health crisis silently taking hold of the capital years before antibiotics or other reliable remedies were available. As she succumbed to fever in Willis Street, a citywide contagion was brewing that continued, unchecked, for another six years. The year Ava died, 85 local residents perished, 63 of them children. By its end in 1892, the body count approached 550.

Katherine Mansfield hinted at this long season of death in her first book, *In a German Pension*. 'A Birthday' tells of a man waiting for his wife to give birth. The setting, identifiable as turn-of-the-century Thorndon, is portrayed as 'an unhealthy hole',[5] not the town of grand residences and shimmering society balls usually associated with her fictionalised Wellington. The narrator, a fictional twin of Harold Beauchamp, stalks the streets, muttering: 'Everything here's filthy, the whole place might be down with the plague and will be too, if this street's not swept away.' He watches a servant polish his shoe with her saliva: 'Slut of a girl! Heaven knows what infectious disease may be breeding now in that boot.'[6]

At times, 'A Birthday' reads like a dispatch from a colonial charnel house. In this early story, Katherine Mansfield unmasks the bacterial city of her birth in all its putrid detail. Then she changes course. Following the death of her brother in World War I, she constructs another Wellington: the glowing landscapes of 'Prelude', 'The Garden Party' and 'The Doll's House'. Her colonial capital emerges, however, as a chimerical, mildly fevered inter-mingling of these elements: the magic past and the rotten past. The most luminous, mature stories are henceforth streaked with darkness; the huddled, contagious poor in their cloth caps and headscarves are never far away.

⚲

I chance on the contours of the epidemic that hung over Katherine Mansfield's childhood when asked to give a talk in 2012 about the capital in the 1890s. Having written an administrative history of the city, I'd drawn on accounts of sporadic, seemingly contained outbreaks of infectious disease set out in the minute books of the municipality. But I'd never grasped the fact that one continuous, lethal epidemic had persisted for upwards of half a decade.

My first piece of evidence emerged in Wellington City Library. On scratched microfilm I deciphered remarks made by Francis Dillon Bell, mayor of Wellington, imploring his city to act after six years of fatalities:

> *Every year, with unfailing regularity, we have at least one outbreak of zymotic disease … all medical experts agree that the existence of the germs of such diseases depends chiefly on defective sanitary conditions … this ghastly list of 548 deaths … does not represent more than a fraction of the sickness and pain … I know it has been the practice to hush such matters and to denounce the man who will hint at them as disloyal to Wellington. I wish I could proclaim them from the housetops … I refuse to be silent.*[7]

I was astonished. It was well known that urban centres like Dunedin and Christchurch suffered a high death toll from typhoid in the late nineteenth century. But Wellington, a city practised at self-promotion, had somehow managed to paper over the traces of its civic calamity. The city council minute books for this six-year period had skirted around it.

After I made a long trawl through council archives, the rest of this woeful story fell into place. By its end, Bell had shaken his city awake. Local citizens had come to see open wooden drains criss-crossing city streets as lethal death traps. And in hindsight and after a close reading, it became plain to me that this crisis underpinned many of Katherine Mansfield's stories. It shadowed her family's views of the world, darkening her memories when she came to fictionalise them. Harold Beauchamp's blend of fear and outrage, for example, is almost audible as the narrator of 'A Birthday' rages, 'I'd like to have a hand on the government ropes.'[8]

So how did Wellington's sanitation get bad enough to start exterminating its population? Over the first half century of European settlement, nightsoil was either collected from houses in iron buckets or tipped via wooden ditches into the harbour. The gentle gradient of the settled part of the central city meant the contents usually stayed put, stinking to high heaven, until disturbed by rain.

The capital's guardian of sanitary health was its Inspector of Nuisances. A kind of policeman/plumber, perhaps moustachioed and squeezed into a brass-buttoned tunic, he was an accepted if comical fixture on the landscape of Victorian England – a minor official with powers to apprehend citizens polluting waterways with their buckets of nightsoil. A homegrown equivalent appeared as New Zealand's municipalities grappled with ridding themselves of 'nuisances': excrement, ashes, dead dogs and similar nasties. In the first years of settlement, the idea of 'nuisance' was still a lark. When Wellington's first inspector was appointed in 1867, the *Post* called him an expert in 'the science of stinks', a man who would 'hunt the smells for £50 a year'.[9]

Victorian sanitary theory was lodged in the nostrils. For most of the nineteenth century, medical experts and Inspectors of Nuisances blamed bad air or 'miasma' from the *smell* of putrefying human and animal waste for causing and spreading disease. Katherine Mansfield touches on the threat of miasma in 'A Birthday'. As the protagonist crosses the Hobson Street suspension bridge, 'a strong stench of fennel and decayed refuse streamed from the gully ...'[10]

Even after scientists famously isolated a cholera microbe and watched it through a microscope, it still took decades for the 'germ theory' – the idea that many diseases were caused by lethal micro-organisms – to be accepted. Nonetheless, councils like Wellington's had begun to suspect that tainted water sickened populations.

In 1871, the municipality asked government scientist and Thorndon resident Dr James Hector to inspect local wells and streams. He concluded, sensationally, that 'no water collected from within the crowded part of the city, from either wells or house tops, is safe or proper for human consumption'.[11]

Elected councillors like prominent businessman John Plimmer responded by rallying to clean up the water. Work began on a reservoir in Karori, to be filled with rain and stream water from nearby bush-covered hills. By 1874, more affluent city households were connected up to Karori water, ferried to them through cast iron pipes. Some even installed prototypes of flushable toilets. House plans show that Harold Beauchamp and his family installed such a 'utensil' at 25 Tinakori Road.

Water quality, however, remained poor. The Hector household below Hill Street coped 'by fixing a piece of flannel over the mouth of the kitchen tap, removing it every evening when it contained a teaspoon of filth that gave off a terrible stench as it decomposed'.[12] This crude filter was not enough to prevent Georgiana Hector and her young son from catching typhoid, as did James Hector himself in 1877: the *Post* issued daily bulletins on the leading scientist's condition. The wife and niece of their immediate neighbours meanwhile died of it.[13] The Hectors were part of the first quiet wave of departures on health grounds, quitting the capital in 1881 for a bushy property in the Hutt Valley hills above Petone.

Construction of sewers to ferry away 'nuisances' became an urgent issue for the council. John Plimmer later promoted himself as father of the city, and is still remembered as such. However, in this early test of leadership, he plumped for self-interest, arguing that comprehensive drainage was simply too costly. A boundless expanse of sea like Wellington Harbour could, he said, take all of the city's raw sewage:

> It is bad surface draining, putrid holes of water and rotting vegetation, from which malaria and fever have their origin. What we want is good water, without limit, good surface draining, and cleanliness at home. Supply these, and put from you that sentimental nonsense of polluting the bay, and you will confer on Wellington a great blessing and make it one of the healthiest cities in the world.[14]

The editors of the *New Zealand Times*, however, disagreed:

> [S]anitary reform admits no further delay, unless we wish to see the inhabitants of this city exposed to the constant risk of decimation by an epidemic. If such a misfortune should befall the city … we may expect to see the city council lynched by the surviving citizens.[15]

Although Plimmer was no longer an elected councillor when he took this stand, he still reflected the interests of city fathers, an elite group of self-made businessmen and property owners whose outlook tended to be closer to that of the average land speculator than to their tenants. A voting right based on property ownership shut out most of the renting population, meaning that only those who paid rates had a say in their community. This tiny pool of Wellington ratepayers shared the Victorian chariness about state intervention, instead embracing the popular *laissez faire* ideology that allowed them, as urban historian Tristram Hunt put it, 'to be dirty but free'.[16] So the city opted for a bargain-basement scheme, based on open wooden ditches. This relied on moving water – not possible in flat areas such as crowded Te Aro at the south of the harbour where working people and the poor mostly lived.

The capital meanwhile boomed: it was home to the colony's busiest port and fastest-growing manufacturing sector. Within a decade, the 1881 population of 20,563 had grown by one-third. Most arrivals could afford only Te Aro's boarding houses or its cramped workers' cottages. Records show that private lanes like Lorne Street off Cambridge Terrace had 30 houses to the acre, matching the densest suburbs of London, a city some arrivals had recently vacated. Egmont Street was called 'a perfect sink of filth and hotbed of disease'.[17]

As waste filled the ditches and piled up around the harbour, the funerals began. In 1885, 63 locals, mostly in Te Aro, sickened and died from acute infectious diseases, including typhoid, diphtheria, scarlet fever, measles, even cholera. Ava Frankland was among 85 who died in 1886. Most fatalities occurred far from her leafy neighbourhood, within the square kilometre bounded by Wakefield, Buckle and Cuba streets and Cambridge Terrace.

Over the following two years the contagion killed 144 more. Fatalities of this kind were not at all uncommon, but such sustained high numbers were rare. Premier Richard Seddon, for one, was cynical about the attitude of city fathers to the poor:

> I say that in the hands of the council are the lives of the citizens; that with no lungs, with unsanitary conditions, with overcrowding comes death; and you will find the mortality in the overcrowded parts of the city – in the slums where these unsanitary conditions exists – the percentage of deaths as compared with other portions of the city is very large.[18]

A municipal official then blew the whistle. Over the summer of 1889, Inspector of Nuisances Alfred Johnson slopped through the back yards and peered under the floorboards of 5697 houses across the city. What he saw shocked him. His report urged the municipality to act. It told of

> open filthy drains … inside yards and under houses … over which the residents have no control at all … [Waste] cannot be properly and efficiently removed till a thorough drainage of the city takes place and the localities freed from the daily fear of typhoid and other highly dangerous disease.[19]

Johnson went out on a limb, blaming the death toll on the excrement tipped into the harbour by the cartload. Challenging the council to fund proper drainage, he left an indelible image of miasmatic, murderous hell by the water's edge:

> Numbers of children … particularly on the sunny days … congregated about the mouths of the main sewers of the city, just where the contents empty into the bay, amusing themselves by fishing etc, and seated in many cases right in the midst of the odours that arise from the drains.[20]

Kathleen Beauchamp's family home across the harbour, in affluent Thorndon, might have seemed a world away from Te Aro. Then, as typhoid struck the area's grandest house, the crisis finally registered with city fathers. The victim was six-year-old Lord Cranley, son and heir to the governor, Lord Onslow. Simply known as The Governor, Onslow was the most powerful person in the colony, Queen Victoria's man. Several months after Kathleen's birth, the young aristocrat caught typhoid fever at Government House. He almost died. Onslow's aide-de-camp, Lieutenant Robert Stewart-Savile, also got sick but survived. The cases brought home the fact that the colony's wealthy and ennobled were not immune.

As Lord Cranley's illness overshadowed the opening of parliament in August 1889, the capital was awash with tales of the 'loathsome state' of the timber taken from the Thorndon drains: 'It was a sniff from one of these dreadful boards close to the museum that gave typhoid fever to the child of one of the caretakers.'[21] Correspondence between Onslow's private secretary, the exquisitely named Rivendell Walrond, and Mayor Bell shows the degree to which the governor involved himself in tracking down the source of the illness:

> His Excellency visited the farm from which the milk is supplied to Government House, and found everything in a clean and sanitary condition … the water supply to Government House … is well and truly filtered before being used. His Excellency further tested the conditions of the drains with the smoke test (for sewer gas) and with a satisfactory result. Finding nothing to account for the outbreak of disease, he now desires to ascertain whether the poison can have been taken from anything outside the fence of Government House [such as] the sewer in Bowen Street.[22]

Finding no clear traces, Lord Onslow and his wife Florence fled Wellington for Nelson. The capital's filthy drains became a national, even international, laughing stock. The *Evening Post* reported how tourists in transit were asking how they could avoid landing in Wellington. The government was mortified: Seddon famously waved his fist at a member of a visiting city council delegation. Seventy-five locals died in 1879, the year the governor's boy became ill. Hundreds more sickened with typhoid, and hospital fever wards struggled to cope.

The council was forced to act, urgently revisiting a drainage scheme based on forcing waste through underground tunnels in the hills and out to Cook Strait. The cost was close to £165,000, or $31 million in today's money. The small pool of ratepayers approved a loan proposal, but their vote was derailed by a technicality and the issue went into limbo. Lord Onslow showed his extreme displeasure by resigning early. 'After the rejection by the ratepayers ... [he] felt that the risks to which his family were exposed through the unhealthiness of their surroundings were too serious to be incurred for any lengthened period.'[23] Wellington would clearly not be fit to live in for some time to come.

As the council prevaricated, Harold and Annie Beauchamp experienced first hand what Frederick and Miriam Frankland and hundreds of other families had suffered. Gwendoline's death in 1891 was one of 104 epidemic deaths that year. Harold Beauchamp urged Mayor Bell to act, as his sheaf of correspondence in support of 'pneumatic drainage' showed:

> Taking into account the enormous death rate from typhoid, diptheria etc, it is a matter of the greatest moment to reduce the time when the sewerage of a city like Melbourne can be accomplished, and we confidently say that three years should be sufficient if this system is adopted.[24]

The municipality, meanwhile, was divided between those like Mayor Bell, who sought action, and those who preferred to look the other way. The *Post* rounded on the city council and the 'dirty but free' philosophy championed by John Plimmer:

> There is a section of ratepayers who not only close their noses to the evil odours which so freely pervade the city during spring, summer, and autumn, but who absolutely cannot see beyond their noses. The idea of a slightly-increased rate call is to them far more terrifying than any danger from diphtheria or typhoid fever. They value their pockets more highly than the health of the community.[25]

≥

I revisit the council archives for a fresh look at the municipal minute books: great 500-page volumes bound in calfskin with gold-embossed titles on their spines. They're wheeled out to me on a trolley. Minute Books 8 to

10 are peppered with alarmed, even hysterical references to contagion. It becomes clear, however, that records from the time studiously avoid adding up the annual death tolls. Mayor Bell's speech to the city is the only place in which the grisly statistic is provided; no council document ever cites it. Only one newspaper, the *New Zealand Times*, will publish his figure; the capital's major daily, the *Evening Post*, appears never to do so. And there it stands in black and white; Bell's toll, so to speak: 548 deaths – 333 in children under five – over a period of six years, roughly one in 50 of the population.[26] Plus an estimated 3000 local cases where a fatality was avoided, as he put it.

Bell, whose name echoes across several of Katherine Mansfield's Wellington stories, had no compunction in using these statistics. He also recruited the local medical officer of health, Dr William Chapple. A new breed of public health activist, Chapple conducted extensive field studies in the inner city, writing in graphic, almost tabloid terms of 'an alarming accumulation of filth and dirt in back yards from one end of the city to the other'.[27] His description of a visit to a house in Holland Street, where a family of 10 slept in two upstairs bedrooms, is memorable: 'The pails [of nightsoil] were only removed once in five or six weeks. I learned from Mrs A that the dejecta from members of the family, after the inception of typhoid, were thrown either into the [water] closet or down the sink.'[28]

The report's low point was Chapple's unblocking of a Tory Street drain stuffed with coils of sheep intestines from a local slaughterhouse. In Holland Street, where 90 people occupied 21 tiny houses, he saw 'evidence of much nightsoil being buried in the yards, some heaped their filth conspicuously against their neighbours' fences'.[29]

Dr Chapple, too, urged proper drainage. The *New Zealand Times* described the document as 'a thorough-paced emetic, a real uncompromising, violent, out-and-outer, read it … you will be even lucky if you can stop without having to seek medical advice'.[30] Mayor Bell called a public meeting at the Opera House, holding up the report. Councillors backed the drainage loan, but another 18 months passed before work began. The Beauchamps had already left.

≥

Route to Karori, circa 1896: '... the big dray rattled into unknown country, along new roads with high clay banks on either side, up steep, steep hills, down into bushy valleys through wide, shallow rivers'. ('Prelude')

Photographer unknown. Ref: PAColl-5671-18. ATL.

A year after losing Gwendoline, the Beauchamps attended family funerals that until now have been missing in accounts of Katherine Mansfield's childhood. In March 1892, Annie's younger brother Henry, 23, suddenly died in Blenheim of an inflammation of the bowel.[31] Harold served as chief mourner at St Paul's Cathedral, and Henry Dyer was interred at Bolton Street within the grave of his father, Joseph. During that year, Harold's brother Charles, also 23, died of typhoid in Wellington.

Many local people concluded that Thorndon was no longer safe to live in. A significant paragraph of Chapple's report noted an exodus of families from the inner city: 'Many of the public [are] panic stricken ...

some … fleeing the district while others are sending their families to more healthy situations while they themselves attend to their business.'[32] The *New Zealand Times* confirmed growing agitation across the city, especially among parents of young children: 'Complaints come from every quarter about the danger of drains … the councillors are accosted at every street corner by importunate ratepayers insisting upon repairs, alterations, immediate improvements.'[33]

In Hawkestone Street, several hundred metres from the Beauchamps, lived Annie's sister Agnes and husband Fred Waters. They, too, were raising small children. Early in 1893 the two families readied to depart the inner city in tandem. The move followed the death in March of Harold's Auckland-based sister Florence Picton, aged 30, from typhoid.[34] If it was good enough for the titled Onslows to flee Thorndon because of lethal microbes, it was good enough for other reputable citizens.

Their destination was Karori, a small rural hamlet several ranges of hills beyond Ahumairangi. Outlying city suburbs had long promoted themselves as 'sites where … children may be reared without the doctor's constant presence'.[35] The borough described itself as the 'natural sanitorium of Wellington – pure air, good water and lovely scenery'.[36] Councillors even came up with a Karori motto: *For Beauty and Health.*

The connection between the move and the epidemic was not made in earlier accounts of Katherine Mansfield's life, probably because the long-running contagion has been forgotten.[37] A closer reading of Harold Beauchamp's memoirs, however, confirms that the shift was made for 'the benefit not only of the children's health, but also of my own'.[38] Successive biographers have not read between the lines. Noting how unconventional the move was for a city businessman, Ruth Mantz suggests Karori was 'a most healthful and desirable place in which small children could grow up'.[39] For Antony Alpers the move amounted to what would today be called a 'lifestyle choice': 'Beauchamp decided to give his daughters a country childhood.'[40] American Jeffrey Meyers writes of a move to a 'rural retreat';[41]

and for Londoner Claire Tomalin 'the family moved to Karori ... to give the children the experience of country life'.[42]

Against the backdrop of the crisis and her family's recent bereavements, Katherine Mansfield's Wellington stories can to some extent be read in a new light. 'Prelude' sees Wellington damned as 'a hole of a town', Linda Burnell stating that at least life in Karori 'won't kill us'.[43] Dread of 'filthy' Thorndon lingers, however. Perhaps this explains, finally, why Stanley Burnell is overtaken 'by a sort of panic ... whenever he approached near home. Before he was well inside the gate he would shout to anyone within sight: "Is everything all right?"'[44]

The fictional Burnells' efforts to keep their children away from the poor have always been interpreted as a comment on their snobbery, their unashamed sense of social superiority. But the recent family fatalities can only have heightened the real-life Beauchamps' anxiety about contact with contagion. The potential for transmission of disease must explain why in 'The Doll's House' Kezia is elliptically informed, 'You know quite well why' the Kelvey children cannot enter the family home.[45] 'The Garden Party' openly addresses the risk of contagion from the 'poverty-stricken' people 'in little mean dwellings ... When the Sheridans were little they were forbidden to set foot there because of the revolting language and of what they might catch.'[46]

Alarm in the capital eventually abated. Over the five years between 1893 and 1898, contractors carved 128 kilometres of sewer tunnels beneath the central city and outlying suburbs. Some 70 kilometres of earthenware pipes, plus a further 11 kilometres of cast iron and steel air and sewage mains, now safely enclosed the city sewage. By 1898, giant hydraulic 'ejectors' forced the waste up the steep hills out to the Moa Point outfall on the city's wild south coast. The crisis had passed.

Part Two

The blast of hell that never rests from whirling
Harries the spirits along in the sweep of its swath,
And vexes them, for ever beating and hurling.
(Dante, *Divine Comedy*: Cantica 1: Hell)

Five: The wind! The wind!

Wellington is a place that everyone passing through or staying in for a couple of days hates like henbane. It's so wind-tossed. And if you stay much longer you get to love it. It's so wind-tossed. – Robin Hyde, 1934[1]

One morning in early 1843, Mary Cottel was out for a constitutional. She was walking along Manners Street, now an inner-city thoroughfare, at that time the white-sanded, flax-shrouded foreshore of Te Aro. She passed a sweep of barnacled private wharves to which flat-bottomed barges were tied. A gale was blowing that day, a wind hard enough to launch a longboat, turned on its back for painting, from the beach. Launch it into the air. Cottel looked up, saw an object dropping. An eyewitness later reported: '[A] flat-bottomed boat lying on the beach here was raised bodily in the air, carried some distance, and fell on a lady passing by and killed her … a gust of wind sweeping up the bay got under it, took it up like a balloon.'[2]

The mother of four died of a head injury. A coroner's inquest heard that, after striking her, the boat 'was carried some distance beyond where the unfortunate woman lay'.[3] The punt was forfeited, destroyed. Mary Cottel's death was set down as an accident. The New Zealand Company's newspaper, the *Gazette*, barely noted it. But the homicidal quality of Wellington's gales was remarked on again in 1888, the year Katherine Mansfield was born – when the wind performed equally malevolent tricks.

It was a far cry from the polite, even fatherly gust of the British homeland, the 'gentle breeze that blows from the green field' of wind-worshipping Romantic poets like Wordsworth or Coleridge.[4] The latter even addressed the gale in 'Dejection: An Ode' as 'mighty Poet'. Those were gales at the tranquil end of the Beaufort Wind Scale, the nineteenth-century speedometer for the tempest. The Wellington wind felled poor

Mary Cottel on one of the hundred days a year it blows at storm grade, two notches below hurricane: whipping up 'very high waves with overhanging crests, sea white with densely blown foam, heavy rolling'.

᠎᠎᠎᠎

As a writer, Katherine Mansfield absorbed the Wellington wind as deeply as the Romantics, making it something like her literary accomplice, even if its vehemence often tested the relationship. She wrote, '[I]t moves me with an emotion I don't ever understand.'[5] The wind stirs beneath her words, snuffling, as she puts it, around the corners of the page. In 'The Wind Blows' she asks: 'Hasn't anyone written poems to the wind?'[6] The Manners Street tragedy is not one she would have been familiar with; it happened decades earlier. But we can guess it is a story she'd be drawn to as a connoisseur, a bard, of her hometown breezes.

Wind adds a feather-ruffling *frisson* to many of her stories. She often uses weather – especially the wind – as a conventional literary device to evoke mood, setting and narrative jumps. In 'Psychology', 'a cold snatch of hateful wind' underlines the anguish of a parting.[7] In 'The Wind Blows' the gale is centre stage, the noisy, lurching main actor. The story 'Revelations' ships the tempest to France where '*un vent insupportable*' roils the protagonist: 'the wild wind caught her and floated her across the pavement'.[8] 'The New Baby' gives the breeze a calmer quality, with 'the soft moist breath of the large wind breathing so gently from the boundless sea'.[9]

In her hands, her hometown wind also gains omnipotent powers, sometimes for better, mostly for worse. 'A Birthday' illustrates its impact on the civic mood. A doctor reassures a patient: '"You're jagged by the weather," he said wryly, "nothing else …"'[10] And like most Wellingtonians, Katherine Mansfield was highly sensitised to the breeze: 'To remember the sound of the wind – the peculiar wretchedness one can feel while the wind blows.'[11] 'The Wrong House' evokes the same mood: 'It was a bitter autumn day; the wind ran in the street like a thin dog.'[12] In 'Juliet', she says of the protagonist: 'the wind always hurt her, unsettled her'.[13]

Wellington's is no ordinary wind. 'A Birthday' outs its gale as pitiless, dominating, even *bullying*: 'A tremendous gust of wind sprang upon the house, seized it, shook it, dropped, only to grip it more tightly.'[14] Katherine Mansfield, however, also understood the odd sense of community that could emerge from shared meteorological outrage, anger softened by the calm luminous dawns and radiant days that inevitably follow. In a well-known section of 'The Wind Blows', she reimagines herself and her dead brother Leslie reunited, literally tossed together, in the gale: 'The wind is so strong they have to fight their way through it, rocking like two old drunkards.'[15]

She of course claimed to have born in a 'Southerly buster', though weather records show it was more likely a garden-variety gale. She first heard handyman Pat Sheehan use the term at Karori to describe 'a big wetness and then a blow'.[16] For novelist Maurice Gee, a later exceptional chronicler of the city's moods, the southerly is 'an honest wind, the true Wellington wind'; he notes how locals 'bend into the southerly and fight back'.[17] Gee's northerly, on the other hand, 'comes behind your back and punches you ... it doesn't even make you decently cold ... but wets you and then, hypocritically, dries you out. It seems to have no source and no direction. Thumps the house, and leaves it still, then gives a sneaky heave ...'[18]

This is the wind Katherine Mansfield met as a toddler in Tinakori Road, a physical presence that in 'Prelude' takes on the qualities of a bogeyman:

With the dark crept the wind snuffling and howling. The windows of the empty house shook, a creaking came from the walls and floors, a piece of loose iron on the roof banged forlornly ... She was frightened ... But IT was just behind her, waiting at the door, at the head of the stairs, at the bottom of the stairs, hiding in the passage, ready to dart out at the back door.[19]

One of the immediate benefits of the Beauchamps' shift to Karori was the absence of the salty gale. Much of the 'strange beautiful excitement' of Chesney Wold resided in the stillness of the air.[20] 'It was a big bare house', her first Karori story, emphasises: 'The sun streamed down, and there was not a breath of wind.'[21]

⚘

Experts insist that Wellington's blowiness can all be excused by geography. The city sits at Latitude 41 South, home to the wild Roaring Forties. As air is squeezed through the 22-kilometre gap between the North and South islands, the local winds explode. Generations of Māori battled to find lasting shelter on the rocky shoreline of the inner harbour, a testament to the inhospitable, some say uninhabitable, nature of the location. The harbour's ability to provide sanctuary for full-sailed English ships, however, made it an attractive option for colonial settlement.

Māori tohunga (priests) believed they could tame the gale, settle it down at times such as when hungry people were heading out to fish. They harnessed prayers to deprive the wind of its power. We can imagine them standing on the Wellington shoreline, at locations like Te Raekaihau, the point on Pipitea Beach where Davis Street now stands. Ngāti Awa called it 'the Place Where One Feeds Upon the Wind'.[22] European settlers, too, prayed for 'warmth and sunshine in place of wind and storm'.[23]

Have the generations who have come ashore at Whanga-nui-a-Tara over the centuries been doing some form of cosmic penance? In Dante's *Divine Comedy*, those who have committed carnal sin are condemned to the second circle of Hell, to be eternally blasted by furious winds:

The blast of hell that never rests from whirling
Harries the spirits along in the sweep of its swath,
And vexes them, for ever beating and hurling.[24]

Within half a century of European settlement, the population had resigned itself to a purgatory of wind with its dreaded seasonal cycles, such as the springtime equinoxial gales. In 'Bank Holiday', Katherine Mansfield coined the term 'flying day' for fine days destroyed by wind: 'a flying day, half sun, half wind. When the sun goes in, a shadow flies over; when it comes out again it is fiery.'[25]

After wind ruined a Wadestown garden party attended by 500 guests in December 1897, a weekly society newspaper raised an eyebrow: 'The day was not a very pleasant one. It was blowing a hurricane, as is usual on these occasions.'[26] The opening of that year's polo season fared no better:

*I looked with supreme pity on the ladies who donned their pretty spring hats
bedecked with chiffon and flowers, for by the time they arrived at the Polo
grounds they were in a very dilapidated state; but the ladies who wore their old
and tried friend, the sailor hat, looked ever so much happier, although even they
were at an angle of 30 degrees. A great many of the young ladies ventured out
on their bicycles ... they arrived very cold and their heads nearly blown off.*[27]

With weather as capricious as this, locals could not – cannot – hope to
plan outdoor events. In her stories set in the capital, Katherine Mansfield
conveys the social, even physical precariousness of the place. Dawn may rise
calm and luminous, but hopes for outdoor activity are routinely dashed:
within hours the wind has risen, even in high summer, ripping lettuce from
the mouths of picnickers.

✀

So why the silence over Mary Cottel's death by gale? Samuel Revans,
a prominent editor who died the year Katherine Mansfield was born,
shoulders some responsibility. He was the noisy megaphone, the 'booster'
for the New Zealand Company. He helped draft its extravagant propaganda
in London: handbills promising a paradise of rolling plains, where 'the
banana and other tropical fruits form immense orchards'.[28] He joined the
thousand who sailed out, ready to settle uncrowded territory. But when
they sailed into Wellington Harbour, many saw only hills covered with
thick primeval forest. They unpacked their tin trunks in Maurice Gee's
southerly. One recalled: 'Disappointment was visible on the countenance
of everyone.'[29] Another wrote of being cast upon 'a barren, dreary and
inhospitable shore'.[30] This was, perhaps, Wellington's founding moment.
History doesn't record whether arriving Māori felt similarly gypped.

So from the moment the settlers realised they'd been conned, that no
bananas were to be plucked from among the flax, keeping people here
became a civic priority if the settlement was to survive. Revans got to work.
Using the columns of the company newspaper, the *Gazette*, he was tireless.
His message – that it was Wellington's destiny, even its birthright, to become
capital – embedded itself. The subject of wind remained *impolite*. Revans
ensured his columns avoided mention of what one early arrival called

Samuel Revans, circa 1860, the noisy megaphone, the 'booster' for the
New Zealand Company. Photographer unknown. Ref: 1/2-038720-F. ATL.

'the plaguey N.W. wind ... the greatest nuisance in this place'.[31] Instead, Anglican Bishop Selwyn insisted 'active habits of industry and enterprise are evidently favoured by the elastic tone and perpetual motion of the atmosphere ... there will always be activity of thought and promptness of action in this battlefield of the north-west and south-east winds'.[32] Less polite was Lieutenant Best, who confided in his diary: 'I have heard of it blowing a gale, and half a gale, but if it ever blew a gale and a half it is doing so at the present moment.'[33] To its credit, the gale fuelled colonial progress, propelling sailing ships in and out of the harbour. Revans was always bullish about the city's 'superior' gale. By the 1880s, however, reliable coal-fired steam was the rising technology, supplanting wind power.

The discovery of microbes also dispelled wind's reputation as a purifier, flushing out disease thought to hang in the vapour over low-lying ground. The old view lingers in 'A Birthday', where the protagonist rails against the 'filthy' Thorndon streets: 'Wind crept round the house, moaning drearily. "We're in for a storm ... Well, there's one blessing; it'll clear the air."'[34]

By the mid-twentieth century, Samuel Revans' successors were still in denial about the capital's vixen climate. A book published to mark the 1970 founding of the municipality noted: 'Wellington's weather is not as bad as it is often painted ... with its freedom from fogs and air pollution ... it is a pleasant place to live and work in ...'[35] Population growth had stalled by then. Fleeing locals openly compared the experience of living with constant gales to an abusive relationship, to being forced to endure the indignities, the humiliations, of being flung like a rag doll down the street, hairstyles and *haute couture* in tatters. Wellingtonians endlessly repeated an unproven story about the city council running ropes along city streets to prevent citizens flying away. But the old conspiracy of silence about the wind continued. When quizzed by outsiders, they still used terms like 'enlivening' and 'healthy'.

When the city was officially designated the world's windiest in 2015, acting mayor Justin Lester held the line, stating how air pollution is non-existent because fumes are dispelled and wind harnessed for electricity. 'Perhaps the best thing of all,' he said, 'it breeds a bunch of sturdy, resilient Wellingtonians who aren't fazed by a little bit of wind.'[36] Citizens grimaced.

Those who pack up the house and head for stiller pastures triumphantly post items on social media about the weather at their new locations. A year later, Lester was elected mayor.

⅃

Just how bad *is* the Wellington wind? The strongest ever gust, 248 kilometres per hour, was recorded high above sheltered Owhiro Bay on Wellington's south coast in 1962. This was pure, uncut hurricane, off the edge of the Beaufort scale: 'air filled with foam, waves over 13 metres, sea completely white with driving spray'.

The year Katherine Mansfield was born, its power gained almost gladiatorial status. The wind whipping the Rimutaka hills between Wellington and the Wairarapa was well known to settlers crossing by coach. Deforestation didn't help; there was less to slow the wind down. To cope with a gale there, they rolled up the canvas sides of their covered wagon like mariners furling their sails. Then in January 1888 the wind plucked a 30-tonne steel locomotive and four wagons off the rails near Pigeon Bush. The train flew into the air; passengers were afterwards unable to stand upright, said the guards. Over the hill in Wellington, newsmen telegraphing the story of flying trains at Pigeon Bush struggled to explain what had happened: 'It is an occurrence absolutely unique and wholly without precedent in railway history,' wrote one. 'It is a wonder and a perplexity that the wind should have been able to exert such tremendous power as to hurl loaded trucks off the rails and to capsize them bodily so that they lay "with their heels" – or rather their wheels "kicking" in the air.'[37]

Wild weather continued into the first half of 1888. An easterly gale flung up a tidal wave in the harbour, the highest in half a century. The waters rose 15 metres higher up the beach than ever seen before, threatening the main street. The *Evening Post* recorded:

> As an instance of the fury of the storm yesterday afternoon, it may be mentioned that a woman was blown off her feet in Hill Street and dashed violently against the footpath on her face. She was raised by several gentlemen, who after a time succeeded in bringing her round.[38]

No mention was made of the woman's attire – or headwear. The paper called for a 'specially invented hat for ladies to wear' during winds.[39] '[I]t is next to impossible to wear the present fashionable high-crowned hats. The angle that everyone has to keep their heads at is trying and not becoming.'[40]

&

After the Beauchamps' return to Thorndon in 1898, wind regularly turned their neighbourhood into a dustbowl. Brown clouds arose from the hills of dirt used for adjacent harbour reclamation. Year on year, from the 1880s until World War I, the citizens endured this almost continuous activity at various points along the harbour's edge. Watering the streets with elaborate contraptions became a daily necessity for the city council. But it was rarely enough. A letter to the *Post* summed up local feeling:

> Could not something be done by our civic authorities to abate the dreadful storms of dust which sweep down Lambton Quay and all our leading thoroughfares on windy Saturday evenings? [We] struggle along with half-closed optics, and reach home powdered with grit from head to foot …[41]

Katherine Mansfield knew this additional unpleasantness well. In 'Ole Underwood', 'the wind filled his mouth and nostrils with dust'.[42] 'The Escape' refers to the 'whirling, twirling snatch of dust that settled on their clothes like the finest ash … "Oh the dust," she breathed, "the disgusting, revolting dust."'[43] There seemed no escape. 'The Wind Blows' describes how: 'In waves, in clouds, in big round whirls the dust comes stinging, and with it little bits of straw and chaff and manure.'[44] In an era before antibiotics, dust from dried horse manure could infect wounds, even cause death.

The wind never stopped stirring Katherine Mansfield; the air quivers on in many stories with European settings. In 'Late at Night', Virginia, 'dowdy and elderly', stares into the fire, recalling the gale as a spritzer of youth:

> … I'm faddy about things now – that's a sign of age, I'm sure. The wind – I can't bear being blown about in the wind now; and I hate having wet feet. I never used to care about those things – I used almost to revel in them – they made me feel so one with Nature in a way.[45]

Joseph and Margaret Dyer, 1855: 'In his photograph he showed severe and imposing – a high brow, a piercing eye, clean shaven except for long "Piccadilly weepers" draping his bosom.' ('The Aloe'). Photographer unknown.

Six: The inventor

One night on Washington Avenue, in Brooklyn, above the city, I'm handed a 'wine box' sloshing with documents – and a gleam of genealogical treasure. Nick Buck opens his BMW, the cardboard carton framed in the light of the car boot. Jenny, his wife, is a Beauchamp descendant and patient family historian.

Back at home, I sift the contents: faded paper inside mottled manila folders smelling of airless kitchen cupboards. And more: carbon copies of typed family trees, embossed birth certificates, elderly newspaper clippings. There's even a cache of mid-nineteenth-century correspondence, originals, crisp as poppadoms, penned in swirling copperplate, some peeking out of black-edged envelopes stamped with young Queen Victoria's head.

Best of all: 800 pages of journals kept up by Henry Herron Beauchamp, brother of Katherine Mansfield's paternal grandfather Arthur. The entries begin in 1870. The first volume recalls his North London roots: seven Beauchamp sons, offspring of silversmith versifier John Beauchamp, known as the 'Poet of Hornsey Lane', and his wife, and raised in the hilly parish of Highgate. Henry, the fourth son, was the first to head to Australia in the 1840s, and soon made a fortune as a merchant. His brothers followed him, less lucratively: Arthur, sixth born, and Cradock, the seventh, later moved to New Zealand. Henry returned to England, thereafter voyaging in luxury around the world, including one leisurely visit to New Zealand. Over 37 years, the journals record his daily life, especially the weather.

Beauchamp's immediate and extended family remained of abiding interest to this sociable, religious moneybags, including, from time to time, the New Zealanders. The male line won most attention. The earliest reference to nephew Harold's family is an announcement of the birth of his only son, Leslie, in February 1894, 'thus breaking the long record of girl producing'.[1] Beauchamp would, however, lay out the welcome mat for his great-niece Kathleen when she came 'home' to England. In 1905 she and her sisters spent Boxing Day in Kent, playing blackjack with Great-uncle Henry, known as 'Dee-pa'.[2]

The wine box's ancestral pay dirt, however, lies in a single, cursory reference deep in volume four. Here, finally, is the answer to a pressing, unanswered biographical question: how did Katherine Mansfield's parents come together? The standard version has always been that Harold Beauchamp met teenage Annie Dyer through her older brother Frank, Harold's fellow clerk at Bannatynes.[3] But the diary indicates that the middleman was Henry Beauchamp, and that the first familial contact occurred as he criss-crossed New Zealand by coach in 1875, calling in on brother Arthur in Whanganui and bonding with his eldest son, 17-year-old Harold. On a squally day in Wellington a fortnight later, Henry Beauchamp, inveterate networker, looked up an old business acquaintance from Sydney days. Accompanying him was Harold. The diary entry for 1 December 1875 is brief:

> Lovely day. With RJD & Harold by 7.20 train nine miles along the Bay to the Lower Hutt … back in town by 10.30 am. Called on J. Dyer – formerly of Sydney – established a branch (central for all NZ) of the Mutual Provident fund here some five years ago.[4]

The connection was made. And Harold, soon to make a permanent move to Wellington, remembered his uncle's kindly, hospitable friend. In time, alone in the capital, he'd take up the offer to call at the Dyer family home on Tinakori Road. And it was there that he'd encounter their pretty daughter, Annie, not quite in her teens, the same woman he'd marry nine years later. He'd become a regular, awkward visitor at the house, much to the amusement of Annie and her father.

⚘

I recognise Joseph Dyer's face from the 1855 daguerreotype with his wife, Margaret, at the front of the journals. Did a more stricken-looking couple ever pose for a photograph? Joseph, in his white waistcoat and 'Piccadilly weeper' sideburns, looks inconsolable. Margaret, her comforting head on his shoulder, pats his arm, looking as if she, too, wants to die. Maybe the long exposure time is to blame.

Dyer sounds like a dear, a sweet nothing, tottering between two worlds: bored insurance executive by day, boiling-brained inventor by night. His nine children adored him but he seems to have been especially close to daughter number three, Annie Burnell, mother of Katherine Mansfield. Born in Sydney in 1864, Annie suffered from birth with chronic heart trouble. She was seven when the Dyers reached Wellington. Biographer Ruth Mantz says 'her hold upon life was curiously slight – just this thin chain of casual delight'.[5]

Katherine Mansfield soaked up the Dyer history, fictionalising her grandparents as the Fairfields in 'At the Bay' and 'The Aloe'. The latter features a Joseph Dyer-like character with a 'passion for inventing highly impracticable things like collapsible umbrellas or folding lamps'.[6] Linda is her father's

> darling, his pet, his playfellow … He understood her so beautifully and gave her so much love for love that he became a kind of daily miracle to her and all her faith centred in him … In the evenings she and her Father would sit on the verandah – she on his knees – and 'plan'. 'When I am grown up we shall travel everywhere – we shall see the whole world – won't we Papa?' … 'One of your inventions will have been a great success – Bring you a good round million yearly.'[7]

English-born Dyer first reached Sydney in 1842. He took a range of editorial and administrative jobs. He was the son of a Baptist minister who had reportedly drowned himself in a cistern. There was a depressive streak here. He then courted and married 16-year-old Margaret Isabella Mansfield, a publican's daughter, famed for her beauty. Although Margaret was born in New South Wales, there was also a family connection to Taranna, a township near Hobart, Tasmania. Katherine Mansfield made 'Tarana' one of several fictional names for Tinakori Road.

At the time of his marriage, Dyer was editing the *Sydney Magazine of Science and Art*. Signs of a desire to escape boredom, or what he calls being 'ennuied', first emerged during a rainy holiday at the beach, babies underfoot. On Trove, the Australian digital newspaper website, I locate his amazing 3500-word manifesto published in the *Sydney Morning Herald*. Entitled 'Bubble Blowing at the Seaside', it sets out his plan to create 'odd schemes for the advantage of the colony that have passed through my head – it will clear my bosom of much perilous stuff'.[8]

Dyer got to work. Sydney and Melbourne newspapers publicised his blueprint for a prismodial (one-line) railway scheme to avoid trains overbalancing – a prototype of the monorail: 'The rail is laid on a wooden prism, the apex of which is just wide enough for its reception, and on the sides of the prism there are grooves into which two side wheels are turned. These wheels clutch the side rails and thus secure the whole train.'[9]

He then invented something unique: the world's first toilet *on the roof*. The Dyers had relocated to Melbourne, at the middle of which was a lake of putrid, semi-liquid waste. Nobody was healthy in the booming metropolis, not even the wealthy. The Dyers feared their young family, too, would succumb to the typhoid raging through the place. Melbourne was undrained, unpaved, and smelled so bad they called it 'Smellbourne'. A local wit asked: 'How many a hot, sultry summer night have I thrown open my window, panting for heaven's pure air, and I have swallowed – a nightcart.'[10]

So Dyer conceived a plan to contain the excrement. It would be forced into an airtight tube of iron bolted along the eaves of household dwellings. Safe above the ground, the nightsoil could then be easily collected by the nightman and his cart. Melbourne's *Age* publicised his plan; the *Sydney Morning Herald*, too:

> The discharge of fluid feculence through our streets is abominably offensive. I wish to propose a new description of house closet, which shall be inodorous in the house, which shall preserve all the valuable excrementitious matter undiluted with water, and which shall admit of its being removed weekly without the knowledge or sight of the owners of the house, or offending their

senses in any way. I propose that the closet should be always in the house, but not as usually placed on the ground floor or the first floor, but as near the roof as possible.[11]

The logistics of getting users to and from the roof was not spelled out. Dyer, as ever, remained undeterred.

By day, meanwhile, he was a rising man in the world of insurance, having served with the Sydney Fire Insurance Company. In 1871 the AMP dispatched him to Wellington as its founding resident secretary. Business was good. Dyer remitted to Sydney upwards of £50,000 per year in premiums (about $7 million in today's money).[12] In 'The Aloe', Mr Fairfield 'ran a small insurance business that could not have been very profitable, yet they lived plentifully'.[13] 'The Aloe' describes '[a] long white house perched on a hill overlooking Wellington harbour – a house with a wild garden full of bushes and fruit trees, long thick grass and nasturtiums'.[14]

Council rate books pinpoint the exact location of the family home: the 1872/1873 ledger names Dyer as the individual paying rates on the property (today the site of 192 Tinakori Road). The house abutted Poplar Grove, one of many private roads at right angles to Tinakori Road and running back to Grant Road. Tiny workers' cottages lined these chilly byways; stables on Poplar Grove were also used as a dance hall.

Dyer was quick to offer his 'house closet' concept to his adopted city, where it was politely turned down. The *Evening Post* reported his presentation to the local municipality: 'The contents, which by their own weight were forced through the hose pipe attached to the pipe, emptied into the cart, and the whole process gone through without any necessity for soiling a hand, the cap fitting the orifice at the bottom of the pipe being screwed on again.'[15]

Annie and her siblings attended the Anglican day school in Thorndon's Sydney Street. In 'The Aloe' the Fairfields are 'quite a "show" family and immensely admired'.[16] The Dyer parents participated in local 'society', including receptions for a new governor. Joseph, however, was more focused on fundraising at his children's school, reciting poems and singing. In 'The Aloe', Linda's father 'had a good voice and liked to sing in public'.[17]

Dyer gained a flicker of fame across the colony in 1874, this time not for his inventions. It came as he urged his Sydney-based board to pay out on the lapsed life insurance policy of a recently deceased Wairarapa customer. Newspapers were united in approval: 'Such an act of liberality is deserving of the heartiest recognition, and is exceedingly creditable to this society, which now stands in the front rank of Insurance Societies in the world.'[18] AMP would not show the same level of compassion to the Dyer family in the years to come.

Annie's older siblings were growing; some were old enough to leave home. 'The Aloe' echoes these events: 'By the time Linda was fourteen, the big family had vanished, only she and Beryl, who was two years younger, were left. The girls had married; the boys had gone faraway ... she stayed at home to be a help to her mother.'[19]

Dyer senior meanwhile continued to invent, honing his idea of a breakwater for Wellington, where sailing ships might be tethered. Politicians and leading citizens gathered in 1876 to learn of his proposed wall of longitudinal iron tubes or 'cells' fronting the waves, the open ends of which would somehow resist the onrush: 'These [tubes] are secured to each other and kept in position by being attached to very strong screw piles which have a vertical section of an acute triangle, so that they oppose no resistance to the attack of the wave.'[20]

The breakwater would be cheaper than concrete, Dyer insisted. 'On the retreat of the wave the air will rush into the orifices from which it has been so forcibly expelled, and then the structure will again constitute an elastic atmospheric wall against which waves may dash in vain.'[21] An engineer gave his blessing. The plan was judged practicable but, like Dyer's 'house closet', quietly ignored.

So what of the courtship between Harold Beauchamp and Annie Dyer? Six years separated the pair when they first met. I speculate Harold first came calling in 1876, the year he shifted to the capital. Katherine Mansfield's sister Jeanne recalled: 'Father fell in love with mother when she was 14. They married when she was 19.'[22] 'The Aloe' places the meeting earlier, and it seems likely the youngsters met when Harold, adrift in the big city, took up Dyer's invitation to the house. Katherine Mansfield imagines the character we can only take to be her father as a ridiculous suitor:

Every evening a stout young man in a striped shirt, with fiery red hair, and a pair of immature mutton chop whiskers, passed their house, quite slowly, four times. Twice up the hill he went and twice down he came ... Who was he? None of them knew – but he became a great joke. 'Here she blows,' Mr Fairfield would whisper. The young man came to be called the 'Ginger Whale'. Then he appeared at Church, in a pew facing theirs, very devout and serious ... every time he so much as glanced in Linda's direction a crimson blush spread over his face to his ears. 'Look out, my wench,' said Mr Fairfield. 'Your clever Papa has solved the problem. That young fellow is after you.' ... 'You know as well I do that I am never going to marry,' said Linda. 'How can you be such a traitor, Papa–.'[23]

In 1877 Annie's father Joseph Dyer suddenly died of nephritis, a kidney disease. Local water quality cannot have helped. He was 58 and, for an insurance man, shockingly financially unprepared. The death – and its catastrophic impact on the family – attracted considerable attention. The *Evening Post* noted: 'We regret to learn that his large family – a widow and nine children – are but slightly provided for, his life having been insured only for £500.'[24] The full quantum, equal to about $75,000 in today's money, went to repaying Dyer's many debts. The *Post* reported how Dyer's employer cruelly denied the family any further assistance:

At the annual meeting of the Australian Mutual Provident Society, reference was made to the late Mr Joseph Dyer ... to whose ability and exertions the remarkable success of the society in New Zealand admittedly is mainly attributable ... The local directors had pressed the claim of this servant on the Central Board and the Board referred it to the meeting; but a resolution proposing a grant of £500 was rejected by a large majority.[25]

Margaret Dyer and her children were penniless. Nothing, not even a widow's pension, was available. For a prominent family like the Dyers to fall so low, so publicly, must have been a humiliation. Which brings us to Harold Beauchamp, on his way to becoming a wealthy partner at Bannatynes. Given her family's financial circumstances, it would have been hard for Annie Dyer to refuse his proposal of marriage, especially when he seemed willing, even happy, to become her extended family's protector and provider. It may explain why she remained grumpy for the rest of her life.

Dyer's death left enduring scars. 'The Aloe' provides clues to a recurring depressive state that sisters Annie and Belle Dyer, fictionalised as Linda and Beryl Fairfield, are known to have endured in real life. One fictional sister challenges the other's remoteness:

> *'Why do you always pretend to be so indifferent to everything,' she said. 'You pretend you don't care where you live, or if you see anybody or not, or what happens to the children or even what happens to you. You can't be sincere and yet you keep it up – you've kept it up for years – ever since' – and Beryl paused, shoved down a little pleat very carefully – 'ever since Father died …'*[26]

Dyer was buried at Bolton Street Cemetery in a modest grave, commensurate with his family's financial state. Once Harold Beauchamp was on the scene, the headstone was attached to an expanded family tomb created in 1892 when Annie's brother Henry died. Margaret Dyer later joined them. But the Dyers' tenure in their adopted city's graveyard would not be a peaceful one: half a century on, their surroundings were smashed apart, their remains exhumed as the cemetery was bisected for an urban motorway. The remains of Katherine Mansfield's ancestors, together with those of 3700 others, were sifted, then shipped in cardboard containers, for final mingling in a large common grave.

Cemetery records suggest that headstones from the Dyer family grave have been reinstated, somewhere in the southeastern corner. But much of the stonework associated with the disinterred bodies is missing. On a sunny Tuesday I go looking, starting at Easdale Street, halfway up the Bolton Street ridge. I crunch down bush-shrouded paths with names like Trustees Crescent and Observatory Path.

The Dyer family tomb, now dismantled, Bolton Street Cemetery. 'Roddie … stood at the graveside … he gave a violent start, turned, muttered something to his father and dashed away, so fast that people looked positively frightened, through the cemetery …' ('Weak Heart') Photographer P.J.E. Shotter. Ref: 35mm-25535-18A-F. ATL.

High on an overgrown ridge known as the Goat Track, I locate the Dyer headstones: three lichen-peppered marble slabs, one above the other, stuck to the back wall of the cemetery. A dozen other stones are cemented to the same rude, ivy-edged retaining wall. The uppermost, belonging to Margaret Dyer, shines above the wild grasses and thick onion weed. A spiny thistle shields the inscription for Henry, bracketed between his parents. Joseph Dyer, the inventor, lurks at ground level, down among the warm roots.

Cradock and Harriet Beauchamp's Anakiwa homestead, 1892. The couple
are seated in the middle row. Arthur Beauchamp is standing at the far right.
Mary Beauchamp is absent.

Photographer unknown. Ref: PAColl-D-0869. ATL.

Seven: Labour of sorrow

It was two days before Christmas, 1879. Arthur Beauchamp, Katherine Mansfield's paternal grandfather and the ancestor she's most often compared to, was in a pickle. The Nelson District Supreme Court was in session at Blenheim courthouse, where Beauchamp, short, blue-eyed and nuggety, was declaring himself a bankrupt. His creditors were circling: the Bank of Australia had an agent in court, hunting £450 (about $20,000 in today's money); a man from Whanganui wanted the £100 he was owed for a small mountain of coal. Wellington retailer Kirkcaldie and Stains, too, was closing in on payment for items ranging from a clothesline to tobacco to a wooden crate of Perry Davis Painkiller, thick in opium. And young Harold, his eldest boy, was also out of pocket.[1]

The bankruptcy came as the colonial economy teetered, ushering in the so-called Hungry Eighties. Many others would face insolvency. But for proud Arthur Beauchamp, auctioneer, merchant and former parliamentarian, it was a resounding defeat, a moment to bow the head. Family histories, especially Harold's memoirs, have never mentioned it: Arthur, to be blunt, was hopeless. His son Harold learned this as a young man. The father Katherine Mansfield depicted as boringly prosperous and complacent had to claw his way up the slippery colonial ladder to firm financial ground. I unearth Arthur Beauchamp's bankruptcy declaration in the reading room at Archives New Zealand. The crisp packet of legal documents reprises the latest chapter of an extended chronicle of rootlessness, business failure and almost ceaseless family tragedy.

The various Katherine Mansfield biographies have always depicted Arthur as an eccentric wanderer. Harold Beauchamp called his father 'a rolling stone by instinct'.[2] He was not exaggerating: over half a century, Arthur shuttled his wife and family between 18 separate locations.[3] Mansfield biographer Antony Alpers says Arthur 'was pulling up stakes with such painful regularity that the family used to say that as soon as his hens heard the sound of packing, they lay on their backs with their legs up, ready to be tied'.[4] It wasn't unusual on the colonial frontier to keep moving in search of opportunity. But even by these standards Arthur Beauchamp was astonishingly restless.

So what made him so peripatetic? He's recalled as larger than life, energetic, joyful and prone to spouting Byron. He was verbally dexterous, a quality Katherine Mansfield inherited: 'a vigorous, picturesque speaker with some wit and an aptitude for punning and versifying'.[5] Yet his childhood seems to have been a crushing one:

> [Arthur] … was always considered the smart, brainy show boy of the family, with his ready wit, wonderful memory and sentiment and pathos. His aunts rather spoilt him by praising his efforts too largely, which our grandfather was always trying to knock out of him to keep him humble. He, I believe, kept Arthur seven years grinding in some dark London office …[6]

We know less about Arthur's wife, Mary Stanley Beauchamp. Family histories have portrayed her as stoical, saintly, perhaps happiest at the piano playing hymns. Another Mansfield biographer claims her godliness helped her survive a half century with Arthur: 'Her body was flexible and sound, strengthened by the tense spirit, hemmed in to itself safely by a ring of belief she had cast about her – a religious belief she was never to lose.'[7]

Katherine Mansfield fictionalises her along these lines in 'The Voyage':

> There was an intent, bright look on her face. Then Fenella saw that her lips were moving and guessed that she was praying. But the old woman gave her a bright nod as if to say the prayer was nearly over. She unclasped her hands, sighed, clasped them again, bent forward, and at last gave herself a soft shake.[8]

Arthur, too, drew strength from his wife's faith. When his brother Henry Beauchamp visited the Whanganui-based family in 1875, he recorded a conversation about the theological meaning of that day's sermon from the Book of Psalms. Mary was busy 'tubbing' the children as the men chatted.[9]

$\mathcal{L}$

She was accustomed to tragedy. Daughter of a Lancashire silversmith, Mary Stanley was orphaned at 16. She then travelled to Australia for work as a governess, meeting and marrying Arthur in 1854. He was 26, six years older than she was, prospecting for gold and running businesses in the Victorian goldfields. Their marital happiness was brief: two sons died of infectious disease in quick succession. The third, hardier child, Harold, survived, but Mary outlived most of the seven more babies she bore.

Harold grew up idolising his long-suffering mother:

> I can truthfully say I never saw her in a temper. She had a serene character and even temperament that enabled her to meet any trouble with perfect equanimity … It must have been trying in the extreme to break up her home so often to follow my father in his wanderings from place to place; but she never questioned the wisdom of that. I can only describe her as an earthly saint.[10]

Arthur called Melbourne's climate 'fatal to his very young children',[11] and the couple quit Australia in 1861. New Zealand was an obvious choice of destination: he and brother Cradock owned shares in valuable sections in Wellington, bequeathed by an English aunt. Arthur chartered a vessel, loaded it with merchandise and sailed with the family to Picton, a thriving township in the Marlborough Sounds. He and Mary bought land there from the proceeds of the sale of the Wellington sections.

New Zealand was in the grip of gold fever. It was no coincidence that the Beauchamps landed the year Otago miner Gabriel Read found gold at Tuapeka. Harold noted that his father could never 'resist the allurements of the gold diggings'.[12] When gold was discovered at Wakamarina, near Havelock in Marlborough, six thousand miners rushed to the area.

Arthur's merchant business boomed. He built a grand house in Picton's Wellington Street and settled into the community. The family holidayed at nearby Anakiwa, where brother Cradock had carved a farm out of the bush.

Arthur had the energy and sociability for politics. He first entered at the provincial government level, gaining attention with a 10-hour political speech described as 'rubbish, ribaldry and Billingsgate'.[13] The working people of Picton then elected him their local parliamentary representative. He called for the subdivision of big estates to benefit the little man – a foretaste of the Liberal policies of a generation later. More radically, Beauchamp opposed confiscation of Māori land. He was also someone with a healthy sense of the ridiculous: '[Beauchamp] then illustrated some remarks by telling an episode in the life of Jack the Giant-killer, and compared the similes of the Colonial Treasurer to soap-bubbles, and concluded after some further remarks of a humorous nature.'[14]

But life as a colonial parliamentarian necessitated a private income. Arthur Beauchamp's business faltered as the Wakamarina goldfield declined. After a year in politics he resigned, leaving for the West Coast where gold had been discovered on the Buller River. Mary remained in Picton with the babies that kept coming every two years.

In the mid-1860s, Beauchamp set up as a merchant and Customs agent in Westport, operating from his private wharf. The discovery of gold was transforming the tiny West Coast river port, and confidence ran high. A lavish banquet held at a local hotel in the spring of 1867 caught something of the bullish, almost manic mood. Arthur sat in the chair that night, hosting the powerful superintendent of Nelson Province, and flanked by senior officials and elected politicians. It is unclear whether Arthur paid for the dinner, but the menu remains tantalising:

Soups: White oyster, Julienne.

Roast: Turkeys à la Montebello, geese and apple sauce, spring chickens à la Française, braised ducks à la Duchesse, saddle of mutton and currant jelly, loin of beef and Yorkshire pudding.

Boiled: Turkeys à la Provençal, fowls à la Tyrolienne, rabbit aux onions, ox tongue, braised ham.

Entrees: Vol au Vent au supréme, salmi of pigeon, lamb cutlets and green peas, Fricandeau of veal, raised pie, fillet of beef à la Marengo.

Vegetables: Green peas and turnips, cabbage and carrots, potatoes, baked and boiled.

Entremets: Plum pudding, Michael Angelo pudding, pudding à la Rubens, pudding à la Neselrode, gateaux Genoise, Savoy cakes, marengues à la crème, fonchonettes, lemon cheese cake, omelette soufflé, jelly à la Victoria, blancmanges, custard, Charlotte Russe, apples à la Condé, vanilla crème, lemon jellies, trifles, French pastry, tartlets à la crème.

Wines: Colonial wines, Hock, Dalwood red, Moselle, No. 2 Champagne, Heidseich, Port, Sherry, Claret.[15]

Beauchamp seemed at the peak of his powers: sociable, witty, launching endless toasts 'until the party broke up at a late hour'.[16] Between songs and bumpers of champagne, the talk was of investment in Westport's future as a port and population hub.

Furious summer storms, combined with a raging Buller River, however, soon dashed those hopes. The *West Coast Times* described the scene on 6 January 1868:

This morning ... the river assumed gigantic proportions and swept to the ocean with terrific force ... During the morning a large quantity of timber had come in contact with Mr Beauchamp's Wharf, and about ten o'clock the T at the end of the wharf went, but was not carried away bodily. Cables were at once attached to it, and with considerable difficulty it was ultimately brought to the river bank ... During the night and this morning the river fell considerably ... The portion of Mr Beauchamp's wharf left standing was examined this morning and found to be very much damaged, but it is thought that by driving down a few additional piles and placing a number of supports on the western side, it will be made as strong and useful as ever it was.[17]

Returning from a Picton family Christmas, Arthur sailed or, rather, steamed into the middle of this chaos. Harold wrote:

… my father saw a portion of his wharf sailing merrily across the bar to the open sea. A fellow passenger in the little coasting steamer remarked: 'Well, Mr Beauchamp, there goes your tee.' My father replied philosophically, 'Well, so long as I can get some supper when I get to Westport I don't care twopence about my tea.' [18]

The West Coast is renowned as wild, pitiless terrain. When the Buller flooded again the following year, the entire river mouth and wharf area were deluged. 'The banks of the esplanade fell in, in tons, and Beauchamp's wharf stood as an island.'[19] Arthur Beauchamp's foray into Westport came to an end.

♀

Arthur returned to Picton. He sold the family home, using the money to buy land at Beatrix Bay, near the entrance to Pelorus, deep in the Marlborough Sounds. According to Harold, '[w]e lived chiefly on fish, mutton, wild pork and birds, such as pigeon, kaka and – I blush to say – tuis, which were most plentiful.'[20] Harold and his father laboured to bring the densely wooded property into cultivation and raised a small number of stock. But this venture, too, ended in failure.

Arthur decided to cross to the North Island and establish a merchant and auctioneering business in Whanganui, beyond which Māori land was available. He was keen for Harold, only 11, to quit school and join him. Harold recalled: 'I protested mildly on the grounds that I had not had enough education, and yielding to my pleading he agreed to my entering Whanganui Collegiate School.'[21] At 14 he did leave school, and spent the next four years helping Arthur on the farm and with other business enterprises.

Harold is always portrayed as painfully respectable. I was therefore surprised to discover that at age 15 he appeared in the Magistrate's Court at Whanganui, charged with 'having wilfully damaged the road known as Shakespeare's Cliff Road, by driving a mob of cattle over the clay and mud embankment'.[22] At the time he was chiefly working as a drover.

Arthur and family spent seven years in Whanganui. In 1875 came Henry Herron Beauchamp's visit, something of a crossroads for Harold, then turning 17. He saw in his wealthy, worldly uncle a self-made man at peace with himself. The two bonded. Harold joined his uncle in Wellington, where he made a second pivotal contact in Joseph Dyer. Henry's visit appears to have shaken up this branch of the New Zealand Beauchamps: Arthur sold up in Whanganui to start a new auctioneering business in the capital.

Harold was, however, determined to strike out alone, and soon took a job with importers Bannatyne and Company. He would remain there for the rest of his working life. Nor would he ever move out of Wellington, except for regular overseas travel.

In 1878 his parents Arthur and Mary returned to the Sounds after Winifred, their 12-year-old son, suddenly died. Then came the ignominy of bankruptcy after Beauchamp's new business enterprise, a sawmill in Pelorus Sound, burned down, leaving him £650 (about $100,000) in debt.

And so, on Christmas Eve 1879, Arthur Beauchamp faced his creditors at the Blenheim courthouse. Among them was 19-year-old Harold, a fact that cannot have enhanced the father and son relationship. The man whose fortune would later support Katherine Mansfield's writing career had sunk his life savings into the failed enterprise: 'I advanced all my accumulated wealth to my father … to purchase sheep for stocking the property. I was supposed to have had an interest in those sheep on a share principle, but it turned out unsatisfactorily, and the whole of my money "went west".'[23]

It is tempting to speculate that this was a second turning point for him.

෫

Seemingly undeterred, Beauchamp senior then headed south and began again. He opened an auctioneering business on Christchurch's New Brighton Road. But the business failures mounted. I uncover details of a second bankruptcy, in 1884.[24] Arthur and Mary were still in Christchurch when a fourth child, Walter, died in 1888, the year of Kathleen's birth. Charles, a fifth son, died of typhoid in 1892; his sister Florence succumbed to the same infection inside a year.

Was it an accumulation of grief that sent Arthur and Mary running? The couple's response to the loss of their children (six out of 10 between

1855 and 1893) was to live out of a suitcase. Arthur, working as a temporary auctioneer, flitted between Picton and Wellington during the 1890s. Even well into their seventies, the couple continued moving around, living variously with Cradock at Anakiwa and their son Stanley in the Sounds.

If the Beauchamp children saw their grandparents only during holidays at Anakiwa, Mary in particular still made an impression. Katherine Mansfield wrote:

> One day I must write about Grandma at length, especially of her beauty in her bath – when she was about sixty. Wiping herself with the towel, I remember now how lovely she seemed to me. And her fine linen, her scent. I have never really described her yet. Patience! The time will come.[25]

'The Voyage' portrays a fictional grandmother undressing: 'Then she undid her bodice, and something under that, and something else underneath that. Then there seemed a short, sharp tussle, and grandma flushed faintly. Snip! Snap! She had undone her stays.' Arthur is also spotted: 'There, lying to one side of an immense bed, lay grandpa. Just his head with a white tuft, and his rosy face and long silver beard showed over the quilt. He was like a very old wide-awake bird.'[26]

❧

By century's end, 40-year-old Harold Beauchamp was already a grandee, a man of wealth and status, a fixer for the Seddon Ministry. Arthur meanwhile had gained minor recognition as a founding Liberal. In 1902, aged 74, he travelled to England, turning up unexpectedly at his brother Henry Herron's residence in Kent, as Henry recalled in his diary:

> Soon after 3.30 this afternoon, just as Rally and I were about starting for Gravesend … to land Arthur and bring him home, he marched up to our front door, having landed there. 54 years next July since he left England … we gave him a hearty welcome: 'You bet'.[27]

Henry's doctor son privately described Uncle Arthur as 'a broken down old man with a bad heart'.[28] Premier Seddon, who met him at a social event, was kinder. In a letter to Harold he wrote:

Your father is looking very well and has increased in weight but your brother's wife told me that her son, who is a doctor, had told her that the old gentleman was suffering from heart trouble and should refrain from any excitement. You would think he had another 70 years before him.[29]

Katherine Mansfield praised Arthur's indomitable spirit, with some reservations:

My grandpa said a man could travel all over the world with a clean pair of socks and a rook rifle. At the age of 70 he started for England thus equipped, but Mother took fright and added a handkerchief or two. When he returned he was shorn of everything but a large watering can which he had bought in London for his young marrows. I don't suggest him as a Man to be Followed, however.[30]

In 1907, a full half century after first arriving in Picton, Arthur and Mary finally slowed, returning to buy a small property there. Arthur died three years later, aged 83. Mary wasn't far behind. I find their grave high on a grassy hillside in the decaying cemetery on the western hills above the town, with views out to the inter-island ferries. They share a tomb as wide as a queen-sized bed and covered with whorls of bark from surrounding gum trees, pea-sized marble stones and a windfall of bright red tree strawberries. The title of a hymn, 'Blessed be the Fountain of Blood', is inscribed on the headstone, ensuring that Mary has the last, martyred word.

Part Three

Chesney Wold, Karori, circa 1880s, subjects unidentified: 'That old house had an
extraordinary fascination for me. I always thought of it as a species of ogre who
controlled all the gardens and the meadows and the woods.' ('My Potplants')

Photographer unknown. Ref: PAColl-5277-1-12. ATL.

Eight: Little brown owl

*I try and make [family life] gorgeous – not hatred and cold linoleum –
but warmth and hydrangeas. – Katherine Mansfield, 1921*[1]

I'm outside Chesney Wold at 372 Karori Road, dinging the electric chimes to what Katherine Mansfield called the 'great old rambling house planted lonesomely in the midst of huge gardens, orchards and paddocks'.[2] Squeezed onto a tiny section, the house is still enfolded by 'the great green shoulders of Makra [sic] Hill'.[3] Current owners Sean Rogers and Julia Rowling open the door. They escort me to the rear of the house, the same space Kezia Burnell glides into the night she arrives here in 'Prelude', holding a 'bright, breathing' kerosene lamp.[4] She'll awaken to birdsong in what feels like an enchanted landscape.

We drink our coffee in the open-plan, north-facing room at the rear: state-of-the-art stainless-steel European kitchen in one corner; low-slung seating, white carpet and plasma TV in the other. In the Beauchamps' time, the dwelling was oriented to the cold south; today sun pours in through French doors. Sean and Julia grumble about the chill; they've installed double-glazing and central heating. It's still nippy, they say.

I look around the high-ceilinged rooms. Can stories like 'Prelude' help us re-imagine the physical layout when the young Kathleen Beauchamp lived here? Successive renovations have rubbed out many Victorian contours: the dining room where, in 'The Aloe', a 'polar bear skin lay in front of the fire place' is long opened up.[5] Harold Beauchamp's Chesterfield dinner table is today a baize billiard table; there's a whiteboard on which Julia's son has scrawled *Chesney Wold Pool Rankings*.

The Karori valley was a far-flung outpost at the end of a long, wet twisted track when farmer Stephen Lancaster bought land here for a dairy farm in the 1860s. He sounds like a poster boy for pioneering vigour, rising daily at 3.30am to lug milk cans into the city on foot; returning home for a full day's work.[6] Lancaster built a 13-room colonial farmhouse in what was termed 'carpenter Gothic' style. Some of Karori's first church services passed under its roof.[7] This was the homestead of rough-sawn timber beneath high gables – spacious but never opulent – where the Beauchamps came to live.

Lancaster named the place Chesney Wold after the stately home on the estate of Lord and Lady Dedlock in Charles Dickens' *Bleak House*. He planned to live here, but ended up in a second, smaller house nearby. The tribute to Dickens wasn't surprising: he was as much a literary giant in colonial New Zealand as he was in England. A 'Pickwick Club' of local gentlemen assembled in 1840s Wellington; an indigenous 'Old Curiosity Shop' opened on Willis Street. Wellington's first mayor, George Hunter, was said to 'exactly resemble Mr Pickwick'.[8] In the 1850s, Charlotte Brontë's friend Mary Taylor and her brother Waring read instalments of Dickens after a long day at their shop on Cuba Street: '[We] don't give over working till bedtime and take a new number of D. Copperfield to bed with us and drop asleep on the second page.'[9]

Karori's Chesney Wold echoed its literary counterpart in ways Lancaster may not have intended. Take the weather. Sad-eyed Lady Dedlock would have been at home in this splashy valley, especially in the gloomy midwinter. In his description of the surrounds of the Dedlocks' home, Dickens could just as well have had Karori in mind: 'The weather, for many a day and night, has been so wet that the trees seem wet through ... The shot of a rifle loses its sharpness in the moist air, and its smoke moves in a little tardy cloud towards the green rise.'[10] A contemporary photograph shows Chesney Wold in its original setting, oriented to the east. Hills shorn of vegetation rise behind it. The surrounding landscape is denuded, devastated: gullies are filled with bleached tree trunks; thick smoke rises from the roots of a smashed tree. Picket fences and young specimens of macrocarpa, the dishevelled pine that flourished here, are also visible.

≶

Politician, orator, journalist and poet James FitzGerald became Lancaster's first tenant. He and his family of 12 arrived from Canterbury in 1867, after the larger-than-life Irishman swapped a demanding role as provincial superintendent for a gold-plated desk job with the colonial government. The setting was never popular with his family: daughter Amy described Karori as 'a very small village arrived at by a very bad road among the hills. It was a cold, bleak place and I found it very dull.'[11] The FitzGeralds attended St Mary's Church, where 'parishioners cannot afford an organ and hymns are sung to the sound of a tuning fork'.[12] And like the fictional Lady Dedlock, Mrs Fanny FitzGerald sank into depression. The family remained for five years, the menfolk distracted by landscaping and the construction of a range of outbuildings, such as stables for James FitzGerald's horse. The children attended an early version of Karori School near where the mall now stands: Mrs FitzGerald called it 'very inferior'.[13] Then, after a particularly bleak fortnight of daily rain that turned the landscape into a sea of mud, the FitzGeralds departed. They returned to the central city, climbing high, building on land above Oriental Bay on the site now occupied by St Gerard's Monastery.

Then came a melancholy chapter in the story of Chesney Wold. The Brown family and offspring arrived with a flourish, planning to turn the house into an elite boarding school for young 'society' ladies. French, German and music were among the subjects on offer. Local notables endorsed the Browns' 'select' establishment. But after a few promising years, the Browns succumbed to what the *Post* politely called 'domestic grievances'.[14] Their expensive furniture, including a massive King Arthur-style round table and marble-topped chiffonier, was carried out of the valley. Mr Brown, government surveyor and Victorian gentleman, walked to a nearby hilltop, tied a silk handkerchief to a post and strangled himself. Social decorum was, however, observed to the end:

There was no sign of drink about the deceased when found; in fact, he had been seen by Constable Ryan … as if coming into the city, so that it is to be presumed he committed the deed shortly afterwards. He … spoke to the constable in the most cheerful manner.[15]

New Zealand Wars veteran Lieutenant Colonel Thomas Porter, along with a songstress daughter, replaced the Browns as the new tenants. Then came the Bagnalls: a retired Birmingham lawyer, his wife and five children.

As the Beauchamps readied to leave Thorndon and take over Chesney Wold, the *Post* advertised for a 'General Servant or Help to cook and wash' at the property. Some domestic help was already on site: an Irish handyman and gardener called Pat Sheehan, who appears in Katherine Mansfield's fiction as himself. He is perhaps her most romantic creation. She pictures Sheehan in 'The Aloe', freshening up the house before the family arrives, rolling out carpet in the dining room. He, however, leaves the most arduous task to fellow servant Alice. She is seen 'lying practically at full length on the bathroom floor laying linoleum. And she is hammering it so frightfully hard that I am sure the pattern will come through onto the dining room ceiling.'[16]

In Europe, years later, Katherine Mansfield resurrected Chesney Wold nail by nail, giving the house and surrounds a living, breathing character. In 'Prelude', the children see it for the first time in darkness:

> *It was long and low built, with a pillared verandah and balcony all the way round. The soft white bulk of it lay stretched upon the green garden like a sleeping beast. And now one and now another of the windows leaped into light. Someone was walking through the empty rooms carrying a lamp. From the window downstairs the light of a fire flickered. A strange beautiful excitement seemed to stream from the house in quivering ripples.*[17]

Reconstructed architectural sketch plans confirm that her account in 'Prelude' of the Burnells' new home in the country closely matches the interior layout of Chesney Wold at the time the Beauchamps lived there. I'm able, for example, to pinpoint the front door Kezia Burnell enters, then a glass door on the eastern side, and the square hall, filled with bales of family possessions, that she walks along. As she crosses the hall, Kezia looks up to see 'hundreds of parrots (but the parrots were only on the wall-paper)'.[18]

I can also locate the dining room on the ground floor that grandmother ushers Kezia into after the night-time coach journey from Thorndon. There, an exhausted Linda Burnell reclines; Kezia's father and aunt are eating, a pot of tea beside them. In real life, this dining space became a family room, a place where the Beauchamp children sipped cocoa and ate knobbly buns with jam.

Across the passage sat a drawing room with its polar bear rug. In 'Prelude' this long room with bay windows opens onto the veranda. Tea was served here and cribbage played. 'It had a cream paper with a pattern of gilt roses, and the furniture, which had belonged to old Mrs Fairfield, was dark and plain. A little piano stood against the wall with yellow pleated silk let into the carved front ...'[19] But it proved a cold corner of the house, and the open veranda was enclosed after the Beauchamps' departure. Off the dining room was a kitchen with built-in pantry and a pine table beneath windows. Servants occupied tiny quarters behind the kitchen. Years later Jeanne Beauchamp recalled that a real-life doll's house stood in the passageway. 'I can see now the little lamp which was full of mystery – it was a real house to us.'[20]

The family slept upstairs, beneath high gables. In 'Prelude', Kezia's elder sisters share a room; Aunt Belle, too, has hers. As Kathleen Beauchamp did, Kezia shares a room with her grandmother. Servant Alice 'lights her to bed': in other words, escorts her by candlelight.

Like other colonial houses, Chesney Wold was lit with a mix of candles and kerosene lamps, often smoky and smelly. Interiors like the Beauchamps' were deliberately kept dim: this was a time of long velvet curtains, thick enclosing fabrics and dark wooden furniture.

Karori at this time had no reticulated water or piped sewage: the Beauchamps relied on wells, running streams and rainwater tanks. They enjoyed one luxurious connection to civilisation, however: the house was connected to the telephone exchange. The addition of a line out to South Karori even warranted a mention in the *Post*.

Chesney Wold in 1893 sat amidst marshy paddocks where Lancaster's cows roamed, bells around their necks. A plantation of bursting pines, always happy in the moist Karori clay, enclosed the spacious grounds, running up the hills behind. Ducks, like the one Sheehan decapitates in 'Prelude' as the children watch in horror, paddled in the little stream flowing beside the grass. A long white corrugated-iron fence with clanking iron gates opened onto Karori Road. An island lay in the middle of the metalled entranceway, dividing it into two arms that met in front of the house. Did an aloe, the elemental tree of 'Prelude', really grow here? They certainly flourished in the valley. In 1889, long-time resident Robert Donald was reported as saying that a specimen he'd planted in his garden 35 years earlier was flowering. Nearly five metres high, the aloe gained 15 centimetres a day.[21]

By the time the Beauchamps arrived, FitzGerald's building and landscaping had begun to succumb to the weather. Outbuildings, including a scullery and washhouse in a lean-to, stables, woodshed, cowshed, piggery and tool house, were falling down. On a paddock beyond the property's edge, a dilapidated stable served as a fowl house.

Kathleen Beauchamp revelled in the freedom of her new surroundings: by 14 she had written her first tribute, a 1903 story entitled 'It Was a Big Bare House', framing up ideas that would later be realised as 'Prelude':

It was a big bare house surrounded with pine trees. A wilderness of a garden stretched away on all sides – no settled beds of flowers, but the whole overrun with weeds, and tall, long grass. At the back of the house were high thickly wooded hills. Beautiful hills where the tui sang all day in summer and the morepork cried aloud in the evenings. But the house looked desolate. There were no dainty window curtains, no creepers to soften its outlines. It was painted white. There was a broad verandah at the back, that was the only 'nice' thing about it.[22]

'About Pat', published in the magazine of her London school when she was 17, was her next attempt to capture the setting:

We had few toys, but – far better – plenty of good, strong mud and a flight of concrete steps that grew hot in the heat of the sun and became dreams of ovens … Well I remember one occasion when we made pies with real flour, stole some water from the dish by the dog's kennel, baked them and ate them. Very soon after three crushed, subdued little girls wended their way quietly up to bed, and the blind was pulled down.[23]

Lancaster's rustic homestead in particular fired her imagination. A less-known story, 'My Potplants', dating from 1906, recalls how 'that old house had an extraordinary fascination for me. I always thought of it as a species of ogre who controlled all the garden and the meadows and the woods.'[24] But it was in 'Prelude' that the wide rolling grounds, with their sections of thick, flowery orchard grass, would be most strongly brought to life:

> [Kezia] had walked away back through the orchard, up the grassy slope, along the path by the lace bark tree and so into the spread tangled garden. She did not believe that she would ever not get lost in this garden. Twice she had found her way back to the big iron gates they had driven through the night before, and then had turned to walk up the drive that led to the house, but there were so many little paths on either side. On one side they all led into a tangle of tall dark trees and strange bushes with flat velvet leaves and feathery cream flowers that buzzed with flies when you shook them – this was the frightening side, and no garden at all.[25]

Young Kathleen appointed resident handyman Pat Sheehan as sovereign of this new green realm, a gruff yet steady counterpoint to the unpredictable grown-ups indoors – even, increasingly, to her siblings. By seven or eight, she found herself alone in the middle: too young for the older, constitutionally biddable Vera and Charlotte; too old for 'the babies', one of whom, Leslie Heron, was born a year after the family arrived. The boy's middle name, a tribute to his great-uncle Henry, was famously misspelt.

In the autobiographical 'About Pat' she wrote, 'our old Irish gardener was our hero', and described Sunday walks with him to a nearby pine plantation. There's a sense that Chesney Wold allowed her to peel off, even withdraw from the rest of the family without it being too noticeable. But Sheehan could be disapproving, too: 'Pat was never fond of me. I am afraid he did not think my character at all desirable … one day [I] committed the unpardonable offence of picking a pumpkin flower. He never recovered from the shock …'[26]

Sheehan's own life story may never be known. The universality of the name prevents genealogical inquiry; he retains a dreamy, almost mystical quality:

Every afternoon he used to brush his old brown bowler hat, harness the mare and start for town, and every evening when he had come home it was my delight to wait until he had unharnessed the mare, then to be lifted on to her back, and start at a jogging trot through the big white gates, down the quiet road and into the paddock. There I waited until Pat came swinging along with the milk pails.[27]

'About Pat' concludes with Sheehan's departure 'to try his luck in the goldfields', the children in tears. He presents each of them with a goldfinch, and the narrator is given two white china vases decorated with forget-me-nots.

More is known about 'Farkey' Anderson (Farquhar Campbell Anderson), an English-born, ex-Indian Army soldier who worked on Karori properties as a labourer and kept birds. Charlotte Beauchamp recalled goldfinches in cages hanging from trees at Anderson's property.[28] Birds, especially canaries, would become a Beauchamp family fixture too. Anderson walked with a limp, and Katherine Mansfield turned him into 'The Man With the Wooden Leg':

There was a man lived quite near us
He had a wooden leg and a goldfinch in a green cage
His name was Farkey Anderson
And he'd been in a war to get his leg.
We were very sad about him
Because he had such a beautiful smile
And was such a big man to live in a very little house.
When he walked on the road his leg did not matter so much
But when he walked in his little house
It made an ugly noise.
Little Brother said his goldfinch sang the loudest of all other birds,
So that he should not hear his poor leg
And feel too sorry about it.[29]

Chesney Wold might have hosted Karori's first church services, but by the time the Beauchamps moved in, local Anglicans worshipped elsewhere.

I'm surprised to discover the extent to which religion, perhaps as a source of consolation, shaped the family's life in Karori. Sundays began with religious instruction for the Beauchamp children: in the morning they attended Sunday School at the Parish (Parochial) Hall on Karori Road, halfway between Chesney Wold and Karori School, followed by a buggy ride to St Mary's for the early evening service. The children continued to attend church twice on Sundays after the return to Thorndon.

Annie and her sister Belle were both baptised as adults at St Mary's late in 1894, in a joint ceremony with baby Leslie.[30] Harold was a vestryman, rarely absent on Sundays; brother-in-law Fred Waters served as the choirmaster. Services could be memorable. Alexander Dasent, the whiskery, half-deaf vicar who baptised Annie, blew noisily on the pages of his sermon to separate them, whacking the pulpit as he did so. The elderly Dasent presided by blending charisma with bombast. The parish history tells of a child who, after a sermon at St Mary's, was prodded by a religious relative: "'Did you see God?' "Yes, I think I did," came the reply, "but he looked very much like Mr Dasent."'[31]

Fresh air and religious worship appeared to shake the Beauchamps out of mourning, even helping awaken an interest in politics. It is possible to imagine Annie Beauchamp in Chesney Wold as a person of presence and vigour, not the shrinking, housebound soul portrayed in her daughter's fiction. New Zealand women won the right to vote in 1893, the year the Beauchamps moved to Karori. I discover that Annie not only joined but was also elected secretary of a group of 25 Karori women working to ensure women enrolled to vote in that year's election.[32] Harold, meanwhile, chaired political meetings on behalf of the Liberal Party, even hosting Premier Richard Seddon and his young children for afternoon tea. He, too, was thriving, batting for Karori's Second Eleven cricket team on Saturdays. A lifelong committee man, Harold also found time to serve as president of the Wellington Horse Parade Association, which held leaping contests in the grounds of the Kilbirnie Trotting Club.[33]

Chesney Wold attracted a succession of visitors, especially Annie's sister Agnes Mansfield, husband Fred, and sons Eric and Barrington, who lived at the other end of the valley. Katherine Mansfield gives a sharp portrayal of visits by the male cousins fictionalised as Pip and Rags Trout: 'The Trout boys had often spent the day with the Burnells in town, but now that they lived in this fine house and boncer garden, they were inclined to be very friendly.'[34]

⁊

There's a telling 1898 photograph of the Beauchamp family in the back yard, a corrugated fence behind them. Kathleen and her mother, side by side, look ready to fly at each other. Annie forces a smile, but her daughter stares down the camera. The unblinking look – what Rose Ridler, the Waters' domestic help, described as 'a penetrating gaze which disconcerted grown ups' – is clearly visible.[35] Perhaps there's a hint of these family dynamics in 'The Little Girl', when a parent snaps: 'Don't stare so, Kezia. You look like a little brown owl.'[36]

To what extent can we tease out other biographical clues, such as the fact that Kezia stutters, particularly around her father? 'She never stuttered with other people – had quite given it up – but only with father, because she was trying so hard to say the words properly.'[37] At nine Katherine Mansfield's self-confidence wasn't improving: she filled out and looked squat alongside her older sisters, especially willowy Vera. She'd later lament, '[W]hy was I stuffed – why wasn't I given lean meat and dry toast – so that I looked less like the Fat Girl from Fielding [sic]. Even my curls were like luscious fried sausages.'[38]

The story 'Maata', however, portrays a character apparently using food to suppress feelings – a sign of what might today be diagnosed as an eating disorder:

> *She cut some rounds of bread, buttered them thickly and spread them with jam, and ate, stuffing her mouth full, washing it down with milk … The same battle was fought every morning between her violent bodily hunger and a wavering sense of shame.*[39]

Does a jibe over weight explain a testy exchange between Kathleen and her Aunt Belle, the Beryl character in 'Prelude', recorded by Tom Seddon during a visit to Chesney Wold?:

The Beauchamp family, 1898. Back: Vera, Jeanne, Kathleen and Annie Beauchamp.
Front: Charlotte, Margaret Isabella Dyer and Leslie. Young Kathleen had 'a penetrating
gaze which disconcerted grown ups'. (Rose Ridler) Photographer possibly Harold Beauchamp.
Ref: 1/2-031204-F. ATL.

*[She] had been doing some mending of the Beauchamp children's clothes. She
held in her hand a skirt of Kas's which she had been altering or mending, and
said 'Kas's skirt – the shape of a potato sack.' I don't think she meant to hurt
Kas's feelings. But a black look darkened Kas's face ...*[40]

In 1898, the Beauchamps departed as the lease expired. But Chesney
Wold would become the most sinewy, fully realised setting of the writer's
childhood and resonates through her fiction. As the protagonist in 'Her
First Ball' awaits her debut at a central-city dance hall, she yearns for the 'old
house': 'And the rush of longing she had had to be sitting on the veranda

of their forsaken up-country home, listening to the baby owls crying "More pork" in the moonlight, was changed to a rush of joy so sweet that it was hard to bear alone.'[41]

Chesney Wold was sold in 1899 after Lancaster died. The new owners enclosed the veranda and removed the gables. The result was the elegant two-storey Italianate mansion with the wide, street-facing upstairs balcony commonly seen in photographs relating to the writer. The alterations didn't stop there. The new owner struggled to find a single-family tenancy, eventually expanding the house into four flats. By mid-century it was badly run down, with three large families reported to be in residence. In 1953 a visiting council inspector found one toilet floor rotted, piles decayed, the roof leaking. An order for demolition was served.

From this time onwards, Katherine Mansfield's name animated all attempts to preserve Chesney Wold. The Historic Places Trust stepped in, calling the house a literary shrine. The Dunedin-based owners agreed: 'Karori has grown around it – through it – from it. Karori needs it. Is it not time the old house spoke in its very own defence? What lead then is the great big Wellington Capital City giving to those who would preserve national antiquities, by ordering KM's favourite home to be destroyed?'[42] The council backed off.

Chesney Wold, however, was crumbling away; its owners neglected to maintain it. Pat Lawlor drew attention to its state in his 1959 review of Beauchamp residences, claiming the family 'would weep if they saw it today'.[43]

> *Like a monstrous giant, a malformed macrocarpa tree extends its stunted arms over the front of the house. Most of the doors swing open to the four winds, the doorsteps are rotten and crumbling, and half the windows are shattered … There were gaping holes in the floor, the yellowed wallpaper was sagging from the roof, old furniture, torn and tumbled, was scattered around each room; on the floor a multitude of newspapers … Desolation upon desolation in every room and there seemed so many of them, more, when I mounted the rickety stairs.*[44]

Lawlor painted Katherine Mansfield's occupancy as a link in a romantic chain of happily roaming Karori youngsters:

Nature had left that little boxwood hedge, referred to so lovingly in 'Prelude'.
The old camellia trees were extant. I did not see 'The Aloe' tree, but perhaps it
is still there. Nature is striving, so it seems, to hold a few precious memories
intact. I saw hope even in the gaunt macrocarpa, even though it looked
forbidding. Apparently children did not find it so, for nailed in neat regularity
up its most massive trunk were a series of steps to a rough haven above.[45]

A builder then stepped in, buying and rehabilitating the house in the early 1960s by converting it into four flats. By 1980, the house was dilapidated all over again. Another, more ambitious, buyer came to the rescue. Today, the internet site Best of Property displays 'before and after' images of this handiwork. The accompanying text states: 'The house captured the imagination of a young man. He purchased the property. And he defied the experts. For he understood the spirit of the place.'[46] The renovation, carried out in a style that might be called 'conquistador meets Liberace', included Spanish-style arches and embossed, throbbing wallpaper of brown and maroon, with dashes of gold and silver. A carpeted staircase the colour of pomegranates, and tipped with a wrought-iron balustrade with Inquisitional flourishes, flew up to rooms where the Beauchamps slumbered a century earlier.

As the twenty-first century arrived, the Mexican ambassador moved in. Current homeowner Julia Rowling, grinning, describes this phase of redesign as 'bordello'. All traces have since been erased. As I leave, I note the staircase of polished native timber, a feature of the latest, more austere makeover. Yet I can just make out Katherine Mansfield sprawling on a chaise longue in the livid bordello.

The McKelveys, South Karori, 1910. Left to right, Elsie, Zoe, Thomas and Annie:
'On the day that Mrs. MacKelvie came to wash, the mistress of the house was likely to
drift down to the wash-house to listen, while the fat red arms splashed in and
out of the foaming tubs, and the voice rose and fell.' (Ruth Mantz)

Photographer unknown. Karori Historical Society.

Nine: The washerwoman's children

I saw Teacher's face smiling at me, suddenly – the cold, shivering feeling came over me. – Katherine Mansfield[1]

Pitiful Lil and 'our' Else Kelvey leave an indelible trail through 'The Doll's House'. Lil shows up at school wearing a ludicrous concoction cobbled together by her washerwoman mother from the hand-me-downs of more privileged classmates:

> *[Lil,] a stout, plain child, with big freckles, came to school in a dress made from a green art-serge table-cloth of the Burnells', with red plush sleeves from the Logans' curtains. Her hat, perched on top of her high forehead, was a grown-up woman's hat, once the property of Miss Lecky, the postmistress. It was turned up at the back and trimmed with a large scarlet quill. What a little guy she looked! It was impossible not to laugh.*[2]

Sister Else is just downright peculiar:

> *[She] wore a long white dress, rather like a nightgown, and a pair of little boy's boots. But whatever our Else wore she would have looked strange. She was a tiny wishbone of a child, with cropped hair and enormous solemn eyes – a little white owl. Nobody had ever seen her smile; she scarcely ever spoke.*[3]

At playtime, the Kelveys are shunned and sneered at. Some parents even bar their children from talking to them. After school, while all the other girls take their turn to visit the Burnell sisters' perfect doll's house, it is clear that this offer cannot possibly be extended to the Kelvey girls.

The world that Katherine Mansfield drew on was Karori School, where the Beauchamp girls began their education. In 'The Doll's House' she describes school as a social melting pot:

> *[It] was not at all the kind of place their parents would have chosen if there had been any choice. But there was none. It was the only school for miles. And the consequence was all the children of the neighbourhood, the Judge's little girls, the doctor's daughters, the store-keeper's children, the milkman's, were forced to mix together.*[4]

And so it was at Karori, where all the children of the valley were thrown together.

It's long been part of the Katherine Mansfield story that a real Kelvey family lived locally. Mansfield's first biographer, Ruth Mantz, described a washerwoman named Annie MacKelvie. I'm keen to find out more about the McKelveys (the correct spelling of their name), perhaps to learn more about why Katherine Mansfield featured the family in 'The Doll's House'. What I don't expect to discover is that the real McKelvey girls may themselves have been an object of envy for her.

Pinning down the family history after all this time proves surprisingly easy. Upstairs at the Karori library are filing cabinets conveniently labelled 'Karori History', material lovingly gathered by the local historical society. Here in manila folders lie the reminiscences of an aged McKelvey aunt, along with written descriptions of the damp South Karori Road where the family lived in the 1890s. A genealogical website, 'Descendants of William McKelvey', provides more clues: an extensive family tree reveals not just parents Annie and Thomas McKelvey, but their three daughters: Lily Maud, Zoe Violet and Elsie Ada Annie.

The same Lily Maud was a contemporary and fellow classmate of Kathleen Beauchamp. She and her little sister Elsie Ada lived with their parents and sister in a cramped, poorly ventilated worker's cottage a 15-minute walk southwest of Chesney Wold, where the road drops into a cold river valley. They'd pass the Beauchamp house every day on the long trudge from South Karori to school.

So what were the similarities between the real-life McKelvey family and the grotesque characters of 'The Doll's House'? While the fictional father is mysteriously absent, even perhaps in jail, the record shows that Thomas McKelvey was a beekeeper and jobbing gardener who regularly helped out at Chesney Wold. He was a man popular, even loved, in the valley.

Annie McKelvey at 40 (extreme right), pictured at South Karori with brother-in-law Samuel (centre), his children and a friend. Ref F-173817-1/2. ATL.

Mrs Kelvey makes her fictional debut in the story 'Autumns I':

… every Monday morning, to the round open space in the middle [of the 'wild' orchard], the servant girl and the washerwoman carried the wet linen: grandmother's nightdresses, father's striped shirts, the hired man's cotton trousers and the servant girl's 'dreadfully vulgar' salmon pink flannelette drawers jigged and slapped in horrid familiarity.[5]

The real Annie McKelvey was an intelligent, vivacious woman who supplemented the limited family income by taking in washing for wealthy households. She was a cheery presence at Chesney Wold on Mondays, boiling up the Beauchamp girls' blue pinafores in a copper heated over an open fire and ironing the family's clothes. She also became a prominent local identity, as Mantz explained:

> She was amusing, and a great talker. Everyone hired her; she knew everything and everyone, and talked to all alike. One of the reasons she was given such free range was that she was either too witty or too wise to gossip indiscriminately. She told a good story and people were always repeating her philosophic comments on life. On the day that Mrs. MacKelvie came to wash, the mistress of the house was likely to drift down to the wash-house to listen, while the fat red arms splashed in and out of the foaming tubs, and the voice rose and fell.[6]

The circumstances of her arrival in the valley are chilling. Annie Howe, a Cockney from the London borough of Enfield, was born in 1855. She'd been orphaned and raised a strict Anglican by an uncle. Still unmarried by her early thirties, she fell victim to subterfuge:

> In the year 1887 she went to Plymouth to board the SS Doric. She thought she was going on a day trip, but when they were out of sight of any land, she realised this may not be so. She went to see the Captain and was told that a second-class passage to New Zealand had been booked and paid for her, and her luggage and sewing machine were in the hold. On arriving in New Zealand she was met by two ladies, and lived in Wellington for three weeks before being married to … Thomas McKelvey who lived at Karori, Wellington.[7]

Within months, Annie was pregnant with Lily, born in March 1888, seven months before Kathleen Beauchamp. Elsie came in 1890; Zoe, believed to be mentally disabled, was born a year later.

Kathleen first encountered both McKelvey parents at her home, as a pre-schooler. Then she and Lily were enrolled at Karori School.

Late nineteenth-century New Zealand has been described a 'world of children', with more than two out of five of the population aged under 15.[8] Demand for compulsory, free and secular education had only risen since a law in 1877 required colonial 'urchins' to attend school. Working-class families like the McKelveys were encouraged not just to send their children to primary school but to keep them there.

In 1895, Kathleen and Lily were just two of 38 new entrants at Karori School, and among 593 new entrants across the Wellington district.[9] Vera and Charlotte Beauchamp were already enrolled.

I'm consulting a Karori School logbook from the time. It spans a quarter-century of school attendances, illnesses, the state of the weather and the punishments meted out to the naughtiest.

Imposing order on the Karori children in the mid-1890s were three teachers, two of them women. Headmaster Henry Dyer was a disciplinarian who had joined teaching after a farming career. A pupil recalled:

> Mr Dyer was a master of the old school with sound ideas about hammering in the 'three R's' and no nonsense about it … he appeared in my child's eyes to be a very gruff and grim old man accompanied by a wholesome smell of tobacco smoke. He always dressed in a double-breasted coat like sea captains wore, with a broad cravat with a pin in it. In school, from the left-hand pocket there projected a supplejack polished by frequent use to a rich golden colour.[10]

Classrooms were lit with kerosene lamps in the darker winter months and heated with open fires. The building had long windows oriented to the west, allowing in a small amount of sunshine. Infectious diseases thrived in this cramped, unventilated setting, and pupils and staff regularly fell ill, especially during winter. The logbook records that in 1893 the school closed for weeks after an outbreak of measles. When the illness returned in the spring, there was 'hardly any attendance'.[11] An epidemic of whooping cough the following year afflicted a teacher for weeks.

The young Kathleen appears to have been sickly and prone to chest and abdominal infections. A former schoolmate remarked on her early propensity for catching colds, resulting in frequent absences from school.[12] Did she later fictionalise her poor health in the story 'Mary'? '[Mary] had a continuous little cough. "Poor old Mary's bark", as father called it.'[13] Either way, it did not bode well. A local doctor who'd known her through music and who'd noted her regular bouts of chest inflammation commented in later years: 'She's doomed [...] You know how often pleurisy spells T.B. later on.'[14]

♫

A Miss Olds was the girls' first teacher in the infant class. She joined the staff as an apprentice 'pupil teacher'. These poorly paid, overworked and undertrained teachers have been described as 'the mainstay of many classrooms, particularly for younger children' in the nineteenth century.[15] Qualifications for the job were minimal: passing the Standard Five exam and being aged over 13. Recruits were apprenticed for five years, teaching during the day and receiving instruction at night. Miss Olds didn't stay: the logbook shows her quitting after a year.

The school day was regimented. In 1894 all infant classes across the colony followed the same teaching regime by the letter and to the minute. At 9.25 Kathleen and Lily would have joined their classmates in two-by-two tiered desks on a low gallery, built up on flat wide steps where Miss Olds stood. Their day began with 10 minutes of physical exercises and ended with drawing classes. Interspersed with 20- to 25-minute periods of arithmetic, reading, spelling and writing were three sessions of 'vigorous' singing. Between 11.25 and 11.45, the children picked up pencils to write on slates. A pupil from the time recalled:

> ... a fair proportion of slates at any one time were frameless or had some broken edges. Slates had advantages over paper ... But they were cold and soon became greasy ... Each of us was expected to provide a cleaning rag and a bottle of water with a pierced cork for the purpose of cleaning our slates ... if we could get away with it we would breathe and or even spit on the surface and then wipe away the moisture with our sleeve.[16]

The timetable was broken up with morning and afternoon breaks and a 75-minute 'luncheon' recess – 'the dinner hour', as it is called in 'The Doll's House'. The Burnells dined on 'thick mutton sandwiches and big slabs of

Johnny cake spread with butter'.[17] After eating, girls and boys streamed to their respective playgrounds: the girls at the rear of the main building; the boys to the north in an area facing Karori Road. Facilities were minimal: swings for the girls, and wooden parallel bars and a fly pole for the boys. This thick pole was capped with a revolving iron plate on which a dozen iron rings each supported a three-metre rope that ended in a loop. One boy at a time would 'fly' high into the air while a dozen others ran in a circle.

Lunchtime in the segregated girls' playground constitutes a crucial scene in 'The Doll's House'. Here the fictional Isabel 'held quite a court under the huge pine trees', gushing about the newly acquired doll's house. It is here too that Isabel and her friends Emmie Cole, Jessie May and Lena Logan round on the Kelveys. Katherine Mansfield had remembered her childhood classmates well. The logbook rolls show three girls in Kathleen's Standard One class with identical first names: Emmie Brogan, Jessie Cathie and Lena Monaghan.

Reading and spelling followed lunch. Like her classmates, Kathleen learned from a dog-eared school copy of the British Royal Reader series, famously distributed to every junior reader in the Commonwealth. Beginner readers started with single letters and letter combinations. From there, they progressed to sentences, starting with two-letter words. By the time Kathleen was learning to read, the Royal Reader featured selections from Dickens' novels, along with flowery English ballads and poetry.

An 'object lesson' followed the mid-afternoon recess, when pupils were at their sleepiest. This revolutionary teaching method involved holding up and discussing 'real' objects such as an apple or a plant. It was seen as positively exciting compared to traditional repetition or 'rote-learning' of multiplication tables, verse and the like.

∽

Kathleen Beauchamp probably didn't know it, but she began her education in the grounds of an old lunatic asylum. The committee overseeing Karori School's 150-year commemorations toyed with calling their publication *From Madhouse to Schoolhouse*.[18] And though she never made reference to this previous function, a chill seems to hang over another depiction of the setting in 'A Married Man's Story': 'School was a tin building, stuck on the raw hillside. There were dark red streaks like blood in the oozing clay banks of the playground ... And it is always cold.'[19] At the time she and Lily McKelvey were taught here, traces of a high perimeter fence used to confine patients were still visible.[20] Were these the 'tarred palings of the boys' playground' in 'The Doll's House'?

The Karori Lunatic Asylum, the colony's first psychiatric institution, became notorious as the place where the matron struck the patients.[21] Mental-health services in the early decades of European settlement were primitive by today's standards, with patients, many suffering from dementia or alcoholism, receiving little treatment beyond having the key turned on them. But Karori's asylum sounds especially unpleasant. A new facility reopened in a more central location when Karori School took over the site in 1875.

The school's first parent committee thought it unlikely that children could flourish in a grim place. For years they fulminated about pupils being taught in the dilapidated ward block where patients once occupied windowless cells. As pupils filed into the repurposed school, described in one report as 'gloomy and unpleasant',[22] officials insisted the site was suitable. Parents were outraged.

The authorities eventually relented: a new school building emerged in 1881 on the clay ramparts bounded by Donald Street and Karori Road, where the main block stands to this day. Pupils entered through a porch where hats and coats were hung. A washroom was provided to remove the mud and mire from children like the Beauchamps and McKelveys who'd trekked long distances. One pupil recalled the boys' playground as 'nothing but a greasy slope in winter'.[23]

In November 1895 Kathleen Beauchamp concluded her infant year. Pupils celebrated the break-up with what the logbook calls 'the usual cakes and tea'.[24] In the New Year she returned to school, a Standard One pupil under Miss Annie Lockett. Karori-born Lockett was a seasoned teacher, first apprenticed at 15. Year on year, she taught Standards One to Three in the same room, each class divided off by thick black curtains.

Kathleen and Lily now entered the education system proper: their year was an extended preparation for springtime exams. They'd be expected to read and spell simple words of one and two syllables, write on a slate, take dictation and count up to 100. And they'd face Inspector Robert Lee, a former British headmaster and stalwart of the Wellington Education Board. Lee came twice yearly to Karori School: once to examine the pupils; the second time unannounced. The headmaster's performance, too, came under scrutiny. The entire inspection process was rigorous and unnerving:

> The inspector generally arrives at about 11am, calls up the classes in their turn beginning with the lowest, and hurries them through a little reading and spelling. After he has disposed of the lower classes, the next undergoes a very short and sharp examination in reading. If a child fails a single word, stops in the wrong place, or passes over a comma, that child is immediately turned down, in some cases with a sharp rebuke.[25]

Lee showed up in the spring of 1896, and once again headmaster Dyer strove to show the setting and the pupils in their best light:

> The afternoon before the great day was a holiday, for the building had to be scrubbed out, and boys had to go into the bush to gather wild clematis and ornamental creepers … the next morning all turned up in their Sunday best. The inspector was Mr Lee, a man of truly Gladstonian dignity. The only means of transport in those days was by Mr Joe Spiers' buses, and Mr Lee arrived in the first bus from town at about 11 o'clock. He was met at the corner by a bevy of girls, who escorted him and his bag to the school.[26]

The inspector sat down to work, examining 141 pupils one by one, including Kathleen Beauchamp and Lily McKelvey (wrongly named Lillian in the logbook). The process ran over two days. Attending to Lee's stomach appears to have been a critical exercise for the headmaster:

> Rumour has it that many a man's academic career depended on that dinner and the tenderness of the roast duck. On the second day we were called to our rooms, and Mr Lee, sitting at the master's desk and looking over his spectacles, passed a few remarks on the work generally. Then came the great moment. Speaking in slow and solemn tones, Mr Lee read the list: 'Thomas Jones has

School Inspector Robert Lee, 1916: 'a man of truly Gladstonian dignity ... [he] arrived [at Karori School] in the first bus from town at about 11 o'clock.'

Photograph by S.P. Andrew. Ref: 1/1-014258-G. ATL.

passed.' 'William Smith – has passed – a strong pass.' 'John Williams has not passed.' The ceremony ended with the announcement of a holiday.[27]

The logbook records that Miss Lockett's class performed especially well. Kathleen, too, impressed Lee: he judged her second equal with Jessie Cathie, and passed 19 of their 20 classmates, including Lily McKelvey, though she was well down the list. The *Evening Post* recognised their achievement.[28]

℈

Kathleen at eight was reading widely, sneaking books to bed, reading by candlelight in her bedroom upstairs at Chesney Wold. The result was that she strained her eyes, and her parents had her fitted with round spectacles with gold wire rims. We can take a guess at what she was reading from Education Board records that suggest the shelves in the Karori School library included *Longman's Fairy Tales*, *Alice's Adventures in Wonderland* and *The Blue Fairy Book*. Other respectable standbys included *A Christmas Carol* and *Macbeth* and *As You Like It*.

Lily McKelvey meanwhile appears to have struggled with the rigours of Mr Lee's examination process during 1897, remaining in Standard Two for a second year. From this time on she'd be a year behind Kathleen (herself not present for that year's exam, according to the logbook, but allowed a pass anyway). Lily was soon to demonstrate her writing abilities in other ways.

Kathleen's second year with Miss Lockett did not go smoothly either. The teacher later recalled her as 'a plump, self-possessed little girl with bright alert brown eyes, always very amiable and well behaved'.[29] But she was already challenging her teacher's authority. There's a story about how Miss Lockett rebuked a boy for dozing at his desk. Kathleen leapt to his defence, explaining 'that he was forced to rise at three o'clock each morning to help with the family milk delivery'.[30] He escaped a caning.

Miss Lockett is remembered as pedantic about clear enunciation. She forced the less articulate to wear a Dunce's hat made of newspaper, a punishment common in colonial classrooms. Kathleen Beauchamp responded with a cheeky limerick:

Old Mother Lockett is full of conceit:
She struts about on her pigeon-toed feet.
Old Mother Lockett by this time must know
If conceit were consumption
She'd be dead long ago. – Kass.[31]

In later years, Miss Lockett admitted she'd struggled to contain Kathleen: 'When she first began to put her thoughts into words, her pencil literally ran away with her and she had to be restrained and taught to put her facts into shorter sentences so as to conform to the stereotyped lower school essay.'[32] If Kathleen was showing aptitude as a writer, Karori School was yet to publicly acknowledge it.

Which brings us to the curious case of 'A Sea Voyage', her long-lost, much-remarked-on essay. Biographers still credit her with winning the 1897 Karori School composition prize for the essay she apparently wrote that year about a trip to the Sounds. Despite its never having been located, it is routinely cited as her literary debut.[33] It is not surprising. One of Katherine Mansfield's earliest stories, 'The Great Examination', concludes with a prizegiving.[34] Another, 'Mary', is about the selfless heroine giving the coveted prize to her sister.[35] And before her death, Katherine Mansfield made a joking reference to that apparent success during her third year at school, signing off a letter to her husband with: 'Prize scholar, English Composition, Subject: A Sea Voyage, Public School Karori.'[36]

The *Post*'s summary of the 1897 school prizegiving, however, shows the overall Composition Prize for Girls going to Vera.[37] The logbook, meticulous in recording all things, confirms the eldest Beauchamp daughter as the recipient. Was Katherine Mansfield's claim of winning the prize an elaborate fiction founded on sibling envy? Was the parental pressure *that* intense?

Charles Dickens, removed from school by his parents at 12, was famously traumatised by the spectacle of seeing his older sister Fanny win a prize: 'The tears ran down my face. I felt as if my heart were rent. I prayed, when

I went to bed that night, to be lifted out of the humiliation and neglect in which I was. I had never suffered so much before.'[38] In later life, Katherine Mansfield, too, was furiously competitive.

ℒ

This chapter ends where it began: with the McKelveys. It appears that despite their difficult economic circumstances, Lily and her sister Elsie were studious Karori School pupils, both proficient in English composition. Their mother Annie remained ambitious for them, spending part of her earnings on painting instruction. The material in the Karori Library describes how Lily would always have a fire going as soon as she got her sisters home from school 'because Thomas would look for smoke from the chimney as he came home from work'.[39] Many other anecdotes suggest material poverty:

> [Lily] used to love her father taking her and her two sisters dressed in long muslin dresses, long haired and [in] pretty sashes into Wellington on his days off, and they would do a little shopping. As the years went on, Lily noticed that her father could not buy much, and it was usually just a bag of lollies …[40]

But I am astonished to discover what the pair achieved during Kathleen Beauchamp's final year at Karori School. Of all people, it was Lily McKelvey who won the writing prize in Standard Three.[41] Elsie took the Standard One writing prize the same year.

Lily's successes didn't end there. Like the Beauchamp girls, she attended the Sunday morning Bible class at the parish hall on Karori Road. The *Church Chronicle and Official Gazette for the Wellington Diocese* notes that in 1898 Lily won third prize in a competition for the best essay about the children's monthly sermon.[42] We don't know whether her classmate Kathleen entered, but records show that Harold Beauchamp put up the prize, so it is likely to have been discussed at home. Could a miffed Katherine Mansfield, in later life, have wreaked some kind of retrospective literary revenge on behalf of her younger self?

Lily then drops from view: the genealogical website records how Karori School 'was disappointed' when she left school early to work in an

Lily McKelvey and husband Sidney Thompson on their wedding day, 1908: '[Lil] … a stout, plain child, with big freckles, came to school in a dress made from a green art-serge table-cloth of the Burnells', with red plush sleeves from the Logans' curtains.' ('The Doll's House'). Photographer unknown. Karori Historical Society.

office.[43] She became a teacher and worked in the Marlborough Sounds before marrying and raising 10, possibly 11, children in Masterton. She continued to paint and in later life entered a competition run by the Kensington School of Art in London. Money in the family home remained, as ever, short. A daughter recalled: 'She did not win the prize, but was very highly recommended to do a course with them [Kensington School of Art]. Unfortunately we could not afford this, but she told her daughter-in-law Doris that she cried when she did not win because she needed the money so badly.'[44]

$$\mathcal{Z}$$

In the second term of 1898, the Beauchamps quit Karori School and were enrolled at a girls' school in Thorndon. Within months of Kathleen's arrival, Wellington Girls' High School had identified her writing talents, publishing her first story, along with a paragraph of fairly mild praise:

> *This story, written by one of the girls who have lately entered the school, shows promise of great merit. We shall always be pleased to receive contributions from members of the lower forms.*[45]

They were words she'd cling to. She'd also find that literary glory can be short lived: her essay in a competition promoted that year by the Society for the Prevention of Cruelty to Animals was merely one of 14 highly commended.[46] Worse, Vera Beauchamp was one of the others.

Chesney Wold in its encircled valley setting, late nineteenth century. Partially obscured by trees (right) is the adjacent home of farmer Stephen Lancaster.

Photograph by James Francis Meadows: Ref: PAColl-7949-15. ATL.

Ten: Their heads in the buttercups: Karori trail

℘

I'm outside the gates of Chesney Wold. It's a shivery grey dawn. Emptied wheelie-bins, lids flipped by the wind, line the footpath. The odd pinstriped office worker in sneakers and dangling earplugs pads past on the long march to the city.

The Beauchamp girls in their hats, ironed pinafores and leather boots with buttons up the side, set off from here through open country to Karori School, almost three kilometres away. I'm retracing one of their midwinter walks in 1896, when Kathleen would have been in her second year at school. I'm hoping to learn what she and her sisters *took in* as they tramped Karori Road, a boggy pathway encircled by 'gorse golden hills'.[1] I'm following a way into her past, hunting for signs of passage. I'll be lucky. Days of rain in July made the track so muddy that Mrs Beauchamp insisted that Karori Borough Council furnish a proper footpath. Her letter to the little municipality is documented in the minute books. At Wellington City Archives I read of the decision of 16 July 1896 to refuse Mrs Beauchamp's request.[2] Councillors, however, agreed to a small metalled section by Monaghan Avenue, halfway to school. We'll be there shortly.

Vera and Charlotte were seasoned ramblers by the time Kathleen started school. Annie Beauchamp insisted her daughters walk every day. Only if it poured would Pat Sheehan fire up the buggy. Karori Road was built to rigorous specifications, say the council minutes: 'formation of 14 feet in width with 12 feet in metal at a depth equal to 9 inches in the centre and 3 inches at the sides, with sufficient culverts to carry off all storm water'.[3] That

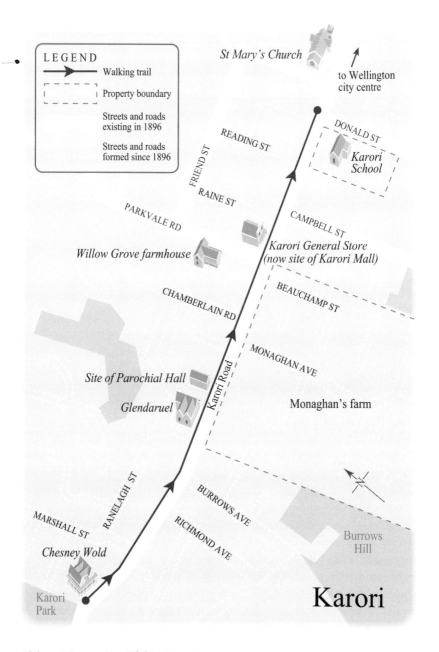

LEGEND

→ Walking trail

Property boundary

Streets and roads existing in 1896

Streets and roads formed since 1896

St Mary's Church

to Wellington city centre

DONALD ST

Karori School

FRIEND ST

READING ST

RAINE ST

PARKVALE RD

CAMPBELL ST

Willow Grove farmhouse

Karori General Store (now site of Karori Mall)

CHAMBERLAIN RD

BEAUCHAMP ST

MONAGHAN AVE

Site of Parochial Hall

Glendaruel

Karori Road

Monaghan's farm

RANELAGH ST

BURROWS AVE

MARSHALL ST

RICHMOND AVE

Chesney Wold

Burrows Hill

Karori Park

Karori

wasn't easy. Runoff made mush of the roadway; borough metal scattered or drowned. On rainy days, water exploded in great silver necklaces down bare Karori hillsides, strewing mud, stones and debris across its ancient valley floor, overwhelming the stream that bisected it. That made the road a long, dreary quagmire, especially on a winter's day like the one I'm imagining in 1896. The girls had to work hard to avoid getting caked in mud.

We'll squelch through the middle of a bowl-shaped valley, a scrawny pastoral landscape being consumed by soaring groves of scented gorse. Farmlets separated by wooden fences occupied the paddocks on either side of Karori Road. Sheep and cattle grazed around their owners' timber cottages. Pine, wattle, broom, sharp bramble and other introduced plants competed with the gorse, flourishing where tōtara, rimu and kahikatea once stood. Colonial explorer and artist Charles Heaphy wrote that the podocarp forest here contained 'the finest timber in the vicinity of Port Nicholson. From one spot in this valley I counted fifty trees around me that would each make a top for a large vessel.'[4] One local man built his four-room whare from a tōtara with a circumference of 1.5 metres.

Sections here, part of the New Zealand Company purchase of 1840, had been quickly released to intending settlers. Ngāti Tama never rated the location; Karori was only a place to pass through on the way to the west coast where food was more predictable. Tribal parties en route to Makara might, however, forage at a famous bird tree:

> … a tall and spreading pine, up the trunk of which they had fastened a ladder of bush vines. The bird-hunter would station himself in this tree, with his long spear or his snares, especially in the morning, and never failed to secure a good bag of kaka or pigeon.[5]

When the Beauchamp girls walked here in the mid-1890s, a thousand people inhabited the valley. Today Karori is home to fifteen thousand; cars crawl in a slow stream into the city, the place locals still call 'town'. Karori Road itself is unrecognisable from the photographs of the rough track of the 1890s.[6] Google Satellite images, however, confirm the road follows the same line in the land; the street grid plan laid down in London by the New

Zealand Company in the 1830s remains intact. The same green hills hem in the walker; the same little Karori Stream gurgles beside the road.

⸎

I squeeze the stopwatch button on my cellphone and take a step east. 'The Doll's House' tells how the three Burnell girls 'brushed through the thick buttercups at the road edge'.[7] I shut my eyes, picturing leather boots plunging into mud, raising scents of wild sage, soft bracken, wet blackberry. The council minutes for July record that roadman Bradnock rolled up to fix a torrent pouring into Chesney Wold. He buried a wild tributary deep. His culvert, a box of solid tōtara, then gave out. Called back, Bradnock instead laid brick pipes.[8] I find myself imagining the roadman laying the 'big red drainpipe by the side of the road' where Lil and Else Kelvey pause at the end of 'The Doll's House'.[9]

As I set off, a rainbird's cry competes with the whir of petrol engines. In 'Prelude', Kezia Burnell awakens to a dawn chorus of introduced species: starlings, whistling mynahs, goldfinches and linnets. A holdout tūī 'sang his three notes and laughed and sang them again'.[10] Native birdlife had mostly scarpered. For settlers planting wheat seed among the stumps, the outstanding problem was the native parakeets. Describing kākāriki as vermin, one local smallholder rejoiced that the 'troublesome' flocks stealing seed from his pastures were quickly cleaned out.[11]

On Karori Road, some 20 metres east of Chesney Wold, what is now Tringham Street drops away to the left. Here the stream is piped below the road, surfacing 100 metres later in the middle of Karori Park. In 1937, a geologist presenting a paper on the valley called it 'a strikingly youthful stream', despite its having been here for millennia.[12] From here, the waters course through the long South Karori valley, out into Cook Strait.

As a 1960s schoolboy I hung on the fence above the Tringham Street tunnel, spat in the water, dropped ice-block sticks. The same waters had floated on through the grounds of Chesney Wold, where a wading barefooted Kathleen Beauchamp trapped squishy things. Her solitary world is echoed in an early story, 'My Potplants': 'If I ever did catch one I always put it in a glass jam jar filled with water and carried it home to keep till it should grow into a whale.'[13]

The Karori Stream was alive with British tadpoles by 1877, noted the *Evening Post*, apparently satisfied with this amphibious dimension of the colonisation project:

> *A good deal has been said about a frog which jumped into Mr Tustin's window on Sunday last … we now learn that Mr Ebenezer Baker, about three years ago, brought five frogs down from Auckland and let them loose at Karori. That 'rural retreat' is said to be swarming with them now.*[14]

The road still runs parallel to the eponymous stream that glides unseen, 30 metres and three rows of houses away, beneath the dank ferny ridges above Ranelagh Street. Teams of workmen with picks spent half a decade here in the 1880s, slicing the terracotta clay hills for the last 120 metres of Karori Road. By 1893, as the Beauchamps arrived, the road was 'formed'.

Seven minutes have passed. To our right stands tall Burrows Hill, from where water and muddy debris smother the road. It is permanent marshland, where no walker can pass without mud stains. In 'Prelude', Katherine Mansfield describes 'a swamp of yellow water flowers and cresses'.[15] Water undermines the soft rutted clay, endangering the coach service that ran to Makara Hill. Bradnock returned to dig roadside trenches to help stem the torrent.[16]

By summer, Bradnock's ditches will have dried out. Enclosed by dock and other greenery, they'll draw dreaming youngsters like Kathleen Beauchamp: warm, shady bowers, corridors to another world. Years later, John Middleton Murry even drew on his wife's memory of these ditches to affirm his love:

> *Don't say you're out of touch with me. Then I feel you are that little girl who used to walk home from school to Karori in the ditch. You are completely hidden in the dock-leaves – and I can't see you anywhere. I have to call: Wig-Wig! Where are you?*[17]

At the foot of Burrows Hill I clock 10 minutes. Thickets of gorse block our way: in 'Juliet', Katherine Mansfield writes how the plant 'spread like a thick green mantle'.[18] Alarm over its dispersal hovers above the council minutes. The stuff vanquished the entire colony, all because an early resident, Judge Henry Chapman, was determined to carve an English garden out of his bushy Karori hillside. In 1844 he sent home for furze (gorse) seed, later boasting: 'I have 2 little furze bushes in my garden. They are about as big as this letter and are a great treasure.'[19]

⅃

Then and now, gorse rules the valley. By 1960 my parents had swapped the rickety house behind the petrol station for a north-facing section on Burrows Hill. For six years I walked from here to Karori School. Gorse encircled our tiny weatherboard house. My childhood was a long-running feud with prickly giants. After a day's gorse cutting with my father, our hands were covered in punctures; I'm convinced quills remain inside my fingers. On top of the hill, beyond the prickle zone, a path led to what we kids called 'the back', a vast reserve of secondary growth soaring several hundred metres up to Wrights Hill. It was our refuge from sarcastic, sometimes violent parents, a hillside garden tangled with shaggy-trunked ponga, māhoe, haukawakawa, coiled cables of supplejack to haul on, and rooftop streaks of crimson rātā above calm trails scented with leaf mould. Prickle-stemmed bush lawyer and tall stinging nettle grew, but they struggled: the thick canopy choked out sunlight. All I knew of birdlife was the occasional tremulous cry of the riroriro, known as the rainbird. One miraculous day when I spied a pair of kākāriki flashing against the dominant green, Mum telephoned the Dominion Museum.

Katherine Mansfield evoked the same scrappy, secondary-growth bush in the 1908 story 'Rewa':

> She climbed quickly, catching at trees and branches, wrenching her hand. A long arm of lawyer pulled her skirt – the leaves brilliantly scarlet, the plant looked as though it had fed on blood. Sticking to the supplejacks, almost swinging herself upwards. And at last the top was reached and the bush behind.[20]

Vera, Charlotte (as Tom Thumb), Kathleen (as Mrs Tom Thumb) and Jeanne,
dressed up for a Karori Parish Hall performance, 1896.
Photographer unknown. Ref: 1/2-028645-F. ATL.

Bruce Glensor knew Burrows Hill as well as my brother and I did. He
scanned the same South Karori dawns described in 'Prelude': 'sharp and
chill with red clouds on a faint green sky'.[21] He ducked the same poisonous
karaka berries Katherine Mansfield called 'Dead Man's Bread' in the poem
dedicated to her brother.[22] Like us, Bruce was a paper boy, who collected
his warm bundles of the *Evening Post* from the Tringham Street depot near
where the Karori Stream vanishes beneath the road. He was shambling, a
bit slow-witted, but no one ever dared have Bruce on about being adopted.
We often found him skylarking up the back, and shared food or insults. His

strict Presbyterian family lived in a weatherboard house at 375 Karori Road, a few doors across from Chesney Wold; he slept in a shed outside. He built things: crystal sets, even a homemade pistol. My brother remembers, 'Yeah, he made a gun, it was a .22 single shot.'

The whole depot knew he left the valley from time to time: there were stories of trouble with the police, spells in borstal. We knew he'd lugged four-by-two planks onto Burrows Hill to build a rough watchtower high in a kahikatea tree. We even climbed the nailed hand-holds; swayed there nervously and downed tinned pineapple from the cupboards at home. One day I met Bruce on the hill with a round-headed blond guy. They'd escaped from borstal. If I told anyone, I'd be dead. They prodded me to their camouflaged 'bivvy', half-heartedly tied me up, fired airgun shots around me. Let me go. I was 11 but not remotely frightened; said nothing to my parents. Next to my dad, Bruce was a kitten.

℘

My stopwatch records 14 minutes. The girls approach the mid-point of the walk. From here they can hear the pealing of the first school bell, rung five minutes before a second ring signalling the start of classes. If they can hear the hand bell from here, they're late and can expect a scolding. 'The Child-Who-Was-Tired' touches on the emotion triggered by the sound of the school bell: '"Hurry, hurry! the second bell's rung," she urged, knowing perfectly well she was telling a story …'[23]

At this point, Karori Road rises, the valley opens out. At number 316, on the northern side of the road, stands Glendaruel, a pit-sawn timber cottage built in the 1870s on a ridge above the stream. It was first a farmhouse, then home to the architect who gave his name to Burrows Hill. The homestead, with its six-paned sash windows and veranda, means we're almost at the parish hall with its bright white fence where the Beauchamp girls attended Bible class on Sundays. They'd call it a community centre now, a place to attend 'entertainments': musical concerts, recitations and the like.

In 1896, Karori churchgoers pondered whether to allow dancing in the hall. The Anglican bishop called the idea improper: '… it ought to be obvious to anyone who reflects on the subject.'[24] More genteel activities continued. A photo taken inside the hall shows a young Kathleen Beauchamp dressed in a 'Mrs Tom Thumb' costume, with a grandmother's cap and an antimacassar apron over her long black dress.

By Eagle Street is a two-room settler's cottage that is practically antique by the time the girls pass by. Today Anoush hair and beauty salon, with its bright red awning, occupies one half. On the southern side of the road, where modern-day Monaghan Avenue stands, is the deepest, sloughiest Karori Road 'marsh', the one that Annie Beauchamp complained of. Here, where the road met William Monaghan's farm, water sluiced in torrents. The culvert still leaves a visible dip in the road. The girls sidle along the footpath Mrs Beauchamp has won for them, trying to keep their skirts from trailing in the mud.

Will Kathleen's classmate Lena Monaghan and her brothers appear? Her companion shielded her from schoolyard taunts about her weight. Years later she'd write of Lena:

> To me, it's just as though I'd been going home from school and the Monaghans had called after me, and you – about the size of a sixpence – had defended me and p'raps helped me to pick up my pencils and put them back in the pencil box ...[25]

After Katherine Mansfield became feted, Lena's mother confided that her daughter's mud-caked pinafore barely lasted two days. She still resented how Annie Beauchamp managed to furnish her daughters with a clean dress every day.[26]

⅊

As we approach central Karori, site of today's small and dingy mall, the valley floor flattens out. In the 1840s a blacksmith's forge operated opposite where the mall now stands. This was Karori's heart, a hub, a gathering place for social and commercial life. On the rise ahead, the school is visible. The Beauchamp name was enshrined here early: in 1906 after the family's return to the city, Harold led a subdivision development, his surname appended to its main street.

Like other colonial byways, Karori was a walking community in 1896; the highway belonged to the pedestrian. But roaming, sometimes charging stock remained a constant threat. The Beauchamp girls often met cattle, sheep, even the odd snuffling pig escaping poorly fenced farms. No wonder Kezia Burnell says in 'Prelude', 'I hate rushing animals.'[27] A fellow walker to Karori School recalled:

> What with dodging through wire fences to avoid mobs of unruly cattle being driven from Makara and being diverted by flocks of sheep en route to the city, it took us all our time to reach our objective to hear the hand bell rung for 'School's in' … we had to run the gauntlet of Johnston's bull ranging along the fence on one side and lowing herds of cattle pawing expectantly on the wires of the opposite fence.[28]

Katherine Mansfield later wrote of accidents involving horse-drawn vehicles and speeding, whip-cracking drivers. In 'Carnation', Eve 'saw the wheels of a carriage … propped up, clear of the ground, spinning round, flashing scarlet and black, with great drops glancing off it'.[29] Carriage driver James Tarr, neighbour to the Beauchamps and sometime Karori mayor, ran down and almost killed Lady Onslow, the governor's wife, as she walked on Karori Road in 1889.[30] Tarr was summonsed for 'furious driving'.[31] Lady Onslow was lucky. Accidents, even deaths were common on Karori Road. A young schoolgirl was knocked senseless when the horse pulling her buggy reared up, overturning the vehicle and sending the occupants flying.[32] A man driving a timber wagon was fatally crushed. Mayor Tarr, caricatured as a mad, greedy colonial in the early Karori story 'Old Tar', himself died on this road in 1905 after falling under the wheels of his buggy.[33]

The girls have arrived at the junction of Parkvale and Karori roads, where the two-storey Karori General Store and Bakery sold currant buns for a penny. It also served as the borough post office. Daily postal deliveries began here in the mid-1890s. A bright blue ANZ bank branch stands here today, next to a Flight Centre and a dry cleaner.

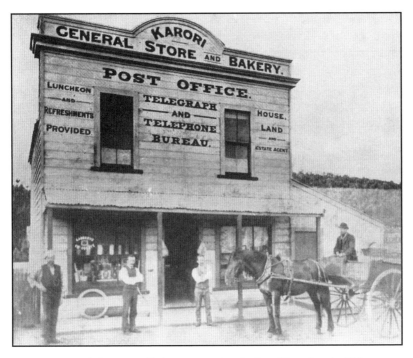

Newcombe's store and bakery, corner of Parkvale and Karori roads, 1893.
Photographer unknown. Ref: 1/4-016214. ATL.

Across the road stood the Karori library, built in the late 1850s and well known to the girls. A boxy, two-storey library with bustling café is not far from the original site; by its entrance is a foundation stone commemorating Mayor Tarr, the furious driver.

Long and flat, Parkvale Road hosted the valley's most intensive agriculture by 1896. Here piggeries and chicken farms were jammed in cheek by jowl. One original farmhouse, Willow Grove, with its steep-pitched roof and sashed windows, remains today near number 11.

Katherine Mansfield sounds wistful when she writes in 'Prelude' of how 'from the paddocks of either side [of the Karori road], there streamed the milky scent of ripe grass'.[34] She wasn't talking about stinky Parkvale Road.

♀

Just on 25 minutes after our departure, the second school bell sounds. As the girls take off, I dally at the foot of Church Hill, by the junction of Campbell Street. High on the ridge to the southwest stands Wrights Hill where Bruce Glensor and I scrambled as children. I'm transported back to 1970, the year I enrolled at university, took a flat in the Aro Valley. Bruce was still living in Karori, married with a child. I'm back to a Thursday in April 1970, visualising him up there in silhouette, tearing through the trees with a gun, still running. The *Evening Post* reported:

> *Police tonight shot and killed 22-year-old Bruce John Glensor in front of the pretty 17-year-old girl he kidnapped last night ... Glensor abducted the girl, Julie Campbell, from her home in Karori, while holding her parents at the point of a shotgun. For most of today, more than 100 police, many of them armed, scoured Karori ... In the evening, police were told Glensor was hiding, and 65 of them surrounded his house. After two hours, Glensor, armed with the shotgun and a pistol, emerged from the house ... He called out, 'I will bring the girl – but I want to die.'*[35]

That night, I poured my heart into verse, devastated to learn such wild horror could erupt on our sedate hills. The valley darkened, took on an aspect of gloom. For me Katherine Mansfield snared something of this dull geography in 'A Married Man's Story':

> *Big crushed-up clouds press across the sky; the rusty water in the school tank is frozen; the bell sounds numb. One day they put a dead bird in my overcoat pocket. I found it just when I reached home. Oh, what a strange flutter there was at my heart when I drew out that terribly soft, cold little body, with the legs thin as pins and the claws wrung.*[36]

I haul myself up the hill. As I pass number 225 on the southern side of Karori Road I stop, remembering from daily walks to school a silver-grey wormwood bush with its distinctive, hateful scent. Further up the road opposite the school gates stands St Ninian's Presbyterian Church. Preacher Denzil Brown's interminable sermons were part of my Sundays as a child, though I was baptised at St Mary's. Years later I learn he ministered to the Glensors that night: 'The night Bruce was killed was one of unrelieved anguish for his parents, Tess and Tom Glensor. Throughout it all Denzil Brown kept vigil with them, an amazing example of pastoral compassion.'[37]

❧

I've been lost in my thoughts. The girls are now 100 metres away, bustling to reach the school gates in time for the final 9.25 bell. One, the shortest of the three, looks bigger from here than the others. A pupil of the time noted the same phenomenon: 'Every morning for several years I used to meet Kathleen Beauchamp (Katherine Mansfield), a fat little girl, trailing along about a chain (20 metres) behind her sister.'[38]

Our walk is over. My stopwatch clocks 30 minutes on the dot from Chesney Wold to Karori School.

> … by the time they had reached the tarred palings of the boys' playground the bell had begun to jangle. They only just had time to whip off their hats and fall into line before the roll was called.[39]

Mrs Agnes Waters, circa 1890s: '... a perfect martyr to headaches. Whole days she spent on the drawing room sofa with the blinds pulled down and a linen handkerchief steeped in eau de cologne on her forehead.' ('The Aloe')

Photographer unknown. Ref: PA1-q-246. ATL.

Eleven: The bride wore black

Wellington East: a Thursday afternoon in the spring of 1882. Guests spilled out of the rimu pews of St Mark's, the wooden church with the Gothic spire by the Basin Reserve sportsground on the foothills of Mt Victoria. At the altar Katherine Mansfield's aunt, Agnes Mansfield Dyer, 23, awaited her groom. Family, friends, bridesmaids rustled. A reverend, in surplice and purple gown, loitered. The choir, shepherded by a half-bearded, sad-eyed man in wire spectacles, fanned out. On the dot of 2pm, the organ music swelled. Just then a carriage drew up. Its passenger leapfrogged the wooden steps, dropped through the open door, whispered to someone on the threshold. As the tidings buzzed above the pews, the bride sank. Guests picked their way out. A doctor with a black leather bag was summoned.

Neither the Beauchamps nor the Dyers – nobody, for that matter – ever talked about *exactly* what happened at St Mark's that day. It was altogether too terrible. Katherine Mansfield and her sisters learned only in later years that groom-to-be William Lewis had jilted Agnes. And that Frederick Waters, the bespectacled choirmaster, eventually ended up as what might today be called the relief groom. But Katherine Mansfield forever savoured this family mystery. And if she never quite managed to solve it, she'd merrily fictionalise its aftermath.

Aunt Agnes was easy meat. In Katherine Mansfield's hands she became Doady Trout, a stricken, half-depressed Victorian matron, a sitter for a pre-Raphaelite painting. In 'The Aloe', she's

*tall and pale with heavy eyelids that drooped over her grey eyes, and rare,
slender hands and feet … a perfect martyr to headaches. Whole days she
spent on the drawing room sofa with the blinds pulled down and a linen
handkerchief steeped in eau de cologne on her forehead.*[1]

Doady is also a closet writer. 'The Aloe' pictures her as a creator of
melodrama:

*… she made up perfect novels with herself for the heroine, all of them ending
with some shocking catastrophe … These dreams were so powerful that she
would turn over buried her face in the ribbon work cushion and sobbed [sic].
But they were a profound secret – and Doady's melancholy was always put
down to her dreadful headaches …*[2]

Could anyone but Agnes be the depressed Mrs Potts, afflicted by 'one
of her mysterious pains',[3] who savages her attentive, doting husband in
'A Man and his Dog'?

*'You only do it because you have to. Don't contradict me. I can see you grudge
doing it' … But the sound of these words frightened her so terribly that she flung
back on the pillow and sobbed, 'Robert! Robert!' Robert was the name of the
young man to whom she had been engaged years ago, before she met Potts …*[4]

ᵶ

So what did happen to cause the bride to collapse at the altar that day? I
type the name Agnes Dyer into the digital newspaper site Papers Past. The
story, lost in a stack of musty newspapers for 133 years, emerges at the click
of a mouse. Here is 'Wedding Tragedy in Wellington', the story of William
Lewis, the groom who cut his throat as the wedding march played:

*Mr Lewis, who has been working very hard for two or three months past, arose
yesterday in his usual health and spirits and continued in a very cheerful
state until one o'clock, at which hour he retired to his room for the purpose
of dressing himself for the approaching ceremony, in which he was to figure
so conspicuously. As the time drew near for him to proceed to the church, his
mother became uneasy at his non appearance, and at length she entered his
apartment, where, it is said, a sad spectacle met her gaze … doctors were
unable to state whether the patient will recover …*[5]

The story, sensational because Lewis belonged to 'Society', was beamed by telegraph around the colony. One South Island newspaper reported: 'Since Friday, the city has been full of rumours as to the injury.'[6] Another speculated that the 28-year-old assistant Crown solicitor was already married. The *Thames Star* suggested Lewis was having a relationship 'of a peculiar nature' with his housekeeper.[7] Much was made of the bride's 'severe shock ... her comatose condition ... Miss Dyer, who is a fine strapping girl ... would have made him an excellent wife.'[8] Lewis did in fact recover, though doctors committed him to a 'private lunatic asylum' and he later quit the colony.

ℒ

We know little of the courtship between the jilted bride and the choirmaster, Frederick Waters, but the events of that day almost certainly precipitated it. The couple wed at Thorndon's St Paul's Cathedral early in 1885, and rented a house in nearby Hawkestone Street, not far from their Beauchamp in-laws. Agnes bore two sons: Eric and Barrington (Barrie).

Waters loomed large in Katherine Mansfield's early life. He'd joined the Postal and Telegraph Department in Greymouth as a clerk, rising through the ranks at its head office in the capital. He was also a busybody, pedant and inveterate letter writer, remembered later for snatching horse manure off the Karori Road for his garden.[9]

Like the Beauchamps, the Waters were raising toddlers in Thorndon during the long epidemic of infectious disease. The family couldn't afford a flushable water closet, and depended on nightmen with horse and cart to carry away their nightsoil. Frederick Waters found these house collections costly and especially resented the charging procedures. At City Archives I discover his revealing, darkly hilarious exchange of letters with the council:

> I must ask you to move the council to protect me from the systematised robbery to which I am at present subjected by the nightsoil contractors ... They charge sixpence for one bucket and simply ignore their obligations. I protest against this ... My receptacle is a four gallon [15 litre] iron bucket. I have measured: that is to say a contract bucket three gallons and a third of another. Plainly

therefore I can never owe by possibility more than three and a third each time. The receptacle is never full: there is never a contract bucketful …[10]

Waters explained his attempts to negotiate with the contractors directly:

I have told these men I am willing to pay more than I even owe: fivepence, equals two contract bucketfuls, for each cleaning, and now they are not satisfied. They are on the contrary, I state my case, violent. They hold your auditing powers as lightly as they do me and my money. I do not want them to scatter their wretched makeshift time: let them do their work cleanly, that is properly. And they satisfy me and my closet. I send you my last bill …[11]

In time he was promoted to chief clerk, and he remained with the Post and Telegraph Department for his entire working life. Waters' true love, however, was singing; his solo baritone, heard at choral festivals around Wellington, was widely admired. He'd lead the choir at St Mark's Church long after the wedding tragedy.

At Easter 1893, in tandem with the Beauchamps, the Waters left for Karori, taking a modest house in Hatton Street at the city end of the suburb, several kilometres from their relatives. Katherine Mansfield called it Monkey Tree Cottage after a monkey puzzle tree in the front garden. Agnes Waters, like her sister Annie, had 'delicate' health and suffered from what would probably today be diagnosed as clinical depression. She too relied on others to assist with childrearing. The Waters' saviour was orphan Rose Ridler, whom they took in as a domestic helper. She stayed with the family for life.

As he had done at St Mark's, Waters served as choirmaster at St Mary's Church, close to the family's Hatton Street home. Katherine Mansfield places a character with an uncanny resemblance to her uncle in 'A Man and His Dog':

At the tail of the procession came Potts in a cassock so much too large for him that it looked like a night-shirt and you felt that he ought to be carrying not

Frederick Waters, circa 1900: 'Wherever he was there was a party ... he loved to get up little theatricals for the children and he seemed to have boundless delight and energy for everything.' (Ruth Mantz). Photographer unknown. Ref: PA1-o-453. ATL.

a hymn and a prayer book but a candle. His voice was a very light plaintive tenor. It surprised everybody. It seemed to surprise him, too.[12]

Waters also relished being a father:

The house simply rang with his gaiety when he was at home; and it seemed an empty shell – without even an echo – in his absence … his real life was lived in his hobbies. He had two. One was music … his other hobby was gardening – or perhaps it was his excuse for playing with his children … they flocked over, when they saw him in the garden, all ready to ride on the barrow, or on his back. The three little Beauchamp girls would drift in, dressed alike in galatea blouses, white or striped; and blue smocked jumper dresses … great times the children had with him in the paddocks. Wherever he was there was a party.[13]

A parent with a similar brand of effervescence is seen in 'The Little Girl':

… the Father with the 'baby Mac' on his shoulders, two little girls hanging on to his coat tails – ran round and round the flower beds, shaking with laughter. Once they saw the boys turn the hose on him – turn the hose on him – and he made a great grab at them, tickling them until they got hiccoughs.[14]

Katherine Mansfield fictionalised her cousins as Rags and Pip Trout, older cousins to the Burnells in 'Prelude' and 'At the Bay'. 'Pip was tall for his age, with lank black hair and a white face, but Rags was very small and so thin that when he was undressed his shoulder blades stuck out like two little wings.'[15] These boys are close enough to be familiar to Kezia and her sisters but visit rarely enough to be a novelty. The Trout boys provide gender ballast to Katherine Mansfield's Karori and Eastbourne stories.

We'll see more of Uncle Frederick splashing about as the free-spirited Jonathan Trout of 'At the Bay'. Here he is favourably contrasted with Stanley Burnell, an obvious representation of the writer's fretful, driven father. Trout embodies a more relaxed approach to life:

Jonathan stayed a little longer in the water. He floated, gently moving his hands like fins, and letting the sea rock his long, skinny body. It was curious, but in spite of everything he was fond of Stanley Burnell. True, he had a fiendish desire to tease him sometimes, to poke fun at him, but at bottom he was sorry for the fellow … To take things easy, not to fight against the ebb

The Waters and Beauchamp families, Chesney Wold, 1898. Left to right: Agnes Waters, Charlotte, Leslie, Fred Waters, Eric Waters (Rags Trout), Kathleen, Jeanne, Harold, Annie (Vera and Barrie Waters absent). Ref: 1/2-044572-F. ATL.

and flow of life, but to give way to it – that was what was needed. It was this tension that was all wrong. To live – to live! And the perfect morning, so fresh and fair, basking in the light, as though laughing at its own beauty, seemed to whisper, 'Why not?'[16]

Trout is even pictured as a singer, a man who performs 'with such fearful dramatic intensity that the meanest hymn put on an unholy splendour'.[17]

In 1921, after completing the story from her sickbed, Katherine Mansfield compared Jonathan Trout, and by extension Frederick Waters, to a figure in a Cézanne painting: 'One of his men gave me quite a shock. He's the spit of a man I've just written about, one Jonathan Trout. To the life. I wish I could cut him out & put him in my book.'[18]

The story's Mrs Trout appears as something of a failure on the domestic front – a fatal flaw for a 'New Woman' of the late Victorian era: 'The Trouts were for ever running out of things and sending across to the Burnells' at the last moment.'[19] Agnes Waters, however, seems to have had some strengths in the kitchen; Rose Ridler kindly recalled that Mrs Waters 'could make soup with her eyes shut'.[20]

❧

Frederick Waters may have enjoyed life but he struggled to support Agnes, effectively an invalid. He compensated by continuing to compose outraged letters to newspapers and local and central government bodies. I locate at least a dozen in the files.

Alarmed at hearing what appears to have been a single audible swear word on the Karori bus, he summoned police to the suburb to probe 'the larrikinism … becoming uncomfortably prominent'.[21] Investigating constables who duly concealed themselves in the bushes around St Mary's noted that Mr Waters gave 'a much milder account' when interviewed in person. He addressed 'the fowl house nuisance … invading our peace in Karori … I wish to provide myself with ammunition preparatory to an attempt on my part to stalk it.'[22] Spitting on trams made him incandescent: 'Last evening an old fellow next to me in the Karori tram spat eighty-seven times in three sections. Imagine what the lady next to me had to carry her skirts over – I assisted her to hold them up – when she got out.'[23]

Sanitary matters in particular preoccupied him:

> *Since, for my sins, I am obliged to come to work on a Saturday morning I have to submit to be smothered in dry dust swept from shops, or otherwise have to walk in the middle of the road. Is dry dust sweeping on pavements allowed? Citizens should not be at the mercy of lazy sweeps … This morning I was the victim of a very flagrant instance. A man swept across the pavement in Panama Street a good sized waste paper basket full of paper, dust and ends of tape with the unnamed filth which such jetsam collects, right against me, trusting to the wind to carry the stuff about and to leave him unidentified.*[24]

Other correspondence shows a streak of humour. One lengthy exchange, seeking a permit for a pair of possums (then strictly prohibited), also highlights his devotion as a parent: 'I want them as a present for a boy of mine. If you will kindly issue a permit … to supply me, I need hardly assure you that you will not be jeopardising any other living creature good or bad.'[25]

Then came World War I and, in its aftermath, a global influenza pandemic that killed 757 people in Wellington City alone. Kathleen's sister Vera Beauchamp returned from England infected with the virus, passing it on to Waters. Their father, Harold, caught it too, but beloved Uncle Fred died aged 58.[26] He was widely mourned. The *Evening Post* wrote: 'A man of ability and conscientious application, the late Mr Waters was recognized as a public officer of sterling worth, his strict integrity, courtesy and general efficiency making an example that was acceptable as a standard.'[27] He was buried in the decaying graveyard on the sunny northern side of St Mary's, memorialised by a pair of stained-glass windows.

Agnes lived on at Hatton Street for a further 18 years, Rose Ridler at her side, before joining Fred in the church cemetery, together with their son Barrie. The Waters remembered Rose generously, leaving her a piece of land at Hatton Street and enough money to build her own house on it.[28] Her headstone, too, lies in the shadow of St Mary's.

Part Four

Drowned cottages, Saunders Lane, in the flood of 1893. The Beauchamp residence is on
the skyline (left): 'They were mean little dwellings painted a chocolate brown.'
('The Garden Party')

Photographer unknown Ref: MNZ-1348-1/2-G. ATL.

Twelve: Moon at the top of the stairs

… one must go everywhere; one must see everything.
– 'The Garden Party', 1922

Number 75 Tinakori Road is a phantom mansion, hovering above six lanes of highway enclosed by high, ivy-draped cement walls. The Ministry of Works demolished the house for a motorway in 1968. All that's left today is a line of scruffy pōhutukawa along a grassed roadside. A shiny information sign on legs directs motorists to Karori. But it was a grand residence when the Beauchamps moved back to Thorndon in 1898.

The departure from Karori was bittersweet: Harold Beauchamp recalled the five years there as the happiest of his life. As a farewell gesture the family hosted a lavish fancy-dress party at the parish hall, attended by hundreds of locals in costume. When the Karori Historical Society interviewed resident Edith Miller in the 1970s, she still recalled the fun she'd had that day at age seven:

> We went as 'Kate Greenaway' children, wearing white frocks down to the ground with artificial roses all around the bottom and mobcaps also covered in roses. We were very sorry to say goodbye to the Beauchamps because we thought there would be no more parties![1]

The new house in Tinakori Road was a fitting address for a 'show' family taking its place among the city's *crème de la crème*. By 1889 Harold Beauchamp was a full partner in merchant William Bannatyne and Co., and had a seat on the Wellington Harbour Board. He had succeeded in giving his family the stability and security he'd badly lacked as a child. City fathers, eyeing him up as a future mayor, even agreed to his suggestion of naming a Thorndon byway (Burnell Avenue) after his wife.[2] And it was clear he'd officially joined the wealthy elite of the city when he demanded – and received – a council rates reduction.[3]

Beauchamp was a rising man. As a personal acquaintance of Premier Seddon and a son of a former Liberal politician, he had close association with the government of the day. There were important social links, too: Seddon and his children had called on the Beauchamps at Chesney Wold. In 1897 the Premier's daughter Phoebe married Annie's brother Frank Dyer, another senior Bannatyne employee, in what was seen as the wedding of the year. Seddon appointed Beauchamp to the board of the ailing Bank of New Zealand a year later.

At 40, then, Katherine Mansfield's father was already a baron of colonial finance and banking, which was concentrated in the capital. A man this powerful (and rich) needed suitable surroundings in which to entertain. It was therefore not surprising that he took over the lease to the grand house from one of a succession of bankers who lived here. With its three entrances (one each for family, visitors and tradespeople), the 75 Tinakori Road residence announced that the Beauchamps had 'arrived' socially. Katherine Mansfield described how the solid iron gates 'clashed and clamoured when Bogey [Leslie] and I tried to swing on them'.[4] In her story 'Sisters', her protagonist eyes 'the florid butcher spanking past in his yellow cart'.[5] It was a privileged, more rarefied place than Chesney Wold.

Tinakori Road, stretching from the gates of the Botanic Gardens to the Beauchamps' original home at the harbour end, was centrally located, just five minutes by carriage to town. Horse-drawn hansom cabs clattered past and gathered at a stand outside the Shepherd's Arms hotel, 200 metres to the south of the new house. It was also the western perimeter of the so-called Sixpenny District, named after the standard cab fare, bounded by Molesworth Street to the north, Vivian Street to the south, and Kent and Cambridge Terraces to the east.

ℒ

The Beauchamp family and others, 75 Tinakori Road, 1898. 'It was a big white painted square house with a slender pillared verandah and balcony running all the way around it.' ('Notebooks')

Ref: PAColl-3320-02. ATL.

Katherine Mansfield came into her own at 75 Tinakori Road. And she also began to write.

To understand how the house and surrounds shaped her, I assemble maps and plans with yellowing bits of sellotape stuck to them, photographs flung in a filing cabinet, faded pamphlets crossed by silverfish and piled in library stack rooms. Here is the reliquary of a white-painted, fine-boned, slender-pillared two-storey house, set well above the road, surrounded by shiny-leaved taupata, purified by sunlight and salt breeze. 'It was high, it was healthy; the sun poured in all the windows all day long,' Katherine Mansfield wrote later.[6] As she and her siblings played in the spacious garden with its lily lawn, tennis court and flower plantings, the setting for 'The Garden Party', Harold entertained the cigar-puffing wizards of colonial finance in the billiard room.

Hand-painted architectural plans at Wellington City Archives show a grand front entrance, a long wide hallway, a master bedroom and dressing rooms, and with formal drawing and dining rooms beyond. Katherine Mansfield recreated the ambience of the place in the 1916 story 'That Woman':

[Aunt Beryl,] Aunt Harrie and Mother sat at the round table with big shallow tea cups in front of them. In the dusky light, with their white, puffed-up muslin blouses with wing sleeves, they were three birds at the edges of a lily pool. Beyond them the shadowy room melted into the shadow ... the cut-glass door knob glittered – a song, a white butterfly with wings outspread – clung to the ebony piano.[7]

Photographs show the house, sheltered behind thick wooden palings and tall hedges, overhung by a massive macrocarpa. Charlotte Beauchamp later recalled

a lovely little dell under the tree ... all shrubs and flowers and so on. It was one of Kathleen's favourite spots. You'd often find her there with a pencil and exercise book, scribbling away at stories ... she was always writing a story ... a friend of hers would often be hidden with her there writing stories too – a Canadian girl named Marian Ruddick who'd come to live in Wellington.[8]

Memories, scents, sounds associated with the house lingered. And Katherine Mansfield pledged to record them all, famously committing herself after her brother's wartime death to 'tell everything, even of how the laundry basket squeaked at "75" – but all must be told with a sense of mystery, a radiance, an afterglow because you, my little sun of it, are set'.[9]

As she recalled in forensic, anguished detail time spent with Leslie, six years younger (and invariably more compliant), the spacious hilltop house and garden become enshrined in her diaries as a bower of childhood bliss:

> *Do you remember sitting on the pink garden seat. I shall never forget that pink garden seat. It is the only garden seat for me. Where is it now. Do you think we shall be allowed to sit in it in heaven. It always wobbled a bit & there was usually the marks of a snail on it. Sitting on that seat, swinging our legs & eating the pears.*[10]

She'd later fasten on the interior of the house, sharing memories with her sister Jeanne:

> *I remember everything … the dining room at [number] 75 to the proud and rather angry looking selzogene [a device for producing carbonated water] on the sideboard, with the little bucket under the spout. Do you remember that hiss it gave & sometimes a kind of groan? And the smell inside the sideboard of Worcester sauce and corks from old claret bottles?*[11]

Upstairs, at the top of a long wooden staircase, lay half a dozen tall-ceilinged bedrooms. 'By Moonlight' describes a climb up the stairs, 'the moon shining through the top landing window … the moonbeam fingers on the bannisters'.[12] The younger girls shared one of these first-floor bedrooms, its windows set so high 'it was like being on a ship'.[13] From here, Kathleen could look down on the harbour and the hills soaring to the east, a view now blocked by tall buildings and separated by a motorway trench.

She described what she saw from up here as dawn rose above the harbour:

> *Four o'clock. Is it light now at four o'clock? I jump out of the bed and run over to the window. It is half-light, neither blue nor black. The wing of the coast is violet; in the lilac sky are black banners and little black boats manned by black shadows put out on the purple wave … Oh! How often I have watched this*

hour when I was a girl! But then – I stayed at the window until I grew cold – until I was icy – thrilled by something – I did not know what.[14]

Beyond the carved wooden front door with its brass knocker, down the concrete steps and out of the gate, lay a less certain world. To the south, a hundred metres along unsealed, manure-strewn Tinakori Road, was the spacious St Paul's Sunday school and church building, once located near what is now the main northbound motorway turnoff. The Beauchamp girls, having attended morning service at St Paul's in Mulgrave Street, joined the throng here on Sunday afternoons to give their 'collects' (short prayers) to the young, glamorous superintendent, Mrs Eliza Balcombe Brown.[15] To get to Sunday school, however, they scurried, hand in hand, past the slum cottages where the poor lived. It was a location Harold Beauchamp tried to shield his children from.

⁊

The light and dark of Thorndon is woven into Thomas Ward's 1892 street map of Wellington. A masterclass in Victorian meticulousness, the map took this surveyor and civil engineer three years to complete. Along with all the buildings, houses and boundaries, street lamps, fireplugs and even individual outdoor lavatories are visible. There's the Beauchamp mansion on Tinakori Road – 12 rooms, long verandas and indoor water closet – smack in the middle of a spacious section. The house to its right is equally large. Directly across the road, tiny cottages are shoehorned into strips of land.

The Beauchamps had dropped into the middle of what city planners now call a 'mixed use' neighbourhood: a mixture of light industry and residential housing, wealth and straggling poverty. From an elegantly turned upstairs balcony, Katherine Mansfield could peer down at another world. She wrote: '... just opposite our house, across the road, there was a paling fence & below the paling fence, in a hollow, squeezed in almost under the fold of a huge gorse-covered hill, was Saunders Lane.'[16]

The lane was named after wealthy contractor Joseph Saunders, whose large house nearby is visible on the Ward map. He assembled eight cramped, rickety cottages on a patch of unstable land behind his house.

Here, 15 families shared a single outside lavatory. Saunders was an early arrival who acquired several acres of land between Tinakori and Grant roads, by the foot of Ahumairangi. He prospered, a prominent contractor and scavenger (rubbish collector), builder of a score of roads around the city. He was also ready to leverage serious housing shortages in the inner city.

The dank, unhealthy atmosphere of Saunders Lane clings to Katherine Mansfield's Wellington stories. Houses at the foot of Ahumairangi lose the sun early, especially during winter, causing what despairing locals still call the 'Thorndon dark'. This absence of sun and warmth is evident in 'The Garden Party': 'It was just growing dusky as Laura shut their garden gates … down below in the hollow the little cottages were in deep shade.'[17] The same story tells of a visit to the family of a dead man who had lived in one of the neighbourhood's 'poky little holes':

> They were little mean dwellings painted a chocolate brown. In the garden patches there was nothing but cabbage stalks, sick hens and tomato cans. The very smoke coming out of their chimneys was poverty-stricken … Washerwomen lived in the lane and sweeps and a cobbler, and a man whose house-front was studded all over with minute bird-cages. Children swarmed. When the Sheridans were little they were forbidden to set foot there because of the revolting language and of what they might catch. But since they were grown up, Laura and Laurie on their prowls sometimes walked through … They came out with a shudder. But still one must go everywhere; one must see everything.[18]

Like Harold Beauchamp, Saunders was a justice of the peace with a semi-judicial role, a man of standing in the community. He'd presided over the 'Rabbit Burrows' case involving a notorious brothel in Ghuznee Street where prostitutes worked out of sack-covered 'hutches' in a garden. He and fellow justices jailed the proprietors – Charles Estall and his daughters – in 1887, and sent the women's children to reform school. The *Post* wrote of 'Dens of Infamy' and 'Black Slums'.[19]

Was Saunders in any position to sit in judgement? When a downpour hit the city and the tōtara culvert running beneath Saunders Lane gave way, the vulnerability of his wretched cottages to flooding became obvious. A photo from 1893 provides a dark snapshot of Victorian Wellington: distant, cloth-capped figures in a rowboat, their oars idle, float past semi-drowned cottages at right angles to Tinakori Road. The water took days to subside. Church-linked 'benevolent institutions' distributed food, blankets and fuel to victims. But in one formerly submerged house in Saunders Lane a woman was found to have nothing to cover her five children; in another, a woman was wrapping her six children in wet blankets and the family lacked coal to warm themselves.[20] The trustees of the Benevolent Society heard that Mr and Mrs Saunders 'had been very kind to the sufferers'.[21]

ℒ

Katherine Mansfield's father had little tolerance for the poor he was forced to share the road with. The presence of such obvious poverty at close quarters must have been confronting for the great man – and he did not handle it well. He became obsessed with the idle urchins of Tinakori Road who had noisily taken possession of the space below his mansion. At Archives New Zealand I unearth a frothing, mildly unhinged sheaf of correspondence showing how Beauchamp pleaded with police to crack down on 'larrikinism' on Tinakori Road:

> I am subjected to an intolerable nuisance by a band of boys and girls who, nightly, congregate in the street and create a perfect pandemonium. In addition to disturbing the peace of the neighbourhood, by yelling at the top of their voices, they, at times, indulge in bad language, smoke, expectorate on the pavement, skylark, and render themselves most objectionable to passersby ... I now write to you in the hope that something might be done ... this Sunday evening there is an unusually large number of these characters just outside my front door.[22]

The files suggest a prompt official response. Aware of Beauchamp's standing as a justice of the peace and wealthy businessman, police cautioned the parents of some of the noisier children. However, privately they had scant sympathy for Beauchamp, identifying him as 'one of those irritable people to be found in every community'.[23] In fairness to Beauchamp, the contrast with quiet South Karori must have been considerable. In the longer hours of daylight, the Saunders Lane children appear to have turned Tinakori Road into their back yard, chasing, squealing and blowing tin whistles.

Police records profiled the young revellers: 'The offenders are boys and girls whose ages range from 5 to 13 years and the road being the only place to play, their voices no doubt annoy people. Mr Beauchamp's house being in an elevated position would feel the noise more than others.'[24]

On 28 December, days from the turn of the twentieth century, Beauchamp penned a second letter of complaint, showing he'd devoted part of his Christmas to remonstrating in person with the children. Their response was to leave a gift of fresh excrement on his doorway.

> I regret to say the nuisance has not in any way abated. For example on Christmas Day, prior to 8.30, several of these juvenile hoodlums, in addition to creating a perfect pandemonium, committed nuisances on the concrete steps within two of my front gates.[25]

The police were quietly unsympathetic. 'I do not think any person who has been young at some time or another during their lives could take exception to the children,' noted one constable:

> I have been living in the Tinakori Road for the past six months, close to Mr Beauchamp's house, and during the whole of that time I have never seen any reason to interfere with the children playing in the street … their games principally consist of chasing one another across the street, and trying to catch each other.[26]

It's hard to resist contrasting Harold Beauchamp's Scrooge-like behaviour with that of his 10-year-old daughter, whose story 'A Happy Christmas Eve' had recently featured in her school magazine. In Kathleen's fantasy Christmas, the urchins are not to be shouted down or turned away: one and all are to be invited to her family's grand house for food, games and a glimpse of the splendid tree. Is she having a dig at him? She quotes her fictional father:

> 'I wonder if they have come,' said Harold to his favourite, Beth, 'do you think they will have?' 'I think so,' said Beth … Such a funny crowd it was that came that night, ragged and dirty, but having a look of curiosity on their faces … The tree was loaded with sweets, fruits and presents and there was a present

for everyone besides the sweets. Then there were games, supper at which the
children ate very heartily, more games, and then they went home.[27]

༄

This was never a happy neighbourhood. Across the road from the
Beauchamps, as the Ward map shows, was the compound of carriers Munt
and Cottrel. Their teams of Clydesdale horses and vehicles were stabled
in a vast yard, and its deep, whiffy manure pits were a target for council
inspectors. Records show that Mr Munt loathed Saunders and his cottages,
constantly complaining to the city council about Saunders' tenants.
Beauchamp, in turn, detested Munt, chiefly because of the 'deadly' gas
pouring out of his sewer. Having moved back to Wellington city satisfied
that a new municipal sanitation system had cleansed the contagious city,
Harold Beauchamp encountered what he considered a fresh threat to his
family. At council archives I discover his claim that sewer gas was polluting
his home:

> *I addressed a memorandum … that a serious nuisance existed in the vicinity*
> *of my premises, 75 Tinakori Road, explained that I had sickness in my house …*
> *I now write to say that the nuisance still exists, and that one of my household*
> *has traced its source today, namely to an escape of gas from a sewer trap*
> *immediately opposite my house. When the wind blows from that direction –*
> *north west – my family and I, therefore, get the full benefit of the poison that is*
> *emitted from this death trap.*[28]

The council resisted the complaint: 'It might be noted that sewer
gas – assuming it to be present – is not dangerous unless inhaled almost
immediately on its escape as the … atmosphere quickly renders it
harmless …'[29] Beauchamp would not accept this explanation.

The occupants of Saunders Lane and its shadowed byways meanwhile
endured these neighbourhood stinks without the benefit of council
reassurances. Perhaps the reputation of this part of Tinakori Road
eventually pricked the conscience of its developer and landlord. Despite
his wealth and standing, Saunders appears to have battled depression and
insomnia. On the morning of 30 May 1906 he bought a revolver and, in the

75 Tinakori Road awaiting the bulldozers, 1968.

Photographer unknown. Wellington Public Library.

shadow of the Palmerston North Post Office, 140 kilometres away, shot himself in the head as bystanders looked on.[30] The Wellington City Council soon stripped his name from this sorry location, changing the name to Little George Street, the name it has to this day.

So much for events across the road. What of the neighbours flanking the Beauchamps? The trials of a mixed neighbourhood were evident here too. Katherine Mansfield describes the occupants to the south:

> ... it was a little trying to have ones own washerwoman living next door who would persist in attempting to talk to Mother over the fence – & then just beyond her 'hovel' as Mother called it there lived an old man who burnt leather in his back yard whenever the wind blew our way ... And further along there lived an endless family of halfcastes who appeared to have planted their garden with empty jam tins and old saucepans and black iron kettles without lids.[31]

The blue-jacketed Stone's Street Directories list the occupants at the time the Beauchamps lived here. The northern neighbour, in his grand dwelling, is named as Frank Allen JP, general manager of an insurance company. On the southern side are three five-room cottages, each with its own outdoor privy. Their occupants' professions identify two of them as likely to have burned backyard rubbish. Isaac Young at 77 Tinakori Road is named as a tanner or leather merchant, as is his neighbour Peter Jensen at number 79. A woman named Mary Wallace lived at number 81. Her profession is not provided but she's described as 'cohabiting' with Frank Cookson, a carter.

Again Beauchamp was fixated on drainage – what he called 'the insanitary condition' of Jensen's house rather than what burned in his incinerator. In another tetchy letter, he informed the council:

> The drainage from no 79 Tinakori Road is at present being discharged upon the footpath, causing great offence to the neighbours – myself and family included. I suggest that you should communicate with the owner of '79' and compel him to abate this nuisance ...[32]

In 1906, some eight years after moving here, Beauchamp sold 75 Tinakori Road to Joseph Mandel, a wealthy Jewish businessman, and his family. The house then became a boarding establishment for Wellington Girls' College, and later residential flats. Mandel's widow named it 'Ledman', an anagram of the family name.

In his 1959 survey of Katherine Mansfield's Wellington homes, writer Pat Lawlor noted of 75 Tinakori Road that 'in aspect it is no longer a theme for the immortal Garden Party'.[33] He lamented:

> The terrain above the fine old concrete gate entrance suggested that a bulldozer had shunted masses of spoil, leaving the job uncompleted. The trees, a mighty macrocarpa predominating, an ancient holly tree and emaciated looking oak, had not been lopped or trimmed for years. The outward aspect of the house is in many ways the same, but has been jig-sawed to meet flat construction exigencies. I went inside the building and saw traces of a fine old home seared, though, with the many partitions and doors, essential for a paying investment in modern flat design.[34]

The damp, rotten cottages had vanished, but in Lawlor's eyes a worse fate had befallen a part of Thorndon sacred to Katherine Mansfield's memory: the hillside had been 'gouged out to make way for the unholy activities of cement and gravel production'.[35]

In 1968 more bulldozers began ravaging old Thorndon. Scores of houses, entire streets and the old city cemetery disappeared as a multi-lane highway was carved through its lower reaches. The Ministry of Works had bought 75 Tinakori Road in anticipation. A spokesman remarked that 'as far as he knew, no one was interested in its preservation'.[36]

The back lawn at 75 Tinakori Road, summer 1898. From left, Leslie, Kathleen, Jeanne, Charlotte, Marion Ruddick and Belle Dyer: three beefy Beauchamp girls and one other, a slender girl in a long white dress.

Photographer unknown. Ref: PAColl-3320-01. ATL.

Thirteen: Fly on the wall

… she looked at me intently and in a low almost tense voice said, 'Do you have parrots in Canada?' – Marion Ruddick on meeting Katherine Mansfield[1]

I'm studying a photograph taken in the garden behind 75 Tinakori Road on a summer's day in 1898, a ragged pōhutukawa in the background. Five children grin for the camera: three beefy Beauchamp girls, their brother, and a slender girl in a long white dress. She's Marion ('Molly') Ruddick, Katherine Mansfield's dear friend and intimate. Aunt Belle Dyer, a picture of slim elegance, sits to the extreme right. Kathleen herself, encased in hot pinafore and thick black stockings, and with unflattering straw boater balanced on her corkscrew ringlets, squats on a garden seat, jammed between siblings. Molly, poised and petite, twinkles for the camera like an envoy from another world.

It was the close of a tumultuous year. Vera, Charlotte and Kathleen were enrolled at Wellington Girls' High School, starting in the second term of 1898 while still at Chesney Wold. On weekdays, the trio climbed aboard the coach and three horses from the foot of Makara Hill for a shuddering, hour-long journey along a steep, winding and muddy road that, in one especially perilous section, required males to disembark and gasp their way to the summit of Baker's Hill above what is now the Karori tunnel. Locals fumed. One correspondent to the *Evening Post* wrote of a 'disgraceful and dangerous' road, of which 'long distances, where the side of the road is most precipitous, are entirely unfenced, or so inadequately as to be no protection whatever'.[2]

The final stage of the journey took the girls down Tinakori Road and across to Hill Street, where they climbed off at Molesworth Street, opposite

Parliament Buildings. From there it was a short walk to the grand wooden school building in Pipitea Street, built across Māori cultivation reserves originally commandeered for a colonial hospital.

At a time when girls' secondary schooling was new, the young, brainy teachers of Wellington Girls' High exemplified the assertive 'New Women' of the day. The headmistress, Martha Hamilton, remembered for restricting the number of male teachers, noted the energised, even driven response of her pupils:

> *Girls are so ambitious, and so hard on themselves that for the sake of gaining a prize, they are willing to lose their beautiful colour and bright looks … It is not the teachers who make these girls work hard. It is the girls themselves; they drive one another.*[3]

As the Beauchamp girls arrived, Wellington Girls' High entered its second decade. Education was booming across the capital: 11 private schools for girls operated locally. Hamilton fretted that Thorndon was too far away from the eastern suburbs, home to much of the city's thrusting middle class. But still they came. The school history relates how 'many walked from Island Bay [eight kilometres away] to Courtenay Place and then along the foreshore to Thorndon, often arriving with their boots and skirts well bespattered with mud'.[4]

Once Kathleen Beauchamp was installed behind an inkpot, she settled, embracing most subjects on offer, including reading, writing, arithmetic, singing, drill and French. Within a few months of enrolling, 'Enna Blake', a slight tale about a schoolgirl's holiday, was written, published and praised in the school magazine, the *Reporter*.

Neither Harold nor Annie Beauchamp was on hand in September to applaud 'Enna Blake'. They were a hemisphere away, enjoying an extended voyage to England by luxury steamer, while the children were left in the care of Annie's mother and sister at 75 Tinakori Road. The couple's eight-month holiday was in part recorded in a shipboard diary kept by 34-year-old Annie, with the occasional contribution from Harold. It is the only diary she is known to have maintained. They mailed it home once RMS *Ruahine* reached London mid-year, keen to keep the family abreast of their experiences. Scholars have noted that each Beauchamp child, except Kathleen, was mentioned therein by name.[5]

Both parents wrote of the beauty and vibrancy of Rio de Janeiro, where they came ashore despite warnings about a looming epidemic of yellow fever. Annie wrote: 'I never remember enjoying a day so much, it was just lovely.'[6] Her happiness was short-lived: Harold caught a nasty dose of fever and for a week was plied with opium. Annie wrote: 'I have been very miserable and anxious … however he is better now.'[7] Other entries highlight how much she was upset by Harold's sickness. Still, she attended the *Ruahine*'s fancy-dress ball. But rather than strut in the bloomers, waistcoat, blue serge jacket and sailor hat of the 'New Woman', as was her original intention, she made a subdued entrance as a 'little girl in short frocks'.[8]

⅃

Kathleen meanwhile was finding her feet in her new school. With the return of her parents came her first genuine friend, Marion Ruddick. The daughter of a Canadian couple who steamed into Wellington aboard the same vessel as the Beauchamps, Ruddick was a unique recorder of Katherine Mansfield at 10. Decades later, she'd craft a 'sketch' of her 18 months in the capital, capturing the privileged world inhabited by both families and offering deft, not always forgiving, portraits of her friend – plump-faced, sweet and sour in turn, with ringlets and round gold spectacles.

The National Library holds the unpublished account, 'Incidents in the childhood of Katherine Mansfield'. It is a well-trodden part of the childhood record: biographers have plucked out Ruddick's choicer observations. Here again is her celebrated cameo of imperious Annie Beauchamp as her children bobbed in Wellington Harbour, having been rowed out to meet their parents' incoming vessel:

> … *she gazed down in a detached way at the group and to my mind didn't seem as overjoyed as I thought she would be after such a long absence. Finally, it was*

to Kathleen that she spoke first, for everyone to hear. 'Well, Kathleen,' she said. 'I see that you are as fat as ever.' And in my first glimpse of Kathleen I saw her eyes flash, and her face flush with anger as she turned away with a toss of her ringlets.[9]

Annie reputedly placated her daughter with a copy of *Elizabeth and her German Garden*. This novel by Great-uncle Henry Herron Beauchamp's daughter Mary, who wrote under the name Elizabeth von Arnim, was a bestseller in England. Kathleen's pride in her own modest publishing success, however, surprised Ruddick:

Kathleen drew me to the book case and producing the last number of the school magazine, invited me to read the foot note, which was to the affect [sic] that this child showed great promise of a literary career and a brilliant future. K looked at me triumphantly.[10]

Ruddick's memoir rewards a close read. Importantly, she confirmed the Beauchamp parents as controlling and disciplinarian: daily dips in cold baths for the children (a common prevention against typhoid, among other things), compulsory matching outfits and hats, even on weekends, and regulation church attendances on Sundays. Neither was Annie alone in having difficulty with her daughter, in turn moody or away with the fairies. Harold, too, was struggling with Kathleen. Ethel Beauchamp, Harold's cousin, noted:

[She] used to irritate her father, and he didn't pay much attention to her. Kass used to sit about in all sorts of positions, dreaming, and he kept at her, trying to make her sit up straight … she was different from the rest of the family and looked different – fat and sallow.[11]

Harold and Annie continued to depend on Margaret Dyer for pastoral care of the children. Ruddick ushers us into the spartan 'day nursery' at 75 Tinakori Road, a room with 'a table, hard chairs and along one wall a bookcase holding some well-worn books'.[12] Here, away from Annie and Harold, Grandma Dyer, brandishing a large brown earthenware teapot, ministered to the children:

Tea was a simple affair of bread, butter, jam and cambric tea – hot water and milk faintly tinged with a pale amber – very pale. Chatter was not encouraged, table manners were frequently corrected and a reply to questions asked was invariably … 'Yes Gran dear' or 'No Gran dear'.[13]

The mealtime gong, which reverberates through 'Enna Blake', was the household enforcer, sounding the serving of dinner for grown-ups and time for the children to begin their homework. At its sound, Ruddick records:

[W]e rushed to the door to watch the house maid pass, the long tails of her cap streaming out behind, as she carried a large dish of breaded lamb chops, each with its frilly petticoat of paper lace, neatly arranged around a snowy mound of mashed potatoes, the whole surrounded with a rich tomato sauce. Groans of envy came up from three of us, only Vera abstaining … the gong was also the signal for play to stop and work to begin and while Vera wrote out her neat exercises, Chaddie vainly tried to learn her spelling and I struggled with pounds, shillings and pence, Kathleen under cover of a pile of books became absorbed in Hans Anderson's [sic] Fairy Tales. Studies ended with the appearance of Jennie, staggering under the weight of a tray laden with cups and saucers, a jug of cocoa and a plate of buns.[14]

Less discipline was enforced at the Ruddicks' residence on Golders Hill, where the family rented a suite in a 15-room mansion. Their host, a Miss Emily J. Partridge, often uttered a world-weary refrain, 'Dear me, how tired I am,' which sent the Canadians into fits of laughter. Ruddick describes her playmate devouring food both richer and more plentiful than at Tinakori Road:

We sat at a table in the huge dining room, which had formerly been the ball room … we were waited on by Bessie, the house maid, to whom life was a perpetual joke. Wearing a stiffly starched apron and cap with long streamers, she plied us with cream buns and thin slabs of bread and butter liberally sprinkled with many coloured 'hundreds and thousands'. Kathleen who enjoyed her food at that time, had two buns and was about to have a third but refrained after a warning look from Vera.[15]

Golders Hill, across from the parliamentary precinct, two minutes from Lambton Quay, was a noted site of European settlement. George Evans, the New Zealand Company's chief judicial authority or 'umpire', built a house there in 1840, naming it after his Hampshire estate. Premier Richard Seddon ensured it was renamed Eccleston Hill to commemorate *his* birthplace. The area became better known as the secluded hilltop abode of the Roman Catholic Church, whose wooden cathedral burned down in 1898 and was replaced with a basilica. The Sacred Heart Cathedral still commands this territory: neighbouring diocesan and parish buildings, St Mary's College and a convent sprawl over a ridge that remains in church hands to this day. The Anglicans are next door.

With its sweeping harbour views, Golders Hill in Katherine Mansfield's day attracted such lofty inhabitants as parliamentarian and sometime mayor Francis Dillon Bell. The Beauchamp girls regularly frequented Bell's vast, hidden and overgrown gardens, entering through a gate in a tall hedge. Here a monkey puzzle tree 'was inhabited by a wicked old witch' and the red-flowered rātā became their 'Fire Tree'.[16]

Ruddick accompanied the Beauchamp girls to Wellington Girls' High. Her memoir records how, on arrival, she removed her coat, hat and walking shoes in the cloakroom, then got into 'house shoes' left at school. After morning prayers in the dark cavernous assembly hall, the girls in the small junior class, including Charlotte and Kathleen, began lessons:

> *The classroom was small with high ceilings and dark wainscoting. It was on the ground floor … A fire burned in a small grate, at which on cold days we were allowed from time to time to warm our fingers … the afternoons were given over to pleasant tasks such as drawing, sewing and poetry. We were often called upon to recite poems we had learned the previous week. One day Kathleen recited one of her own and although it was slightly difficult to understand, we were duly impressed.*[17]

Thanks to Marion Ruddick, notions of Kathleen Beauchamp as droopy or even sedentary at age 10 can be set aside. In the school gymnasium, a wildly physical side emerges. Miss Hamilton would have approved. Her *Reporter* article entitled 'How to be Strong and Handsome' urges pupils to keep fit: to run, play and laugh. She helped promulgate progressive

Moturoa Street, Thorndon, circa 1890s, showing Wellington Girls' High School, the grand wooden school building in Pipitea Street, built across Māori cultivation reserves.

Photographer William Henry Whitmore Davis. Ref: 10x8-2091-G. ATL.

'bloomer uniforms' for gym classes, an alternative to the constrained girls' dress wear of the day. She ensured the gym at Wellington Girls' was well appointed, with Indian clubs, dumbbells and jumping apparatus. The swing ropes in particular brought out Kathleen and Marion's competitive side:

> [W]e had our own game with the long ropes knotted at the ends and which hung suspended from the middle of the ceiling ... What a thrill it was to swing back and forth from one end of the gym to the other. One particular morning Kathleen and I both scrambled up at the same time. 'My turn first,' Kathleen cried. 'No, it's mine,' I said and settled the question by leaping off the mantel. Kathleen furiously followed suit, with the result that we crashed in mid air and I, being the lightest in weight was hurled to the hard floor of the Gym, where I lay stunned. Frightened, the others gathered round ... Kathleen dumb with misery, was relieved when I sat up ...[18]

Miss Hamilton, remembered for her red-gold hair and blue eyes, was an upright Scot. She remained watchful for slackness and, worse, slanginess among pupils. Her most notorious punishment was to force miscreants to collect 20 snails from the arum lilies in her private garden, located in a corner of the grounds. Miss Hamilton was also renowned for her pet, a white cockatoo which she kept in her office. She resigned in 1900 to marry the male French teacher, Charles Cosmo de Naverne, a tall black-haired man with a pince-nez who murmured in French to his charges: 'All great men have their weakness. Mine, young ladies, is that I cannot bear to see the ungloved hand.'[19]

Other teachers seemed to incite bad behaviour. When 'poor meek and mild' Miss Isabel Ecclesfield came to teach history to Kathleen and her classmates,

> ten well-behaved little girls became so many hooligans ... Vida drew a frivolous picture on the board, we put the fire tongs and poker in the middle of the room and turned the desk chair upside down. We greeted Miss Ecclesfield with shouts of glee and her mild remonstrances only brought forth fresh demonstrations. One by one we were sent from the room until there were more in the corridor than in the classroom.[20]

Kathleen and Marion Ruddick became inseparable. Ruddick tells how Kathleen turned to her one day and said: "'I'm so glad you're the kind of girl you are." And I said the same to her. We decided to shorten our names to Katie and Molly.'[21] Increasingly they retreated to Bell's secret garden, immersing themselves in fantasy literature, especially the fairy tales of Grimm and Hans Christian Andersen. They scribbled verse. The older Beauchamp girls' disapproval of this activity only brought them closer, fostering a conspiracy of imagination:

> To us, every tree in the Golders Hill garden contained a wood nymph and every flower was a fairy in disguise. We wrote 'poems' and I well remember our struggles over 'An Ode to a Snow Drop'. We were so elated over our creation that we read it to Vera and Chaddie and while Chaddie scoffed, Vera explained that it was only a rhyme and could not possibly be called a poem. Downcast and infuriated, we vowed never to confide in anyone again and from then on kept our imaginings to ourselves and lived in a world of our own.[22]

Ruddick's account is at times self-serving but usually plausible. It sees her endlessly cajoling 'Katie', persuading her, for example, to climb a tall acacia tree growing on Golders Hill:

> I went first to one of the higher branches where I had my own special seat. Katie with much difficulty and puffing, managed to find a comfortable place on a slightly lower branch. From this elevation we had a view of the harbor which, on warm, calm days was like a mirror and on days where there was a slight wind, seemed like rippling silk of steel blue. On the other side we looked down into the convent garden ...[23]

The hilltop location appears to have been part inspiration for Katherine Mansfield's story 'Taking the Veil':

> [Edna] smiled wisely, sadly, as she turned into the gardens of the Convent of the Sacred Heart and mounted the path that led through them to Hill Street ...

> Edna had reached the top of the path. There under a new-leafed tree, hung with little bunches of white flowers, she sat down on a green bench and looked over the Convent flower-beds.[24]

Marion briefly became part of the Beauchamp family when she joined them for Christmas 1898 in a cottage at Island Bay. Premier Seddon, in top hat, frock coat and diamond stud, called by for a drink. Her memoir, full of irresistible close-ups, snaps Kathleen Beauchamp on the brink of adolescence. A house entertainment at 75 Tinakori Road for visiting sailors shows her friend gaining heart as a performer, a role she would relish in later life:

> Kathleen would recite one of her own poems about a fisherman who didn't return … announced beforehand as the author of her poem, she brought down the house. A fashionable audience would have appalled her, but she liked these rough sailor lads; she associated them with brine and tar and holly stones and did her best.[25]

Throughout 1899 Kathleen made regular appearances at lunchtime school poetry recitals, often alongside her sister Charlotte.[26]

Whether due to Ruddick's influence or not, Kathleen's time at Wellington Girls' High School appears to have been enlivening, even transformative. A programme for a 1973 American exhibition of childhood memorabilia included her class copy of *Longman's School Grammar* with the inscription: 'Kathleen Beauchamp Girls High School Wellington New Zealand. Southern Hem. Pacific Ocean. The Space S of the North Island Capital of New Zealand Antipodes and British Isles 75 Tinakori Road.'[27] It is touching to imagine her writing something so universal, even mundane, in an attempt to pin down her place in the world.

And writing she certainly was. In 1899, as she won coveted class prizes in English, French and arithmetic, the *Reporter* printed 'A Happy Christmas Eve' – a second published story and early intimation of 'The Doll's House'.

Midway through 1900 the Ruddicks returned to Canada. There is some evidence that Marion stayed behind to board at a Christchurch school. Ruth Mantz quotes Kathleen as saying, 'You lucky girl to be going away to school!'[28] The Beauchamp girls then transferred to the nearby Fitzherbert Terrace School. Seventeen years passed before the pair reunited in Soho,

London. Ruddick recalled that Katherine Mansfield was ill and almost unrecognisable as they reminisced over a meal of spaghetti. Reminded of her boasts about 'Enna Blake' in the first hours of their friendship, the now published author marvelled, 'What a little horror I must have been.'[29] Ruddick saw her friend one more time, briefly, in 1922.

Vera Beauchamp helped engineer Ruddick's memoir. After her move to Canada, where Ruddick was living, Vera, then known as Mrs J. Macintosh-Bell, prodded her sister's friend to record her memories, assisting with Māori phrases and other New Zealand detail. Her close involvement assured a layer of authenticity. When Ruddick died in 1970, the manuscript was bequeathed to Vera and later deposited at the Alexander Turnbull Library.

6522. THE U. S. S. Co's "PENGUIN" NEGOTIATING THE "FRENCH PASS" N. Z.

Muir & Moodie

The 'Picton boat', the SS *Penguin*, Marlborough Sounds, circa 1900: '… there is no snugger place than a warm cabin, a warm bunk. Tucked up with a rug, a hot water bottle and a piping hot cup of tea …' ('Six Years After')

Photographer unknown. Ref: 1/2-091856-F. ATL.

Fourteen: A place in the sun

Lying beside the dark wharf, all strung, all beaded with round golden lights, the Picton boat looked as if she was more ready to sail among stars than out into the cold sea. – Katherine Mansfield, 'The Voyage'[1]

Katherine Mansfield knew the Cook Strait crossing well. The Beauchamps appear to have been ardent holidaymakers, early, deep-pocketed adopters of the leisure boom that defined the decades before and after 1900. Moreover, they had relatives to descend on in remote, idyllic spots like Anakiwa in the Marlborough Sounds, home to Great-uncle Cradock with the long white beard, and on regular occasions the wandering Beauchamp grandparents as well. The Sounds became the home turf of the Kiwi Beauchamps following Arthur and Cradock's arrival in the 1860s. Harold was raised in tiny portside Picton, attending local schools and spending summers at Anakiwa. Today a 30-minute drive from Picton, this finishing point of the Queen Charlotte Track was once accessible only by sea.

Katherine Mansfield insisted that she first landed at Picton aged six months.[2] In fact she was five weeks old: shipping records show that 'Mrs Beauchamp and children' arrived on 20 November 1888.[3] Within a month, Annie Beauchamp 'and infant' returned to Wellington, leaving the elder girls in the care of Cradock, his wife Harriet and their nine children.[4] But the visit had a recuperative element for the infant Kathleen, who was born with jaundice. Her cousins remembered 'a yellow, ill-looking baby'.[5]

Later, she and her siblings ('the Misses Beauchamp', as the *Marlborough Express* called them) spent many school holidays at Anakiwa. I make out a long, clear trail of their comings and goings in the digitised shipping records of the *Express*: as saloon cabin passengers they are automatically identified, unlike the hoi polloi in crowded, low-ceilinged steerage. I'm able to conclude that the 'Picton boat' featured in stories like 'The Voyage' was the SS *Penguin*, used for the inaugural inter-island service after 1895. For a generation the 67-metre steamer, with its polished green hull, white navigation bridge and red and black funnel, was a familiar presence in and around Cook Strait.

Then, as now, first-class travel was expensive: a return fare in one of the *Penguin*'s luxury cabins at the rear of the vessel cost about 30 shillings, or $280 in today's money – twice the price of steerage. The little steamer throbbed between the two islands at a speed of 12 knots, meaning voyages took about four and a half hours. I think Kathleen coveted her cosy berth within the ladies' cabin. 'Six Years After' recalls the private joys of a saloon crossing: 'there is no snugger place than a warm cabin, a warm bunk. Tucked up with a rug, a hot water bottle and a piping hot cup of tea …'[6]

She'd associate the strait with calm weather. Pat Lawlor, however, found a reference to a rough journey:

> *Katherine Mansfield came bustling along the deck after the boat had left the Picton wharf. 'You know, Mother,' she said, 'this seasickness is all in the brain – all in the brain. We are not going to be seasick.' Half an hour later, Katherine Mansfield came tottering back to us with the words, 'I'm afraid, Mother, that sea-sickness is not in the brain, but entirely in the stomach,' and she fled to her cabin and was not seen for the rest of the voyage.*[7]

Her best-known evocation of a Cook Strait crossing, 'The Voyage', climaxes with the boat's arrival at the Picton wharf, where a man with a cart meets Fenella and her grandmother. They rattle along the road to a 'shell-like house … up a little path of round white pebbles'.[8] In fact, Arthur Beauchamp and his wife Mary, both in their sixties, were on the move, shuffling between Anakiwa, Pelorus Sound and Wellington. As we've seen, they'd return to Picton in their final years only, giving the Beauchamp children fewer chances to experience Arthur's garrulous humour or to hear Mary sing at the piano.

By the time Kathleen holidayed in Anakiwa, Great-uncle Cradock's place was a spacious homestead in wide paddocks planted out with established chestnut, oak and walnut trees. Some of them stand to this day. Here the children could fish from a boat, swim and explore the tangled bush.

Indigenous and introduced plants and animals intermingled: a weeping willow hung over the dairy, and a population of native bats occupied its roof. She'd write of the shoreline: 'There were exquisite small shells to be found on these beaches, a small greeny-blue kind, coral spirals and tiny yellow ones like grains of maize.'[9]

Biographer Mantz mentions the profusion of native birds at Anakiwa: '[Katherine Mansfield] could hear them at daybreak from the room that she shared with the grandmother under the honeysuckle vine … innumerable different notes.'[10] She also notes how Cradock's children and grandchildren had their favourites among the visiting 'townie' cousins, and that Kathleen was not one of them: 'To see Vera was to love her [...] to see Katherine [Mansfield] was to remember her.'[11]

Kathleen appears to have become bored with her country cousins fairly early, preferring to isolate herself or to talk to adults:

> They were happy little girls, but Kass was mostly the silent dreamy one. She was fat and appeared rather dull, but her big 'mossy' eyes lighted with interest when one of the grown-ups took the trouble to speak to her … the grandmother spoke sharply to her at times. Yet Kass loved her. She always called to her when she came to the house: 'Gran, dear, where are you?'[12]

Anakiwa was no longer the wilderness Cradock and Harriet contemplated when local Te Āti Awa first rowed them to their newly purchased 80-hectare block in 1862. Harriet never quite accepted the brutal isolation. Henry Beauchamp, visiting from England, recorded the family struggles to eke out a living here. On a wet December day in 1875, Cradock rowed him in darkness the 12 kilometres from Picton. (Kathleen and her sisters would arrive by the same means.) Henry Herron's journal records:

> … their clearing, a flat in a pretty little bay at the head of an arm of the Sound and backed by thickly wooded hills 600 to 1200 ft high … took a hand with Crad at the churn – he makes 7lbs butter a day besides supplying themselves … Crad has about 150 turkeys which he never feeds or cares for in any way. He will shear directly and expects seven bales wool – worth tenpence per pound – half of which belongs to Arthur [Beauchamp] … Crad says he never had a doctor for

either himself or children but once at Picton where one lived next door. He looks gaunt and overworked but is active and gets through a good deal.[13]

Beauchamp was soon desperate to leave:

… such a relief after poor Crad's establishment, cows, calves, pigs, 8 babies, 15 cats, fowls, turkeys etc all jumbled together. He has not the faintest notion of business, reckless, improvident, happy and with golden visions of a comfortable future which will never be realized. Spent already 14 of the best years of his life and upwards of 2000 of his and other people's money – besides 1000 of Harriet's, on this wretched, out of the way place – which would probably not fetch 500 if sold now. No galley slave works harder than he and his wife, and all their labour for the most part misdirected. Poor things![14]

His visit came at a difficult time. Cradock and Harriet's first homestead had recently burned down. Cradock and his son Herbert would build a second home nearer the hills, a large spread encircled by English trees. In 1900, Herbert's daughter Ethel came to live there with her grandparents, then both in their seventies. Her memoir chronicles the sober daily rituals at Anakiwa that were familiar to Katherine Mansfield:

All the winter and in any cool weather, a huge log fire was kept burning in the open fireplace at the end of the long dining room. [Cradock] would sit there most of the morning, writing his diaries, his poetry, his philosophies … dinner was never informal. Granny wore a stiff black frock that rustled, there was white lace at the throat and wrists. A spotless white cap on her head. Grandpa wore a brown velvet coat, the aunts their pretty dresses … the uncles always wore their dark suits … everyone helped with the clearing away and washing up of dishes … someone lifted the heavy Family Bible off the shelf beyond the mantelpiece and put it at the head of the table. The family, the men who had had their meal in the kitchen, sat round while Grandpa said the Lord's Prayer, then Granny read from the Bible.[15]

Ethel Beauchamp Hazelwood later became a writer. Katherine Mansfield remembered her as 'a pale girl, very thin, with flaxen hair'.[16] Half a century later, Hazelwood recalled the 'sombre brown eyes' of her famous cousin, stating, 'I never saw her smile. My grandmother's verdict was that she was sulky, but we can all be misunderstood.'[17] Ethel Hazelwood later ran a successful guesthouse from the old Beauchamp homestead at

Anakiwa. The Outward Bound Trust bought the property and still owns it. Katherine Mansfield is commemorated in its brick courtyard, along with her celebrated aphorism: 'Risk, risk anything.'

By the time she crossed Cook Strait, the SS *Penguin* had endured bumps, scrapes, even strandings, in the narrow, rocky Sounds. Worse was to come. Some 20 years later, in 1909, 'the Picton boat' came to grief in what was to be the country's worst maritime disaster of the twentieth century. With a noise 'like the rending of a gigantic piece of calico', the *Penguin* foundered in wild seas on the rocks by Cape Terawhiti on Wellington's south coast.[18] Many of the 75 dead are buried at Karori Cemetery, including four of the five children from one family.

~

In time, the Beauchamps came to prefer holidays closer to home. First, a rented cottage at Island Bay; then a bungalow at Eastbourne, a popular location on the eastern side of Wellington Harbour. On any weekend the family might also be out picnicking around the region with friends and family. The marriage of Annie's brother Frank to Premier Seddon's daughter Phoebe proved a social catalyst. The two families, including Phoebe's brother Tom, often picnicked at Frank Dyer's fishing lodge in an old farmhouse by a stream at Wainuiomata, over the hill from the Hutt Valley. Sandwiches of egg, lettuce and pressed tongue, followed by a brew of tea, were the usual fare.

Tom Seddon's memoirs offer a rare portrait of the Beauchamps at leisure:

> *A large brake [horse-drawn carriage] was ordered and my family and Frank's relatives, Mr Harold Beauchamp and Mrs Beauchamp, who was Frank's sister, and the Beauchamp children, Aunt Belle Dyer and Kitty Dyer, Frank's other sisters, all had a happy day at the old whare. It is strange that I remember quite well in the course of conversation somebody said it was a 'lovely' party – someone said it was a 'lovely' day – someone said a trout just landed was a 'lovely' fish and then the discussion continued about the misuse of the word 'lovely'. 'Just slovenly thinking' someone remarked. Oh yes, the Beauchamps were keen on the right word to express the right meaning.*[19]

~

The Beauchamps first holidayed on the long, rocky coastline on the eastern side of Wellington Harbour, below steep, bush-choked hills, in the summer of 1898. They crossed the harbour from the city by passenger steamer, landing at Days Bay. The white-sand beach was a daytrippers' paradise, thanks to the efforts of entrepreneur J.H. Williams who, having bought up the bay in its entirety, funded a deep-water wharf and operated ferries. A Brighton-style pavilion with encircling verandas offered seating for 800. David Johnson's history of Wellington Harbour describes the city's enthusiastic response: '… in its first month as Wellington's new playground, THE Bay needed no name. Everyone knew. On New Year's Day 1896, "The Bay" had 3000 visitors.'[20]

As a child, Iris Wilkinson, later known as the writer Robin Hyde, also came here to picnic under the trees. The Bay inspired her fiction, just as it did Katherine Mansfield's. In her 1938 novel *The Godwits Fly*, Hyde describes leaving the city aboard the *Cobar*, the ferry known in Wellington as the 'Holy Roller':

> *On the far side of the wharf a notice says, 'Danger! Twelve Feet Deep'. Boys with dark gold bodies, wearing only Vs, jump on the stanchions, steady themselves, then plunge down like gannets. In a minute their dark heads bob up, they shake water and laughter out of their eyes, ears and noses, swimming leisurely overarm to the wharf steps.*[21]

The Beauchamps first rented at Muritai, beyond what is today Eastbourne township, a quiet spot of sandhills, meadows and a few beach houses. The owner of their rented bungalow was Sydney Barraud, a BNZ bank manager and one of Harold's fellow Anglican elders. Days Bay was long thought to be the setting for 'At the Bay', but the consensus now is that Muritai (Crescent Bay), to the south of Days Bay and more private, inspired the story. The sultry, almost mystical atmosphere of Anakiwa is another element Katherine Mansfield wove in.

Wealthy families like the Beauchamps flocked here. 'Summering' at sunny Muritai became *de rigueur* among the local elite. The *Evening Post* noted in 1897 that 'as much as three pounds [$500 in today's money] has been offered for the use of a four-roomed house at Muritai for Easter week'.[22] A residence for the Beauchamps needed to accommodate Annie's

The Glen at Muritai: 'The green blinds were drawn in the bungalows of the summer colony. Over the verandas, prone on the paddock, flung over the fences, there were exhausted-looking bathing-dresses and rough striped towels.' ('At the Bay')

Photographer unknown. Ref: 1/2-040430-F. ATL.

sisters and her mother. The Glen at 283a Muritai Road was ideal, with its eight rooms, large front veranda, bathroom, scullery and what were termed 'conveniences'. The half-hectare property, fronting what was then the main road, also offered a stable, trap shed and summer house. Advertisements from the time boasted that it sat 'in a wealth of native vegetation and commands a magnificent panoramic view. A splendid stream runs through the property ...'[23] Today the white wooden bungalow, shorn of its veranda, perches on the shady hillside. Surrounded by bush and houses, it looks over the same little stream now constrained beneath a slatted wooden bridge.

Katherine Mansfield strove to be accurate in her fiction. The veranda shading the front rooms of the Muritai bungalow is recreated in detail in 'At the Bay':

The green blinds were drawn in the bungalows of the summer colony. Over the verandas, prone on the paddock, flung over the fences, there were exhausted-looking bathing-dresses and rough striped towels. Each back window seemed to have a pair of sand-shoes on the sill and some lumps of rock or a bucket or a collection of pawa shells. The bush quivered in a haze of heat; the sandy road was empty.[24]

The blazing sun proved a mixed blessing. Hours at the seaside, even draped in neck-to-knee bathing costumes, always carried the risk of sunburn. Robin Hyde was an early chronicler of the sunbathing fad at the turn of the twentieth century, describing in *The Godwits Fly* how 'rather than swim most people prefer to lie on the beach, turning on the gramophones and slowly cooking themselves the colour of raw steak'.[25] Long, exposed hours making sandcastles and swimming had serious, painful consequences, Vera recalled years later: 'We got very sunburned … we even had to have the doctor to see us. We had enormous blisters on our legs.'[26]

Dawn was a safer hour. The celebrated pattering, dew-covered sheep in the opening scene of 'At the Bay' were no pastoral fantasy. Kathleen is likely to have seen drovers guiding flocks along the beach. Since the earliest Māori settlement, beaches had been used as roadways around New Zealand's rugged coastline. The first sheep to reach the Wairarapa in 1844 passed this way, en route to Palliser Bay. Around the corner at Mukamuka, where the route became inaccessible, men lugged sheep through the surf. Flocks continued to be herded across the sand for at least another century, especially on the North Island's east coast, until roads were carved through the landscape.[27]

Early-morning swimmers were probably a rarer sight at the turn of the century. Although so-called 'natation' was a popular colonial pursuit, beaches were still seen as places to be treated with caution, as this contemporary report suggests:

There is at this time of the year a certain indefinable fascination in the mere sound of the word beach. It suggests a soothing monotone of cool sea waves, and a luxurious reclining on cool sand. As a rule, however, the sand is anything but cool, and the beach is exposed to the glaring sun, making it quite impossible to read, or even sleep, in comfort. Under these circumstances the beach, on closer inspection, loses half its charm.[28]

The Muritai bungalow was some distance from the beach: a rough calculation shows the swimmers in 'At the Bay' had to cover 300 metres:

... a figure in a broad-striped bathing suit flung down the paddock, cleared the stile, rushed through the tussock grass into the hollow, staggered up the sandy hillock, and raced for dear life over the big porous stones, over the cold, wet pebbles, on to the hard sand that gleamed like oil.[29]

Katherine Mansfield described with similar clarity the long summer twilights on this side of the harbour: 'the day had faded; the gorgeous sunset had blazed and died. And now the quick dark came racing over the sea, over the sandhills, up the paddock.'[30]

The bustling general store in 'At the Bay' was based on an equivalent shop on Muritai Road operated by Herbert Martin and Edwin Jones. The memorable Mrs Stubbs was a version of the owner's wife. Harold Beauchamp confirmed the connection: '[Katherine Mansfield] ... made the acquaintance of a Mrs Jones ... who lived only a short distance from the seafront. She was quite an original character, and I fancy my daughter made some use of her in one or two of her sketches.'[31] Edwin Jones would later be accused of illegally selling alcohol in the dining room at the back of the store.[32] The place closed during the 1930s.

The success of the 'summering' at Muritai inspired Harold Beauchamp to acquire a section at Days Bay, several kilometres to the north – the 'Daylight Cove' of 'At the Bay'. In the early 1900s he bought at Downes Point on the bay's northern tip. A rough two-room holiday cottage with a spartan sitting room and adjacent bunkroom was constructed. Next door stood an outhouse with a cast-iron tub. Even though it was used by teenaged Beauchamp children, the room clearly inspired the washhouse scene in 'At the Bay' when the children talk of spiders 'as big as a saucer' dropping from the ceiling.[33]

Despite its size, the cottage remained a haven for the Beauchamps. It served as a bolt-hole for Katherine Mansfield during her brief unhappy return from Europe in 1906:

> I sit in the small poverty stricken living room – the one and only room which the cottage contains with the exception of a cabin like bedroom fitted with bunks, and an outhouse with a bath, and wood cellar, coal cellar complete. On one hand is the sea stretching right up the yard, on the other the bush growing close down almost to my front door.[34]

℘

A new harbour ferry, the *Fairmile*, was carrying daytrippers to Days Bay in 1951 when Darryl Coburn's grandmother, Minnie Lamb, acquired the cottage. The Beauchamps were long off the scene, having sold up before World War I.

Today, Coburn, an architect in his seventies, sits at the kitchen table of his self-designed apartment in central Wellington eating a vegan lunch of beetroot on wheat crackers. He recalls idyllic childhood summers of boating, bathing and fishing from the wall in front of the house, as the Beauchamps did. The facilities were still basic, conditions harsh:

> Staying at the house was modest living. You had to go outside to go to the toilet. My grandmother bought it because she knew her four grandkids would like to go there. Anyone who knew about the storms in the harbour there wouldn't have bought it. For me the main attraction was the bush. We'd be up there every day, doing the circuit. Climbing the hills to get out of the wind. I'm sure it was the same for Katherine Mansfield. The wind that hit that point was just horrendous.[35]

Coburn says that for decades the family was unaware of the literary connection:

> No one really knew who Katherine Mansfield was when she [his grandmother] bought it. Later [biographer] Gillian Boddy came by and talked about her and the house. We used to swim from the concrete platform in front of the house over to Days Bay. We'd fish from there too. I remember catching flounder. We'd row around offshore in a clinker boat. We'd stay on there after the summer

holidays, taking the ferry across the harbour to town, then catching the bus out to primary school.

High tides finally destroyed much of the old Beauchamp cottage. The Sims family, residents for 11 years, reported in 2013 how a wave 'took out the dining-room window … the kitchen bench had been lifted, cupboards ripped off, the oven was outside and the fridge was in the lounge'.[36] A local newspaper carried the lament: 'Katherine Mansfield bach "all gone now"'.[37]

A single bidder was on hand when the site was auctioned: local developer Chris Stevenson. He acquired the site, with ambitious plans for an 'At the Bay' boutique bed and breakfast. Known as 'Whitebait', Stevenson is best remembered in the city for a succession of jokey messages on the billboard above his Basin Reserve car yard in the 1980s. 'My best friend stole my wife and he's still my best friend' is among the less offensive offerings.

The same irreverence was apparent as Stevenson began the enterprise at Days Bay.[38] As he started salvage work on the cottage, he persuaded his builder to make a sign saying: 'Welcome to the Resurrection of Jane Mansfield House'. (He meant Jayne.) Aligning our principal literary lioness with an American sex goddess raised a few weak smiles and quite a few frowns. Katherine Mansfield's reputation remains sacred on this side of the harbour: locals indicated via social media that they weren't amused. The builder, feeling the heat, removed the sign.

Stevenson, however, insisted he was making a subversive joke, one that Katherine Mansfield would enjoy. He may be right. He claims to have since spent $2 million rebuilding and modifying what's now cautiously named 'Katherine Mansfield House'. The cottage has been lifted by two metres in the hope of staying ahead of rising sea levels, and a second storey has been added to create four bedrooms. Stevenson says he unearthed some of Katherine Mansfield's footwear under the floorboards. He shakes his head at the weight of the Beauchamps' cast-iron bath in the adjoining boathouse. But dreams of creating a bed and breakfast at Daylight Cove are on hold: Whitebait's son needs a place to live.

Thorndon Esplanade and baths on a calm day, circa 1900: 'The wind is so strong that
they have to fight their way through it, rocking like two old drunkards. All the poor little
pahutukawas on the esplanade are bent to the ground.' ('The Wind Blows')

Photographer unknown. Ref: Eph-B-POSTCARD-Vol-6-028-1. ATL.

Fifteen: Ablutions: Thorndon trail

*... the feeling of the Thorndon baths, the wet, moist, oozy ... no,
I know how it must be done – Katherine Mansfield, 1921[1]*

May Street is up in the air, a grey ribbon of bitumen flying above the Thorndon motorway. Today it's thick with cars, no longer the quiet residential by-street where Kathleen Beauchamp ambled to school. Nor are there any traces of the spreading cedar tree she passed at the corner where May Street joined Tinakori Road, and that dropped a soft coat of greenery on the pavement. 'It was dark and hung over the street like a great shadow.'[2] Today it's a street in name only: the sign is bolted to a motorway off-ramp where ten thousand cars a day curve from Molesworth Street onto Highway 1 below.

Katherine Mansfield vowed to say more about her Thorndon cartography, the city ways of her adolescence, making a commitment in the final months of her life to describe 'the baths, the avenue, the people in the gardens, the Chinaman under the tree in May Street'.[3]

She'd manage an imperishable sketch of Tinakori Road at dawn in 'A Birthday'. Though set in Germany, its terrain is recognisably, unerringly Thorndon. The squalid quarter her narrator traverses is silent, empty. The milkman, another early riser, materialises: 'A milk cart rattled down the street, the driver standing at the back, cracking a whip; he wore an immense geranium flower stuck in the lapel of his coat ...'[4] Andreas Binzer picks his way along the paving stones, past the Princess Hotel on the triangular intersection of Molesworth and Murphy streets:

... there was nobody about at all – dead and alive this place on a Sunday morning ... The shutters were still up before the shops. Scraps of newspaper, hay, and fruit skins strewed the pavement; the gutters were choked with the leavings of Saturday night. Two dogs sprawled in the middle of the road, scuffling and biting. Only the public-house at the corner was open; a young barman slopped water over the doorstep.[5]

♀

I'm here in the Mojo coffee shop, all oak joinery, steel and glass, on the corner where the Princess Hotel once stood. As cars pour by on either side I'm musing on what Kathleen Beauchamp made of these streets. Did she pine for rural Karori? I suspect not. Rough, bustling, gritty Thorndon, traversed daily in her school days, offered an apprentice writer peeps into other worlds. Her playmate, Molly Ruddick, often accompanied her. Inspired by Ruddick's memoir, I'm imagining one of their rambles to school, retracing their steps along roadways edged with rustling cabbage trees, past lodgings of thin pine and corrugated iron. The girls will cool off with a swim. It's a fine day in December 1898, sunny but blowy.

Our starting point is 75 Tinakori Road, a white wedding-cake house on the ridge above Tinakori Road. Accompanied by the three eldest Beauchamp girls, including 11-year-old Kathleen, Ruddick describes the street as it was:

In navy serge and sailor hats, our books carried by a strap, we set out for school. Mrs Beauchamp and her sister 'Aunt Belle' waving goodbye from the veranda and calling out last minute instructions. To Vera and Chaddie, it was just a walk, a means of getting to school, but to Katie and me it was an adventure, the unknown lurking round every corner.[6]

We descend the concrete steps to the unsealed street. Ruddick makes no mention of the slums below the road from the Beauchamps' front entrance: the workers' cottages of Saunders Lane. Today the area is a service depot for sleek European cars. Nor does she seem to remember the manure pits in Munt's yard between Saunders Lane and George Street. Dozens of horses and carrying vehicles were stabled here. Instead she recalls 'a

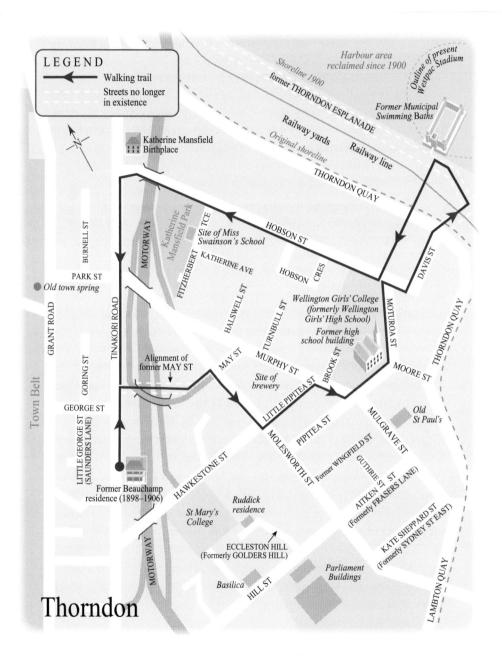

LEGEND

← Walking trail

Streets no longer in existence

Harbour area reclaimed since 1900

Outline of present Wetpac Stadium

Shoreline 1900

former THORNDON ESPLANADE

Railway yards

Railway line

Original shoreline

THORNDON QUAY

Former Municipal Swimming Baths

Katherine Mansfield Birthplace

N

PARK ST

Old town spring

BURNELL ST

MOTORWAY

Katherine Mansfield Park

FITZHERBERT TCE

Site of Miss Swainson's School

KATHERINE AVE

HOBSON ST

HOBSON CRES

DAVIS ST

GRANT ROAD

TINAKORI ROAD

GORING ST

HALSWELL ST

TURNBULL ST

Wellington Girls' College (formerly Wellington Girls' High School)

Former high school building

MOTUROA ST

THORNDON QUAY

Alignment of former MAY ST

MAY ST

MURPHY ST

Site of brewery

BROOK ST

MOORE ST

Town Belt

GEORGE ST

LITTLE GEORGE ST (SAUNDERS LANE)

HAWKESTONE ST

LITTLE PIPITEA ST

PIPITEA ST

Old St Paul's

MULGRAVE ST

Former Beauchamp residence (1898–1906)

St Mary's College

Ruddick residence

MOLESWORTH ST

Former WINGFIELD ST

GUTHRIE ST

AITKEN ST (Formerly FRASERS LANE)

KATE SHEPPARD ST (Formerly SYDNEY ST EAST)

MOTORWAY

ECCLESTON HILL (Formerly GOLDERS HILL)

Basilica

HILL ST

Parliament Buildings

LAMBTON QUAY

Thorndon

delicious scent of moist earth and growing things, as it had rained during the night and the air was almost muggy, giving a promise of warm days to come ...'[7] Maybe the wind was blowing in the other direction.

The girls head north down Tinakori Road, what Katherine Mansfield calls Tyrrell Street in some stories, but usually Tarana Street after the Tasmanian settlement where her grandmother lived. Here Victorian-era villas are today interspersed with modern townhouses.

Her story 'Weak Heart' portrays a row of modest but well-manicured wooden dwellings tucked among grander homes,

> *... beautiful in the spring; there was not a single house without its garden and trees and a plot of grass big enough to be called 'the lawn'. Over the low painted fences, you could see, as you ran by, whose daffys were out, whose wild snowdrop border was over and who had the biggest hyacinths, so pink and white, the colour of coconut ice. But nobody had violets that grew, that smelled in the spring like Bengels.*[8]

By number 51, a dozen houses to the north, we reach May Street, dipping rightward to Molesworth Street. Singing teacher Madame Rosaly Merz lived at number 7. Other genteel types occupied a row of tidy villas, with a few cramped workers' cottages between. Vera and Charlotte press on, but the younger girls pause here beneath the cedar: 'There was a tree at the corner of Tarana Street and May Street. It grew so close to the pavement that the heavy boughs stretched over, and on that part of the pavement there was always a fine sifting of minute twigs.'[9] It was 'the velvet tree', a place where 'lovers parading come into its shade as into a tent'.[10]

From here on the corner of May and Molesworth streets, the bulbous wooden tower of Wellington Girls' High School is visible. To our right is the weathered Princess Hotel, an establishment of 22 rooms. Premier Sir George Grey once held his Cabinet meetings upstairs, asking that the wooden floor be packed with sawdust to ensure discussions were not audible below. Grey also conferred from the windowsill with Māori chiefs gathered below. Today it is our busy Mojo coffee bar, filled with police sergeants from their adjacent headquarters and networking public servants.

The Princess Hotel, Molesworth Street, Thorndon, 1950s. 'Only the public-house at the corner was open; a young barman slopped water over the doorstep.' ('A Birthday')

Ref: 1/2-075071-G. ATL.

The girls are already halfway across the crowded carriageway, Kathleen trying to keep her schoolbooks from slipping out of their holding strap:

Today the dash through the traffic when we reached Molesworth Street was even more exciting than usual as Katie dropped her books and there was a scramble on the part of all four of us to pick them up while the traffic good naturedly stopped …[11]

Molesworth Street of an early weekday morning is an eddy of pounding, jingling one-horse carts and wagons: four-wheeled chaises without hoods, drags, omnibuses, dog-carts, leather-curtained hackney cabs and other battered, lurching vehicles, many with rubber tyres. The air crackles with the sound of whips. Horsemen, some in frock coats, top hats and riding boots, duck in and out, negotiating the unsealed, rutted roadway. A bitter smell of hops from a nearby brewery hovers. Horses pace slowly, however; after a grocer's cart killed a cap-chasing child in Cuba Street, the council came down on furious driving. Traffic is in flux as the girls sidle past. William McLean, a wealthy local, imported the colony's first two motorcars in 1898: a pair of Daimler Benzes.

This is a wholesome commercial and residential neighbourhood, edged with fruit shops, fishmongers, florists, parlours and hot kitchens catering to parliamentarians and soft-handed officials. The Parliamentary Hairdressing Saloon, across from the House of Representatives, specialises in daily trims for bearded gents. It is also a place of lodging houses. Many members rent rooms for the entire session of parliament in one of the half dozen hotels lining the street. The cosy Shamrock Hotel bills itself the 'general resort' of parliamentarians and is famed for its roast beef and hot toddy. Premier Seddon occupies a spacious section at number 22 Molesworth, between a cabinetmaker and a tinsmith. His gabled two-storey wooden house has a glasshouse, poultry yard, and stables in which he houses the great white horse on which he rides to work in the wooden Government Buildings on Lambton Quay.

By night, however, Molesworth Street takes on a lawless, even libertine look, the hangover from which we see in 'A Birthday'. Sailors from the nearby docks and free-spending arrivals from the Thorndon railway station swarm through the noisy saloons, billiard halls, oyster bars, brothels and disreputable boarding houses that festoon this old city gateway. The quarter gained a reputation in the 1890s as the 'Barbary Coast of Wellington', after a bawdy quayside area in San Francisco.[12] Most of the capital's sex workers operated out of rickety back rooms and garrets here.[13] Frasers Lane, where a row of brothels operated behind the Provincial Hotel, today provides a generous site for the National Library. 'Fallen women' appeared, blinking, in court after an 11pm raid on Philomena McHugh's rival bawdy house in adjacent Wingfield Street. McHugh fought back with a decanter.[14]

The fleshpots of this part of Thorndon also draw their share of liquored-up grandees. Search parties were called after a reveller locked Seddon's Speaker, Sir Maurice O'Rorke, in a back room at the Metropolitan Hotel.[15] Another sozzled MP who mistook wharf lights for a chemist shop window was fished out of the harbour.[16] Frasers Lane and adjoining streets were later demolished as part of civic slum clearance.

Prominent on the corner of Hill and Molesworth streets is Barraud's chemist and druggist, a shop Kathleen Beauchamp often passes. In 'A Married Man's Story' the narrator's father, a chemist, serves local prostitutes:

> In the evening his customers were, chiefly, young women; some of them came in every day for his famous fivepenny pick-me-up. Their gaudy looks, their voices, their free ways, fascinated me. I longed to be my father, handing them across the counter the little glass of bluish stuff they tossed off so greedily.[17]

The bells of Wellington Girls' High are sounding. We speed up. Molesworth Street today is a sterile corridor of daytime lunch bars and Asian food outlets. Yet the short cut the girls take to school along Little Pipitea Street remains, squeezed now between the Thai Embassy and a supermarket carpark. They join a queue outside Mrs Temperance Kirkby's dairy on the corner of Mulgrave and Pipitea streets, keen to spend some of Molly's money on changing balls, licorice buttons, bullseyes and other treats held in tall glass jars.

Despite a stiffening breeze, the scent of hops from the nearby brewery is intense. Beer was first brewed in Thorndon in 1866, and the industry continued until 1988. A disused brew tower stands today at the entrance to the supermarket complex.

The yeasty air of Thorndon is familiar. When I came here from Karori in 1973, the brewery was still a link to the Victorian streetscape Katherine Mansfield knew. What was different, however, were the cars humming down a motorway through Thorndon's heart. And there was a pile of settlers' bones from the excavated cemetery, including those of Katherine Mansfield's ancestors, ready to be reinterred in a mass grave.[18]

I was similarly out of place. My father, the gorse-cutter, died suddenly in 1972, leaving our family devastated. Over several years, I occupied ('crashed at', as we called it) a succession of student flats. There I'd be, squeezing a suitcase and a banana box of university texts – Rimbaud, Baudelaire – around bannisters. I'd pin a gestetnered copy of Picasso's Rimbaud lithograph to walls repainted chocolate and purple; there'd be a double mattress on the floor, butts floating in cold Nescafé.

We kept one foot in high-flown literature, the other in the counter-culture with its new tingly sensations. Nothing made more sense to us than Rimbaud's call to 'derange the senses' with opium and hashish. My first room was in old nuns' cloisters in the Catholic quarter below Golders Hill, the blue front door shrouded in wet hydrangeas. Then up the rimu staircase at nearby Collina Terrace to a music teacher's mansion where my mother lived in the 1940s. Finally, 119 Hill Street, a white two-storey house of wood. I unpacked my banana box, wrote the odd essay in longhand but mostly poetry in felt-tipped pen. Decades later I learned that our flat concealed a second, sharp connection to Katherine Mansfield's city. Thorndon historian Dinah Priestley informs me that Mrs Margaret Dyer briefly lived then died here.

I'm far behind the girls, daydreaming. School is breaking up for the year. Many pupils, Molly and Katie included, are celebrating with a dip at the esplanade baths out on Pipitea Point. Dozens spill out of the gates, past the row of tidy two-storey villas on Moturoa Street, a name Katherine Mansfield will retain. Today a tall mirrored building housing the country's electronic spy agency overshadows the college.

We turn right into Hobson Street, then Davis Street. Between old villas now stands a Steiner kindergarten. The Free Ambulance headquarters is across the road. At the intersection with Thorndon Quay, the Westpac Stadium building crowds the horizon. Then as now, this is the railway precinct, half a dozen tracks criss-crossing land reclaimed for railway yards, sheds and sidings, a rusting precinct on the edge of the city.

The girls tear on, a copper penny in their hands, making for an opulent four-domed wooden building. The great saltwater baths hang off a long gravelled strip of coastline, 'beautified' by laurel plantings and flowerbeds, iron seats and a band rotunda where orchestras play on Sundays. Inside are tidy changing sheds, galleries and vast refreshment rooms. Chilly harbour water flows in and out through openings in the exterior, creating shallow pools at the front where lessons are taught. Inside, in deeper water, experienced swimmers splash about.

Swimming is not only seen as healthy; Victorians believe it instils habits of cleanliness and sanitation. This is probably why activists like William Chapple, the doctor who peered into the Tory Street drains, later chaired the Wellington Swimming Club. At the baths' 1897 opening he said, 'There is absolutely no exercise at once so pleasurable, so invigorating, so healthful and so productive of physical development.'[19]

Molly and Katie materialise in elaborate swimming gowns: 'long tunics with short sleeves made of navy blue (very occasionally) red serge trimmed with white braid, and worn over navy-blue bloomers'.[20] Their hair is tucked into bathing caps that look like sponge bags. They're soon romping in the water. Both owe their water skills to 'Professor' Joseph Pannell, a former stationer turned celebrity swimmer. (Another attraction at the baths was a tame penguin. Ruddick recalled its antics.) Pannell is the buffed, grumpy and usually drunk instructor who rules the baths. In her memoir, Ruddick refers to 'a big man who roared at us. He stood for no nonsense and wasn't in the least concerned if we went under in the process of learning to float.'[21] The propriety of a male teaching schoolgirls raised eyebrows at the time, but the professor's ability was unquestionable.

Learners donned a leather harness with reins attached to a pole. Pannell dragged them from shallow to deeper water, tightening or loosening the

Swimming instructor 'Professor' Pannell, bearded and in black costume, rear centre.
Photographer unknown. *New Zealand Graphic and Ladies' Journal*, 1898.

reins according to whether they sink or swim. Council records show Pannell
was almost certainly Kathleen Beauchamp's instructor. Ruddick wrote of
her persistence. 'Kathleen made hard work of it, alternately puffing and
panting and holding her breath, but she persevered and triumphed at the
end. Soon we were as at home in the water as on land.'[22]

The 'professor' exemplified the physical culture craze of the day,
where strongmen like Eugen Sandow were lionised. His drill exercises and
dumbbells classes were taught at Wellington Girls' High School.[23] Katherine
Mansfield pictures the cult of athleticism in 'Prelude', as the narrator hears
her father 'bending and squatting like a frog and shooting out his legs.

He was so delighted with his firm, obedient body ...'[24] She'd later mock women's adoption of this fad, writing of 'the most Physical Cultured men and women. I shuddered at the women. Great, tall gaunt looking figures, and all angles ... they had a hungry look in their eyes.'[25]

Known as the 'Water Wizard', Pannell was famous for intricate swimming feats. By day, however, he taught swimming to hundreds. After being found intoxicated at work, he was stood down. He offered to take the pledge to abstain, but left Wellington by the early 1900s.[26] His wife's divorce petition claimed he was 'constantly addicted to drink'.[27]

Katherine Mansfield kept her promise to describe this 'oozy' harbour setting, capturing elements of 'the coldness, the blueness of the children, her size in the red twill bathing dress trimmed with white braid. The steps down to the water – the rope across.'[28]

We visualise how the protagonist in 'A Cup of Tea' 'shivered as though she had just come out of the water'.[29] 'A Married Man's Story' tells how the narrator's dying mother 'looked like one of the boys at the school baths, who sits on a step, shivering just like that, and wants to go in and yet is frightened'.[30]

But we're back at the baths, on the last day of term. Perhaps today Katie gets a fit of jealousy after Molly frolics with another friend:

> Suddenly someone bumped into me rather violently. To save myself from falling back, I clutched the railing and turning, discovered that it was Kathleen who had bumped into me. It flashed on my mind that she resented my friendship with Winnie and at the same time I was hurt to think that she would have done what she did intentionally. We never referred to the incident ... K was jealous of her friends; her likes and dislikes were intense, there was no half way.[31]

Our visit to the pool over, we climb the hill to Hobson Street and home. The gale is in full cry, creating whitecaps on the harbour. 'The Wind Blows' immortalises Thorndon Esplanade on such a day:

Over by the breakwater the sea is very high. They pull off their hats and her hair blows across her mouth, tasting of salt. The sea is so high that the waves do not break at all; they thump against the rough stone wall and suck up the weedy, dripping steps. A fine spray skims from the water right across the esplanade.[32]

Molly and Katie are pressing Vera to take a more adventurous route. There's fennel, two metres high, growing in the weed-covered wasteland beyond the esplanade. There's a reference to it in *Pat Lawlor's Wellington*, where, as a youth, the writer explored the 'wonderful forest of fennel, six feet high, with many intriguing pathways'.[33] But many homeless people lived here: '… police once made a clean-up of the place and found a miniature dossers' city there. They even had a "city square" there from which they branched off their sleeping quarters.'[34]

Today I locate the spot where the girls might have clambered up through the scrub to reach the seaward side of Hobson Street. Between Meter Reading Services at 133 Thorndon Quay and Field Smart Technology at 137 is a small lane crammed with cars, leading up to 10 Hobson Street. The elite gravitated here to 'Snobson Street' by the late nineteenth century, building pillared mansions on original town-acre sections.

I'm flagging. The girls approach the Tinakori Road end of Hobson Street, ready to cross the infamous gully behind the original Beauchamp home. Ruddick: 'We persuaded Vera to walk home by Fitzherbert Terrace and the suspension bridge. The suspension bridge, swinging above a steep gorge lined with feathery trees was most exciting … It was always a relief to find the ground solid beneath our feet on the other side.'[35] Lawlor and his friends were braver: 'A great game on this suspension bridge was for a half dozen boys to commence a united swaying motion.'[36]

Unaccompanied children on the quieter edges of Thorndon were not always safe, even in daylight. The city's homeless, most of them male, some of them aggressive, frequented the inner city then as they do now. One of the best known was 'Jess' Underwood, a weathered man with black flowing hair and gold earrings, a likely habitué of the fennel forest by the

Esplanade. In 1899 Underwood was charged with 'using an obscenity' in Molesworth Street. Magistrates heard he'd been 'in the habit of abusing and threatening children on, and in the vicinity of, Wadestown Road for some time past'.[37] He was jailed for seven days.

Katherine Mansfield portrays this courtly alcoholic in her story 'Ole Underwood'. Her close, almost affectionate observations suggest he was well known to her: '"Ah-k!" shouted Ole Underwood shaking his umbrella at the wind bearing down on him, beating him, half strangling him with his black cape. "Ah-k!" shouted the wind a hundred times as loud, and filled his mouth and nostrils with dust.'[38]

We're back on Tinakori Road now, on the homeward stretch. Near the intersection with Hobson Street, where townhouses now stand, the girls cluster around number 29, the setting of what the papers call a 'romantic suicide'.[39] Maybe they've heard tell of recent events in the house, pointing up to the room where they happened. It was here that Annie Clark, an unmarried 25-year-old, fired a bullet through her 'bare bosom'.[40] Her lover, William Jacks, had spurned her after the death of her child from a previous relationship. Annie's farewell note was widely remarked on:

> *It seems rather hard to die just yet … You said all men are not alike, but I see they are … Dear Will, I do not know where they bury people who take their own lifes [sic], but if they bury me in the Karori Cemetery, bury me near my little baby. The number of its grave is 193, on the side of the hill. Now, I want you to keep my ring in memory of me. Will you do this – it is the only thing I ask?*[41]

At 75 Tinakori Road, the Beauchamps mount the concrete steps. Ruddick continues up the road, turning into Hill Street. Kathleen often returned to the esplanade. Pat Lawlor spied her there, 'looking out to sea longingly. I was tempted to speak to her for there was something just "different" about this admittedly plain girl. I was too shy and she was older and more mature than I.'[42]

Rats in a rowboat, sneaking plague into the country.

Cover illustration. *New Zealand Graphic and Ladies' Journal*, 1900. Wellington Public Library.

Sixteen: Picked out in primroses

I have such a pretty garden. The border is double purple primroses, and my initial
'K' is in white primroses in the centre … – Kathleen Beauchamp, 1901[1]

T he cover of the *New Zealand Graphic and Ladies' Journal* for 24 March
1900 pictured three whiskery rats in a rowboat, sneaking bubonic
plague into the country. With a new century came a fresh sanitation
panic. Fears of plague, the infamous medieval 'Black Death', replaced
typhoid and cholera as the epidemics *du jour* when a few cases broke out
in Sydney, Fiji and even, possibly, Auckland.

As the spectre of disease hung over the country, Wellington city
councillors spent the equivalent of $10 million on an 'exuberant' town
hall, infuriating Seddon and his fellow ministers. Standing supreme as
the country's commercial, financial, administrative and transport hub,
its economy and population booming, the capital was in such bullish
heart that one commentator even suggested that moving the seat of
government elsewhere would be 'no crushing disaster'.[1]

In response to queries from the *Evening Post*, Harold Beauchamp
reassured citizens that no vermin lurked in his harbourside warehouses
where incoming cargo was stored. A local ship's captain, however, claimed
he'd seen rats peeping out from bunches of bananas.[2] The municipality
ordered ships be moored 'away from the wharves after five o'clock in the
evening, so as to prevent rats leaving from them'.[3] A threepenny bounty
was paid on each rat taken to the great city furnace – or destructor – that
flamed around the clock where Waitangi Park now stands. Attention
turned to insanitary buildings, and the council ordered demolition of
decaying houses in Te Aro. The noisome slums of Saunders Lane and

adjacent George Street in Thorndon, on Katherine Mansfield's way to school, were overlooked.

At 11, she was already a witness to the wealth and poverty in the streets of her city. By day she and her siblings sat in the well-appointed classrooms of the nearest thing the colony had to a finishing school. Here, at their new school at Fitzherbert Terrace in the leafiest part of Thorndon, they mingled with the offspring of the class that ruled the colony. Kathleen happily donned the school's straw boater with its blue and green ribbon. She enjoyed the braided frocks of dark wool. Besides, she was on familiar ground: behind the wooden school building lay the gully that backed onto her old home. School principal Mary Swainson might have been a daring smoker who favoured 'mannish' clothing and short-cropped hair, yet here the elite paid for – and got – a traditional private-school education for their daughters and a few sons, including young Leslie Beauchamp.

At school Katherine Mansfield connected with other bookish types, joining the select Ante-Room (AR) club, which mulled over production of the school magazine in a room at the top of the back stairs. In a fundraiser she played Mrs Jarley, the colourful owner of the waxworks in Dickens' *Old Curiosity Shop*.[4] Dickens remained as popular as ever. She archly recalled the principal reading him aloud:

> There is something so fascinating in her voice that I could listen for years & years. She is reading David Copperfield. When there is a full page illustration she passes the book around for us to look … The headmistress herself is exactly like one of these illustrations – so tiny, so spry … What does she remind me of? She reminds me of a bird and a donkey mixed.[5]

Her recollections of school life suggest a hankering for freedom: she observes a tall girl named 'Rhody' 'break from the "crocodile" (line of girls in pairs) when they walked in the park'.[6] Her early friendship with Maata Mahupuku, of Ngāti Kahungunu, a fellow literary type, was also represented as a voyage to a less constrained world. The story 'Kezia and Tui' imagines Maata's shabby, untidy Thorndon home, with Kezia 'stepping over a saucepan, two big cabbages and Tui's hat and coat'.[7] Tui's urban Māori domain is fictionalised as homelier and less starched than 75 Tinakori Road, though its fashion sense does not go unnoticed: 'White muslin curtains made out of an old skirt of her mother's adorned the bed, and everywhere Kezia looked there were pink sateen bows.'[8] In fact, Maata appears to have been a boarder at the Fitzherbert Terrace School at this time.

Kathleen was pulling back, even mildly rebelling in a way she'd never considered at the more egalitarian Wellington Girls' High: she'd developed the Edwardian equivalent of an attitude problem. One teacher remembered her probing questions on 'free love', a scandalous topic.[9] Another, a Mrs Henry Smith, described her as 'surly'. Worse, the compositions she'd beavered over were dismissed as 'too prolific, poorly written, poorly spelled and careless'.[10] Her story 'Juliet' touches on this period: 'She had been, as yet, utterly idle at school, drifted through her classes ... and all the pleading & protestations of her teachers could not induce her to learn that which did not appeal to her.'[11] In fact, Kathleen was anything but idle: scribbling at home, chronicling the passing life – and death – outside her front door.

✀

The rats depicted on the cover of the *Graphic* spooked the population. At the height of the panic, on 29 March 1900, the occupant of one of the wretched cottages below the Beauchamps' residence sickened. Henry Samuel Scott, a healthy 40-year-old, collapsed while gathering parcels on Lambton Quay, and died hours later in hospital. The authorities wouldn't rule out plague, said the *Evening Post*: an inquest was ordered. A paragraph about the parcel carter, or modern-day courier, 'well known about town', noted the suddenness of his death. This was said to be a calling card of the plague.[12] Scott was interred at Karori Cemetery. Days after his burial the *Post* noted, anti-climactically, that in fact 'the cause of death was heart disease and a tumour in the intestines' and that no inquest was necessary.[13] But the death set the capital on edge.

This Henry Scott, I believe, was the starting point for Katherine Mansfield's 'The Garden Party', her unforgettable story of rich and poor on Tinakori Road. In the story, the Sheridans reside in a grand house and throw a garden party. In the midst of the revelry they learn that Scott, the father of 'five little ones' in the nearby slums, has suddenly died, and gauchely take party food to the mean little cottage where he's laid out. The baker's man asks Laura Sheridan: 'Know those cottages just below here? There's a young chap living there, name of Scott, a carter. His horse shied at a traction-engine, corner of Hawke Street this morning, and he was thrown out on the back of his head. Killed.'[14]

The cause of the real-life carter's death has long confused scholars. But after a trawl through newspaper and cemetery records I'm able to ascertain the circumstances of Henry Scott's death and its tragic aftermath. First, as we know, he died of natural causes. Second, the victim and his widow Lillia had two children, a boy and a girl, not five as in 'The Garden Party'. Third, his widow almost certainly could not have afforded to bring the body home: the undertaker's basic fee of £1 8s 6d (nearly $300 in today's money) wouldn't stretch to that. Lastly, the death sent Scott's family into penury, forcing them into a tiny cottage in Saunders Lane.

So what did Kathleen Beauchamp make of this death and the accompanying spoor of plague? Did she know Scott's daughter, Lily Amelia, a girl of the same age? Might she even have been a classmate at Wellington Girls' High? Was Lily one of the urchins from Saunders Lane pursued by her father? Either way, the death in the neighbouring house appears to consume her.

Within months of Scott's death, she'd be submitting for publication a story of life and death in the slums, a fragment of overlooked juvenilia clearly inspired by the melancholy events across the road.

I'm on the top floor of Wellington City Library, inside the rolling stacks, a state-of-the-art shelving system that glides on rails at the turn of a wheel. These roof-high, fast-moving walls of books (beware the vanishing aisle!) hide some of the library's brittlest, brightest treasures. Librarian and polymath Gabor Toth and I are retrieving a unique collection of the *New Zealand Graphic and Ladies' Journal*, an Auckland weekly popular in the fragrant drawing rooms of middle-class 'ladies' at the turn of the twentieth century. I've taken up his suggestion of a dip into the world's only remaining paper copy of a periodical that chronicled the Beauchamps' world, a periodical yet to be examined in its entirety a century after its demise. These bound, azure-coloured volumes are so heavy that Toth balances them on my shoulder.

The *Graphic* flourished between 1890 and 1908. Its swirl of elite gossip, royal bulletins and moody pictorials of Māori maidens was an irresistible confection for local rumps of colonial society fixated on rank, wealth and fashion. What made its broadsheet pages unusual was the fact that the weekly never shied away from traversing – in a genteel way, of course – debates about women's emancipation: dress reform, bicycling and smoking.

These volumes look as good as new here in the Wellington library's newspaper room, which today is crowded with readers at wide tables. Cloth-capped men or women in shawls could come here to the library a century ago, curl up by the fire grate, and look in on the closed, glittering world of the local urban and rural gentry.

I start my reading, turning pages, pausing at stories with headlines like 'The Art of Enjoying the Beach' and 'Why Women Ask Questions'. I'm hoping that a read of the *Graphic* can help me understand 'society' in turn-of-the-century Thorndon, the world of the Beauchamp family.

The family was ushered into these select purviews when Annie's brother Frank Dyer wed Phoebe Seddon. The happy couple were stars of the issue of 23 January 1897, which devoted three pages, a splash of luminous photographs and a gushing commentary to what it called THE society wedding of the year:

> *Wellington elbowed and jostled and fairly trod on its own heels in a struggle to witness the marriage celebrated in St Paul's Pro Cathedral, Mulgrave Street … a large arch stood in the centre aisle, decorated with ferns, bamboo and white agapanthus. From the centre hung the initials of the bride and bridegroom beautifully designed in silver thread tinsel.*[15]

The Beauchamps had linked arms with the political and social elite, with Kathleen's little sister Jeanne a bridesmaid in cream silk trimmed with pink, and a broad-brimmed picture hat.

The family name henceforth was embedded within the *Graphic*. Here was Harbour Board chair Harold farewelling the Duke and Duchess of Cornwall and York in soaking weather. 'He hoped that their Royal Highnesses would regard it as emblematic of the public regret at their departure from Wellington.'[16] Here was Tinakori Road hostess Annie, in a 'pretty gown of soft cream voile, tucked, and the bodice softened with lace and pale blue silk',[17] rehearsing the quaint 'At Home' ritual, imported from England, based on formally receiving guests and leaving cards. The highlight of her 'At Home' at 75 Tinakori Road in 1900 was a singing performance. Magnate T.G. McCarthy's wife was more daring: she amused her guests with a fortune-teller. And an adjacent room at her Boulcott Street mansion was devoted to the 'new craze of ping pong'.[18]

'Society' in the capital tended to be plucked from the ranks of saloon passengers aboard the first waves of New Zealand Company vessels, people whose names stand out like blue veins on a city map. A self-styled gentry, with its house parties, hunt balls in the Wairarapa and teams of servants, was at first 'tightly knit and very small', according to historian Roberta McIntyre.[19] Many gravitated between New Zealand and 'Home'. By 1900, a businessman like Harold Beauchamp, once looked down on as 'trade', could find a seat. It was in part self-interest: as Seddon's Liberals shook up the political landscape after working men, then women, got the vote, the landowning 'plutes' found themselves out on the margins.

But their rarefied world glittered on, perpetuated in such outposts as Kathleen Beauchamp's finishing school. It was said of Wellington that 'there is society and a school'.[20] Not surprisingly, the Fitzherbert Terrace School was a fixture in the *Graphic*'s society pages, with paragraphs devoted to a charity bazaar run by pupils in aid of the Maori Girls' School in Auckland. Expensive prizes handed out to the winners of the best-dressed doll and other competitions included silver-backed brushes and combs, gold brooches and pins.[21] Even the *Graphic*'s reporter sounds envious.

Week by week, the *Graphic* lovingly covered this terrain, with vats of ink devoted to 'At Homes' in Parnell and Thorndon. Readers could stay apprised of the latest London and Paris fashions: Marguerite's weekly 'World of Fashion' showed engravings of 'A Coming Hat', 'Yet Another Bolero of Unmistakeable Grace' and a solemn edict that 'Epaulettes Should not be Pleated'.

If Seddon and his Liberal government were ushering in a more egalitarian age for New Zealand, the writers of the *Graphic* seemed unaware of it. Domestic servants still mattered a great deal to its readers, although 'help' was to vanish within a generation. This is made clear in a pictorial spread, the first page of which is entitled: 'This is the sort of servant we should like to have'.[22] Captions (with accompanying black and white photos) include: 'As for scrubbing and scouring, she says she rather likes it', 'She is up early and gets a bright fire going' and 'Breakfast is on the table at 8am sharp'. The second page, however, is entitled 'This is the sort we usually get', along with the following complaints (and photos): 'She reads all our private letters interestedly', 'She is a holy terror in the matter of breakages' and 'She listens at keyholes'.[23]

℘

After several days of leafing through these drawing-room trifles, I'm bored. But I keep reading. The Children's Pages at the back of the *Graphic* prove a bright distraction. I'm drawn into what page editor Cousin Kate calls the 'cousinhood': the community of young misses (and a few masters) who read the paper on a rainy Saturday afternoon. Younger contributors are entitled to a 'cousin's badge' in red satin for a published letter or story. Cousin Kate encourages contributions ('write on one side of the paper only') and devises bright competitions. Cousins are urged to raise money for the Cousins' Cot Fund 'for maintaining a poor sick child in Auckland Hospital'. The cousins send large amounts after Kate reveals 'the poor little chap in the Graphic cot suffers from eye trouble'.[24]

I feel I'm getting to know Cousin Kate. Erratic contributions from her New Zealand readers often force her to draw on British material and other fillers. This brings out her martyred side – her occasional complaint that 'you have, most of you, been rather lazy about writing lately, and really do not deserve many competitions'.[25] She urges more input: 'You will easily understand that if only four of five cousins try for a competition, it is not possible for me to get the proprietor to give nice prizes.'[26]

I'm getting the most peculiar feeling. Without understanding why, as I turn through each week's issue I make straight for Cousin Kate's pages. I'm now figuring Kathleen Beauchamp *must* have been reading this paper, because her family and her world feature in it so prominently. And if she read the paper, would she have been able to resist contributing something? The girl who'd rushed to show Molly Ruddick her story from the *Reporter*? The one who later skewered classmates who had had more success at writing, and who pretended to have won her sister's prize? I keep reading, hour after numbing hour, driven on by a weird, nettlesome hunch.

Several hundred editions in, the Children's Pages start to pall; Cousin Kate is just another editorial steward of tedious copy. There is nothing here. What was I thinking? But I keep turning the pages. I open the edition of 8 June 1901. Ho hum. There's yet another caricature of politician Joseph Ward on the cover; the first instalment of Rudyard Kipling's *Kim* begins. Then, boom! Here, in the middle of the Children's Page, is a letter signed by a Kathleen Beauchamp. The writer is shamelessly flattering Kate, working hard to ensure publication and secure a red satin badge. (Later, John Middleton Murry remarked on his wife's ability 'to assume a personality to please … I suppose we all do it to some degree. But in her it was very pronounced.'[27]) Either way, the letter is a hoot, and Kate's lengthy reply shows she's been won over.

> *Dear Cousin Kate, – What beautiful competitions you are now having. My great chum, Irene Jameson, is staying with me for the term holidays, and is now, as you see, writing to you. We have a dear little kitten called 'Jimmy', pure black except for a white tip to his tail. Every morning he comes upstairs with the morning tea, and expects to be rewarded with a piece of bread and butter. This dear little puss is on the table beside me now, and is playing with the blotting paper. He had pulled over the ink, so excuse the smudge. I have such a pretty garden. The border is double purple primroses, and my initial 'K' is in white primroses in the centre. We have been having very good weather, which is most unusual for the May holidays. Might I write another story for*

the 'Christmas Page'? I was very pleased that my mother met you in Auckland. I really must conclude now as Irene and myself are going to make toffy [sic]. Love to all the cousins and the same to yourself.

I am your loving cousin,

Kathleen Beauchamp

PS – We are sending the pictures which we coloured.

Dear Cousin Kathleen, – It is quite a long time since I heard from you, but I was highly delighted to be told all about your lovely little garden and also that dear little puss. She must be very clever and amusing. I hope you will try another story, and be sure if it is a nice one I shall be only too glad to publish it in our Children's Page at Christmas. Did that toffee turn out well? I used just to love making it before I became a 'grown up' – I like it best when it is not quite cold, but in the state we used to call stick-jaw. Do you put almonds in your toffy [sic]? and how do you flavour it? I like a very little lemon, but it makes an awful spluttering when you squeeze it into the boiling toffee. – Yours, Cousin Kate.[28]

Young Kathleen's initial 'K' in white primroses! What tosh. I chortle out loud, sit back, overcome, disbelieving. I make a series of low, garbled noises at librarian Ann Rewiti, seated at an adjacent desk. She looks nonplussed, as does a second librarian when I repeat what I've found. They're used to eccentrics here in the reading room.

I contact a friendly authority on Katherine Mansfield. The reply is encouraging yet terrifying: 'Sent in high excitement! … almost certainly KM must have had an earlier story published in that same magazine, so if you could find that!!! It is also earlier by two years than the first letter in the Collected Letters …'[29] I close the laptop feeling queasy, aware that my immediate priority is to track down a story. It will not be easy. Would any contribution by Kathleen Beauchamp even bear her name? Would I recognise her style if it was unnamed? From what I know of Cousin Kate, she's a fickle, even erratic editor: sometimes she cites the names of contributors, but not always.

By the following morning I'm hanging my head, certain I'll never find what I'm looking for. Nevertheless, I join the throng outside the library front doors, half sprinting up the escalator to the third-floor reading room where my volumes are piled on a trolley. I try to look nonchalant. Could someone, after 115 years, have rumbled my find overnight?

I scour the Children's Pages in a hundred editions, examining everything Cousin Kate ever handled, back and forward, retracing my steps. Nothing. After three hours my eyes hurt. I try to keep up morale. I'm aware that apart from short pieces in school magazines, Katherine Mansfield was not formally published until 1907. A *Graphic* debut in 1900 would be little short of revelatory.

By midday, I'm pretty sure the library angels have flown. I'm perusing the issue of Saturday 13 October 1900. Richard Seddon, busy annexing the South Pacific, appears on the cover, caricatured as a Fijian chief. I note a story about the twin evils of hurry and work. Hmmm. I'm back on the Children's Page, two-thirds of the way down. Suddenly, wondrously, I spot the name 'Kathleen M. Beauchamp, age 11, Wellington'. I can't bring myself to read further; I crumple in relief, disbelief. Eventually, exhaustedly, I start to focus on the accompanying story, a piece entitled 'His Little Friend':

In a quiet little village in S— there dwelt an aged couple, whose names were John and Mary Long. They had a small cottage standing far back from the road, with a large garden in front, both of which were scrupulously neat and tidy. Mary had married John when she was nineteen, and they had lived in the same little cottage ever since. Now she was past sixty, and he was seventy-three. Mary took in sewing, while John sold fruit and vegetables to the villagers.

It had been a hot day, and John had been picking fruit and digging up vegetables nearly all day. It was six o'clock now, and Mary had called him to tea. He put his tools in an out-house and went in.

'Have you wiped your feet, John?' said a sharp voice, and Mary looking up from the toast she was buttering glanced at the boots in question.

'No, Mary, I have not,' he answered meekly; 'but I'll go and do so.'

He went to the mat, wiped his boots carefully, returned to the kitchen and sat down to tea. There was never any conversation between them at meals. John ate his tea, returned to his garden for half an hour, read the paper, and went to bed.

'I am going with you to the village today, John,' said Mary, 'as I have to take Mrs Gage the dress she gave me to make.'

At nine o'clock they started, John with his kit of fruit and vegetables, and Mary with her parcel. When they reached the village they disposed of their goods, bought a few supplies, and wended their way home. They had nearly reached there when they met the village parson.

'Oh, good morning,' he said pleasantly. 'I have not seen you in church with your husband lately, Mrs Long.'

'No, sir. Last Sabbath I had neuralgia so bad I couldn't move, so told John to go.'

'I am sorry you had neuralgia,' the minister replied gravely; 'but I hope I shall see you next Sunday. Good-day! Oh, by the way, Mr Long, could you supply me with fruit and vegetables?'

'I should be only too pleased sir,' John answered.

'Very well; come on Mondays and Thursdays.'

And they went on. Next Monday John set out with the best of his fruit and vegetables for the minister. He sold his things and was just out of the gate when he heard a noise as though someone was sobbing. John, though he did not look it, was very fond of children. On looking back he beheld a little boy sobbing piteously.

'What is the matter, my little man,' said John.

The child lifted a tear-stained face to his. 'Oh, please sir,' he said, 'mother's ill and we hasent got nofing to eat.'

John remembered that Mary had gone to the village to spend the day with some of her friends, so he said kindly: 'Come along with me, and we'll see what we can do.'

The child ran forward, and clasping his tiny hand in John's big one he said: 'I fink you's very kind. My name's Bobbie; what's yours?'

'My name is Mr Long,' John answered.

After that they trudged along quickly, the child amusing John with his prattle. They reached the cottage, got some provisions, and went to Bobbie's home, which was a miserable enough abode:

'Come in and see mother,' said Bobbie, who had quite regained his spirits.

'I think I must be going,' said John.

He put the provisions on the table, and promising to make him a boat out of a piece of wood he had, he went home. When he reached home John set about making the promised boat, and he really fashioned it most skilfully. The rest of the day John spent in his garden.

It was not till the following Thursday that John saw his little friend. He had the boat with him, and they met at the same spot. Bobbie rushed up to him and welcomed him most cordially.

'I fought you was never comin'. I'se been waiting for you every day,' he said.

'Here is the boat I promised you,' replied John, unwrapping his present.

He was quite rewarded for the pains he had taken in making it by the look of admiration and pleasure which filled the small boy's eyes.

'Oh, Mr Long,' he exclaimed, 'is it weally for me?'

'Yes,' said John, and he held out the present to the delighted child.

'Fankshu' (thank you), he said, 'and next time you come, Mr Long, I'll have a pweasent for you.'

'I'll be here on Monday,' replied John, and then they parted.

John was very curious to know what Bobbie would have for him, so he went to the minister's a little earlier next Monday, but Bobbie was there before him, and in his arms he held a tiny black and white kitten.

'Here, Mr Long,' he shouted, 'here's a pweasant for you.'

John accepted the gift with many expressions of thanks, but when he got home he took care that Mary should not see his little pet. So every Monday and Thursday John saw Bobbie and a great friendship sprang up between them.

John's love for Bobbie increased every day, and by denying himself comforts to give little gifts to him he won the child's affection. One morning John went with his goods as usual but Bobbie was not there. He thought there must be some reason for it, and was looking round when he perceived a woman running towards him.

'Oh! Please sir,' she gasped, when she reached John. 'Bobbie's very ill, and he keeps callin' for Mr Long. Where does he live?'

'I am Mr Long,' said John; 'let us go at once. What is the matter with him?'

'He's been ill since Monday with the cold and the doctor says he can't live past to-day.'

They had reached the cottage by this time, and as they entered a girl came to meet them.

'He's just awake,' she said, so John passed in.

What a different little Bobbie it was that lay there.

'Mr Long,' he whispered feebly, 'I have wanted you so. I so glad you here.'

John whispered words of love and tenderness to the little lad. Suddenly a smile illuminated his face. He stretched out his arms. 'Yes, I'se tumin,' was all he said. Then he fell back on the pillow. John's little friend was dead.

CHILDREN'S CORRESPONDENCE COLUMN.

Any boy or girl who likes to become a cousin can do so, and write letters to 'Cousin Kate, care of the Lady Editor, 'Graphic' Office, Auckland.

Write on one side of the paper only.

All purely correspondence letters with enelope ends turned in are carried through the Post Office as follows:—Not exceeding ½oz, ½d; not exceeding 4oz, 1d; for every additional 2oz or fractional part thereof, ½d. It is well for correspondence to be marked 'Press Manuscript only.'

Please note, dear cousins, that all letters addressed to Cousin Kate must now bear the words 'Press Manuscript only. If so marked, and the flap turned in, and not overweight, they will come for a ½d stamp in Auckland, but a 1d from every other place.

COUSINS' CORRESPONDENCE.

My Dear Cousin Kate,—Is it not grand news that has been quickly sent along the silent wires? The Duke and Duchess of York have accepted the invitation of the Government to visit this colony. Coming with the roseate dawn of a new century—for we hope it shall see the complete dispersion of the clouds that have darkened our skies of late—such royal appreciation will linger long in the mind of the people of Britain's far-off colony. This gracious act of the Queen shall be for us of the Land of Aotearoa, the greatest event of the longest and most glorious reign in English history. The love borne for her by her people, and the knowledge that she is still dearer to them to-day than she ever was before, must make all desirous to give a loyal welcome to her grandson, who may one day wear the Royal crown. It is said that France is considering the contingency of war with England. I think we need not take a gloomy view of such a position, or think seriously of the chances of a French invasion, but rather sing with Alfred Austin:

And, though the world togetner band,
Not all the legions of the land
Shall ever wrest from England's hand
The Sceptre of the Sea.

The war in South Africa is drawing to a close, and I am sure the termination of the twelve months' strife will be hailed with the wildest delight throughout Great Britain's vast dominion. All should determine to do their best to show the loyalty of our small colony to a great Empire, and an historic throne, and mark in a befitting manner the auspicious occasion when Britain furls her battle banners, twines the peaceful olive round the sword, and rings the bugle call of victory.—Your loving Cousin, Jack.

[Dear Cousin Jack,—Thank you very much for your very eloquent and scholarly letter. It will be read with pleasure by all the Cousins. It only arrived just as we were going to press, so I will ask you to excuse a brief reply.—Cousin Kate.]

⊙ ⊙ ⊙

Dear Cousin Kate,—We are indeed getting a large, happy band. I am very glad to be welcomed as one of the Cousins. Could you tell me about how many there are? I have an air gun with which I practise shooting at a mark. All our fruit trees are in blossom, and we hope to have a good crop this year. Would once a month be too often for me to write to you? My father thinks it is very good practice. He wishes me to be a doctor. I like going down to the beach to fish. Summer is coming, and I will be able to continue my lessons in swimming.—Cousin Oscar, Thames.

[Dear Cousin Oscar,—You must write just as often as ever you like, and not regulate yourself by any fixed time. I am afraid I could not spare time just now to send you a list of all the Cousins, but we must count ourselves by hundreds now, I think. I hope you are very careful with that air gun. They are rather dangerous toys, I consider. I hope you will be a doctor, too. It is a noble profession.—Cousin Kate.]

⊙ ⊙ ⊙

Dear Cousin Kate,—I wrote to you in June, and it is now the 24th of September. I have had no answer to my letter either in the "Graphic" or a private one, so I am wondering what has happened to you. I read the Cousins' page every week, and from your answers to their letters I see you are still alive and well, so I cannot understand why I have not heard from you. The letter about the coleuses has not arrived here yet. Mother cut the coleuses down and put them by the fire every night, but two of them died. Was not that a terrible thing about the blacks in N.S.W. murdering the people? We were told that they were in the country that Rolf Boldrewood wrote about in "Robbery Under Arms." Did you ever read it? I think it is a splendid book. What has happened to the "War Competition"? There has been nothing about it in the "Graphic" for a long time now. The last South African war news we hear is that Kruger has got away to Holland after all. When we last heard from our brother he said he believed Oom Paul would be too many for them yet. Have you ever seen an Australian magpie, Cousin Kate? There has been one about here for the last three or four days, such a pretty big black and white bird; but the poor thing was lame. Some people tried to shoot it, and they must have lamed it, and the poor thing came down here. I have not seen it to-day. I have read the book you sent to Dora for a prize, "Polly, a New Fashioned Girl." There is one very amusing piece in it about a little dog that is always biting, and two of the children, one an Australian boy and the other an English girl. They dig a hole in the ground, hide the dog (they do it at night, so that they will not be seen), and then the boy sells it the next night, and puts the money in its owner's purse. Its owner is a very crabbed old woman, so you can imagine what the result is when it is found out what they have done. One of the Cousins (a Wellington Cousin, I believe, it was) said she had read a book called "Elsie's Motherhood." I suppose it was one of the "Elsie" series, by Martha Finley. I have read a lot of them, right from the first one, to the one called "Elsie's Kith and Kin." I liked them, and wish I could get some more. I am looking forward to seeing those photos you have been promised for the "Graphic." I, like you, could not understand Cousin Norman's letter about his photo. As far as I could make out you had put the wrong name under one of the photos. All the last photos that have been in the "Graphic" of Cousins I have put in my book that I told you about, with ferns round them. I liked Mr William Satchell's patriotic verses that were printed in the "Graphic" a little while ago. The one called "Mafeking" I liked best. That letter from Lord Roberts to Dorothy Cummings was not written by him. It was begun and signed by him; but the rest was not his hand writing. Anyone could see it was two different writings. Now, I expect this is long enough, and I must not take up two much of your time and space. Good bye.—I remain, your Cousin, Anna.

Dear Cousin Anna,—I cannot imagine what became of your former letter. Certainly I never saw it. It must have got lost or perhaps you forgot to post it. I have done that once or twice myself and found the letter ages after in a blotting pad or a drawer. Most certainly you have not offended me. I am very glad you like to write and take so great an interest in our cousins' page. Your letter was a capital one, and I hope you will soon write again. I should not think the fire was very good for the coleuses, but perhaps you may save the second one. I told you in my letter that it was very difficult to keep them save in a greenhouse but to give them a nice warm window, and not too much water. You must excuse a short answer, as I have several other cousins to write to.—Cousin Kate.]

⊙ ⊙ ⊙

Dear Cousin Kate,—Wellingtonians are experiencing very funny weather just now for the mornings begin with being very pleasant and sunshiny, and then quite unexpectedly it begins to pour with rain. At the Opera House this week Donald Macdonald has been delighting us with his lectures on the war. The first night there were 2000 people present to hear him, and for the four succeeding nights there were very large audiences. The ever-amusing Pollards are coming here again on Monday, and will open with "Paul Jones." We are having plenty of amusement here now in the way of variety companies, for there is another one opened in Wellington now besides Dix's and Fuller's; it is called Hooper's, and promises to be as great a success as the former ones are now. The spring fashions are now in full play, and we see the fascinating cherry-trimmed hats and toques with their billowy heaps of chiffon. Some of the dresses worn now are very beautiful, and the fashions this year are the prettiest and most expensive we have had for some time. Dear Cousin Kate I have not yet received my card. Hoping to do so, I remain, Cousin Winnie, Wellington.

[Dear Cousin Winnie,—I have just posted you your card. I am sorry I overlooked it before. The weather here has been horrible, and everyone is ill with influenza. I am glad you liked Donald Macdonald. I thought him a capital teller of war stories. Have you chosen your spring dress yet?—Cousin Kate.]

⊙ ⊙ ⊙

Dear Cousin Kate,—I should like very much to become one of your cousins. We take the "Graphic" every week, and I am always very much interested in the children's page. I think it would be very nice if the cousins who collect stamps, crests, or monograms would put their whole address to their letters when they write, because then we could write and exchange stamps, etc., with each other. Cousin Roie who writes to the "Graphic" is a real cousin of mine, though we have never seen each other. I am fourteen, and go to Pepitea private school. My favourite subject is French. A French master comes to teach us. Cousin Aileen goes to the same school as I. Will you send me a collecting card please. I must now close my letter.—I remain, your affectionate cousin, Zaidee Nathan, Wellington.

[Dear Cousin Zaidee,—What a very quaint and pretty name you have got. I am most delighted to have you for a cousin. There is a letter you see from Cousin Roie in this "Graphic" too. I think your suggestion about the stamp collecting cousins a capital one. Perhaps some other cousins will take the matter up. I am sure you will find French very useful, especially when you go home to Europe. Write again soon.—Cousin Kate.]

⊙ ⊙ ⊙

Dear Cousin Kate,—I received my badge quite safely, and please let me thank you for it. My holidays are now ended, so I am at my lessons again. Has it not been nasty weather lately. Mother took my little sister and myself for a drive yesterday out to Mt. Wellington. We had a lovely blow. There were such a lot of dear little lambs on the way in the paddocks. Was there not a big hailstorm this morning; we got a big basin full of it. I hope this letter will be in time for next week's "Graphic." Are there not a lot of new cousins? I am trying to write a little story, and if I ever finish it perhaps you may think it good enough to put in the "Graphic." I think that is all I can think of to say. With love, I remain, your affectionate cousin, Roie.

[Dear Cousin Roie,—I was so sorry this letter arrived just a few minutes too late for last week's "Graphic." I hope you were not very much disappointed. It is a very nice drive out to Mt. Wellington, is it not? I have ridden and driven there several times. I shall be so very glad if you send me in a story for the cousins' page, and it is capital exercise for you to try. You will see by a letter just before this that a real cousin of yours in Wellington has joined us. Are you not glad?—Cousin Kate.]

His Little Friend.

(By Kathleen M. Beauchamp, age 11 years, Wellington.)

In a quiet little village in S—— there dwelt an aged couple, whose names were John and Mary Long. They had a small cottage standing far back from the road, with a large garden in front, both of which were scrupulously neat and tidy. Mary had married John when she was nineteen, and they had lived in the same little cottage ever since. Now she was past sixty, and he was seventy-three. Mary took in sewing, while John sold fruit and vegetables to the villagers.

It had been a hot day, and John had been picking fruit and digging up vegetables nearly all day. It was six o'clock now, and Mary had called him to tea. He put his tools in an out-house and went in.

"Have you wiped your feet, John?" said a sharp voice, and Mary looking up from the toast she was buttering glanced at the boots in question.

"No, Mary, I have not," he answered meekly; but I'll go and do so."

He went to the mat, wiped his boots carefully, returned to the kitchen and sat down to tea. There was never any conversation between them at meals. John ate his tea, returned to his garden for half an hour, read the paper, and went to bed.

"I am going with you to the village to-day, John," said Mary, "as I have to take Mrs Gage the dress she gave me to make."

At nine o'clock they started, John with his kit of fruit and vegetables, and Mary with her parcel. When they reached the village they disposed of their goods, bought a few supplies, and wended their way home. They had nearly reached there when they met the village parson.

"Oh, good morning," he said pleasantly. "I have not seen you in church with your husband lately, Mrs Long."

"No, sir. Last Sabbath I had neuralgia so bad I couldn't move, so told John to go."

"I am sorry you had neuralgia," the minister replied gravely; "but I hope I shall see you next Sunday. Good-day! Oh, by the way, Mr Long, could you supply me with fruit and vegetables?"

"I should be only too pleased sir," John answered.

"Very well; come on Mondays and Thursdays."

And they went on. Next Monday John set out with the best of his fruit and vegetables for the minister. He sold his things and was just out of the gate when he heard a noise as though someone was sobbing. John, though he did not look it, was very fond of children. On looking back he beheld a little boy sobbing piteously.

"What is the matter, my little man," said John.

The child lifted a tear-stained face to his. "Oh, please sir," he said, "mother's ill, and we hasent got nothing to eat."

John remembered that Mary had gone to the village to spend the day with some of her friends, so he said kindly: "Come along with me, and we'll see what we can do."

The child ran forward, and clasping his tiny hand in John's big one he said: "I fink you's very kind. My name's Bobbie; what's yours?"

"My name is Mr Long," John answered.

After that they trudged along quickly, the child amusing John with his prattle. They reached the cottage, got some provisions, and went to Bobbie's home, which was a miserable enough abode:

"Come in and see mother," said Bobbie, who had quite regained his spirits.

"I think I must be going," said John.

He put the provisions on the table, and promising to make him a boat out of a piece of wood he had, he went home. When he reached home John set about making the promised boat, and he really fashioned it most skilfully. The rest of the day John spent in his garden.

It was not till the following Thursday that John saw his little friend. He had the boat with him, and they met at the same spot. Bobbie rushed up to him and welcomed him most cordially.

"I fought you was never comin', I'se been waiting for you every day," he said.

"Here is the boat I promised you," replied John, unwrapping his present. He was quite rewarded for the pains he had taken in making it by the look of admiration and pleasure which filled the small boy's eyes.

"Oh! Mr Long," he exclaimed, "is it weally for me?"

"Yes," said John, and he held out the present to the delighted child.

"Fankshu" (thank you), he said, "and next time you come, Mr Long, I'll have a pweasant for you."

"I'll be here on Monday," replied John, and then they parted.

John was very curious to know what Bobbie would have for him, so he went to the minister's a little earlier next Monday, but Bobbie was there before him, and in his arms he held a tiny black and white kitten.

"Here, Mr Long," he shouted; "here's a pweasant for you."

John accepted the gift with many expressions of thanks, but when he got home he took care that Mary should not see his little pet. So every Monday and Thursday John saw Bobbie and a great friendship sprang up between them.

John's love for Bobbie increased every day, and by denying himself comforts to give little gifts to him he won the child's affection. One morning John went with his goods as usual but Bobbie was not there. He thought there must be some reason for it, and was looking round when he perceived a woman running towards him.

"Oh! please sir," she gasped, when she reached John, "Bobbie's very ill, and he keeps callin' for Mr Long. Where does he live?"

"I am Mr Long," said John; "let us go at once. What is the matter with him?"

"He's been ill since Monday with the cold and the doctor says he can't live past to-day."

They had reached the cottage by this time, and as they entered a girl came to meet them.

"He's just awake," she said, as John passed in.

What a different little Bobbie it was that lay there.

"Mr Long," he whispered feebly, "I have wanted you so. I so glad you here."

John whispered words of love and tenderness to the little lad. Suddenly a smile illuminated his face. He stretched out his arms. "Yes, I'se tumin," was all he said. Then he fell back on the pillow. John's little friend was dead.

Janey's dolly had met with an accident, and broken her head, and mother was trying to take the broken head off and put on a new one, but could not manage it.

"I'm afraid I can't manage it, Janey," said mother; "the head won't come off."

"Never mind, mummy dear," said Janey, "Just take the body off; that'll do."

A Hideous Monster.

One would scarcely expect a "devil fish" to be a pleasing animal, and, indeed, of the several wholly different species of fish which bear the name, all are more or less repulsive; but the one encountered in his boyhood by Mr. Frank T. Bullen, which he has described in a recent article, was particularly unpleasant, and represented a little known variety, found only in the Gulf of Mexico. "When I was a youngster," he writes, "I was homeward bound from Santa Ana with a cargo of mahogany, and when off Cape Campeche I was one calm afternoon leaning over the taffrail, looking down into the blue profound, on the watch for fish. A gloomy shade came over the bright water, and up rose a fearsome monster some 18 feet across, and in general outline more like a skate or ray than anything else, all except the head. Then what appeared to be two curling horns about 3 feet apart rose one on each side of the most horrible pair of eyes imaginable. A shark's eyes, as he turns sideways under your vessel's counter and looks up to see if anyone is coming, are ghastly green and cruel, but this thing's eyes were all that and much more. I felt that the Book of Revelation was incomplete without him, and his gaze haunts me yet. Although quite sick and giddy at the sight of such a bogey, I could not move until the awful thing, suddenly waving what seemed like mighty wings, soared up out of the water soundlessly to a height of about 6 feet, falling again with a thunderous splash that might have been heard for miles. I must have fainted from fright, for the next thing of which I was conscious was awakening under the rough pontoring of my shipmates. Since then I have never seen one leap upward in the daytime. At night, when there is no wind, the sonorous splash is constantly to be heard, although why they make that battike leap out of their proper element is not easy to understand. It does not seem possible to believe such awe-inspiring horrors capable of playful gambolling. That is a kind of monster sufficiently hideous to form a fitting companion to that most frightful of all monsters—and one often called a devil fish—the gigantic octopus, well known and remembered by readers of Victor Hugo's 'Toilers of the Sea.'"

Mamma: "Freddy, what are you going to buy mamma for her birthday present?"

Freddy: "Why, momay dear, I've thought and thought about that, and I decided that the best thing I could get for you would be a new bat and ball for your little boy."

"What tiny little eggs, mamma!" said Edie, the other day at breakfast-time. "Wouldn't it be better to let the hens sit on them a little longer?"

It was the first t'me Dorothy had seen a cart for watering the roads in use.

"Oh, mother," she exclaimed, "do look what that man's got on his waggon to keep the boys from hanging on behind!"

THE BITER BIT.

Cat Murderer—Now, then; one, two, three and off she goes; right out into the deepest parts!

"Let 'er g-g-go, then!"

The Cat—Any port in a storm!—Ally Sloper.

HOW HE WENT FOR A DRINK OF WATER

THE ADVENTURES OF GENTLE JACOB.

The day was hot, the sun was strong,
And Jacob had been walking long,
With swift and steady song.
"I'll hie me down and get a drink,
Right glad he was at last to think,
My thirst is very ——."

Then to the pump he gaily went,
His dipper in his hand, content.
(He was a thirsty ——.)

And held it close beneath the spout
Where cool the water bubbled out,
And filled his —— with joy.

But though he pumped with all his might
He could not fill that dipper bright.
He tried it —— and ——

Where'er he would have drunk his fill,
Held to his thirsty lip it still
Was empty, as before!

Then puzzled sore, he smiled to see
Dear Susan coming o'er the lea,
Serene from anood to slipper.
She saw, she heard, she shook her head.
"Dear Jacob, don't you see," she said,
"The hole that's in the ——?"

Pages 224–225

An electrifying find: The *New Zealand Graphic* Children's Page featuring 'His Little Friend'.

New Zealand Graphic and Ladies' Journal, 13 October 1900. Wellington Public Library

. . . .

So there we have it: a splash in a national weekly, a thrill for any 11-year-old apprentice writer and a full seven years earlier than the publication of 'Vignettes' in the *Native Companion* (Melbourne) in 1907, previously thought to be her earliest story published outside school magazines. The story itself: a tragedy of Saunders Lane, an intermingling of the real-life death of Scott the carter and the fictional passing of Nell Trent in *The Old Curiosity Shop*. There's a character named Lord Bobbie in Dickens' novel. But what strikes me is the attention she pays in the first half of the story to the relationship between the Longs (an embryonic version of the Burnells, the Sheridans and other Beauchamp varietals). Kathleen Beauchamp is already rendering the people around her into copy, down to Mrs Long's age at marriage, her hectoring treatment of her husband and the detailed state of her health.

'His Little Friend' shows her grappling with harsh, bleak truths at a young age, paving the way for much of what was to come. It's the earliest – and previously unknown – example of the so-called 'baby' stories, mostly sentimental and featuring lonely, often ill children in miserable situations, and predates the others that Katherine Mansfield produced after 1903. 'Misunderstood' is one, obviously inspired by the Cousins' Cot Fund in the *Graphic*: 'In the front ward there was only one cot which did not have a visitor. This was occupied by a child of about eight years of age.'[30] She'd also write the dark, death-obsessed tale 'Two Ideas with One Moral'.[31]

So how would publication in the *Graphic* late in 1900 have affected daily life at the Fitzherbert Terrace School? Was it a talking point in the classroom? Cousin Kate's decision to publish can only have boosted Kathleen's confidence. She turned 12 the day after the story appeared. Criticism of her literary abilities from Mrs Henry Smith or other teachers would now, surely, have appeared irrelevant. A writer was on her way.

I'm not finished either: I reach for a fresh volume. Within hours I find a second letter, published weeks after 'His Little Friend':

Dear Cousin Kate, – I must apologise for not writing to you for so long. When are you going to have another story competition? I should very much like to go in for one. We have been having very bad weather, raining or else a howling gale of wind. I have just finished The Lady of the Forest, by L.T. Meade. I have enjoyed it very much. We are having a play at school called 'Alice in Wonderland'. I am to be Tweedledum. Might I write another story for the Children's Page? I was very pleased to see mine in print. We are having an asphalt tennis court made. Do you play tennis? I do not collect stamps, but postcards. I know Cousin Zaidie very well. She has a splendid collection. My sister collects also. We have a museum at school, and a society called the Natural History Society, and on fine Saturdays this society goes for expeditions to the seaside and collects shells etc. It is very interesting. We have four canaries at home. Their names are Buller, 'Bobs', Kitchener and Major Robin. They (the birds) sing beautifully. I think that Jungle Jinks in the Graphic are very comical. I went for a trip lately to Timaru. We were two days outside the harbour waiting for calm weather. When we were there we went for a drive and both horses fell down in the middle of the road. However, nothing very terrible came of it, for the driver touched them with his whip and they went on again perfectly all right. I must close now. – Hoping to see my letter in the Graphic, and with much love to the cousins. I remain your loving Cousin Kathleen.[32]

Kathleen Beauchamp sounds chatty and contented enough. The Irish-born, London-based author of *Lady of the Forest*, L.T. Meade, wrote rollicking yarns for Victorian girls, producing some 300 books in her lifetime. I note the reference to the *Graphic*'s Jungle Jinks feature. A young girl called Jinks is the star of 'One Day', a nursery tale from 1905, written at school in London. There's confirmation here, too, that the Beauchamps were canary fanciers, showing why father Harold was a patron of the local Poultry Pigeon and Canary Association. Katherine Mansfield also makes a canary the subject of her last published story.

For another entire day I sluice the *Graphic*, but the literary treasure appears to have evaporated. A consolation prize of sorts turns up: a pair of letters by nine-year-old Jeanne Beauchamp, stuffed with rich detail of life at Tinakori Road. The first is dated 24 August 1901:

Dear Cousin Kate, – this is the first time I have written to you. I have been reading your letters in the Graphic. We had such a nice old dog for a few days and he ran away and never came back again. His name was Boson. I have a cat named Woody; he is yellow. His mother is dead. My sister writes to you. My little brother has got croup. I have a canary of my own; it came from Las Palmas. I hope you will excuse the writing and allow me to be one of your cousins. My name is Jean [sic] Beauchamp, and I am 9 years old. I have been at school a year. Goodbye. – Your loving cousin JB.[33]

Jeanne's second letter, dated 21 September 1901, like her sister's letter of 17 November, portrays family members making regular trips out of town:

Dear Cousin Kate, – Mother and my three sisters have gone to Nelson. I am going to stay at home to take care of granny and my little brother. We have holidays for three weeks. My aunt has got three puppies. I went to such a nice bazaar on Monday. It was so nice. It was at Miss Freemon's on the Terrace. We are going to have one at our school. Our servant is at the hospital. She is very ill. We have had such lovely weather. – Jean.[34]

And that, sadly, was that. I close up – with a snap – the last of my tall, azure volumes of the *Graphic*. Like a typical bumblebee adolescent, Kathleen Beauchamp had moved on. A year after the glory of publication, she'd already graduated from the cousinhood. She'd not forget 'His Little Friend', of course; it would all be filed away. In it lie the sharp, dark seeds of 'The Garden Party'; and the clumsy phonetic dialogue to denote lower-class voices will later echo in 'The Doll's House'.

⌇

By 1901 Kathleen's focus was shifting to school exams and good works, as she announced in her prayer book: 'I am going to be a Mauri missionary.'[35] Her next known written effort, dated 4 June, even exposed her as a bit of a swot. 'The Great Examination' is a tale of three sisters (Phoebe, Bessie and Kitty) readying for exams.[36] Kitty, who 'bit the handles of two pens down to nothing' during the exam, wins a school prize – leather-bound books.[37] Prizegivings were never far from her mind.

She approached 13, symbolically crossing into adolescence with her first painful menstruation. Thereafter, she called the monthly cycle 'Aunt

Martha'. The family physician prescribed painkilling drugs. The moment came back to her in 1918 when she was again forced to take drugs for serious pain: 'They are the same things that good old Dr Martin gave Mother to give me when I was 13 and knew myself as a woman for the first time.'[38]

Music, not writing, became the preoccupation, the teenage craze. Edwardian Wellington had a feast of *al fresco* music on offer: orchestral music floated from band rotundas in public parks, gardens and on Thorndon Esplanade. The city council subsidised no fewer than four local orchestras and, in 1910, underwrote a 45-strong municipal orchestra, an Australasian first.

Chamber music, too, was wholeheartedly validated across middle-class Wellington households: young men and women took up piano and string instruments in vast numbers. The 1901 census showed no fewer than 1400 music teachers employed nationally.[39] National piano imports topped 4000 by 1901 – so many that one building in four hosted its own instrument.[40] Musical luminaries from Europe undertaking arduous but lucrative Australasian tours drew packed houses. Crowds applauded in 1901 when, as the *Graphic* put it, 'Wagner's strange, weird music was introduced to the Wellington theatre-goers on Wednesday in *Lohengrin*.'[41]

The Fitzherbert Terrace School put music at the heart of its curriculum; resident piano and singing teacher Robert Parker was judged the 'most outstanding' in the city.[42] The school history records: 'From the before-breakfast practising until bedtime, the house was rarely without the sound of music, and the girls were given every encouragement and incentive to hear music and study it.'[43] Katherine Mansfield's story 'The Singing Lesson' shows the senior forms, full-throated, in the music hall:

> *The noise was deafening … a sea of coloured flannel blouses, with bobbing pink faces and hands, quivering butterfly hair-bows, and music-books outspread.*[44]

Parker taught Kathleen during school hours in a music room dominated by a grand piano, but she was unmoved by an instrument that both her parents played. The desultory experience of a one-on-one piano lesson with an older male is remembered in 'The Wind Blows':

She likes this room. It smells of art serge and stale smoke and chrysanthemums … there is a big vase of them on the mantelpiece behind the pale photograph of Rubinstein … over the black glittering piano hangs 'Solitude' – a dark, tragic woman draped in white, sitting on a rock, her knees crossed, her chin on her hands.[45]

Besides, there was now a boy. Well, sort of. At the start of 1902, Kathleen discovered the cello. She'd fallen for Tom Trowell, a gifted musical prodigy of the same age who lived in the central city. He and his twin brother Garnet were the sons of Thomas senior, a music teacher and accomplished violinist, an Englishman with a long drooping moustache.

He was a sad man. In 1894 he and his wife lost Lindley, their firstborn son, to what was termed 'an infection'. The eight-year-old's death certificate records that heart inflammation (pericarditis) killed him in three days. Thomas Trowell survived by directing energy into the musical education of his remaining twins, cajoling the boys to practise for eight hours a day.[46] Pat Lawlor, who frequented the family home in Buller Street for violin lessons, witnessed Trowell's single-mindedness: 'I spent many hours there playing games with the boys, but never can I forget the dogged devotion of my teacher to his sons, teaching them music. He would appeal in a pathetic voice and manner to them to practice more.'[47]

Tom (stage name Arnold) and Garnet Trowell, performing in public by 15, were the redheaded musical idols of their day. When Kathleen first met Tom in 1901, she was just another teenage fan. But the 1906 story 'Juliet' details the protagonist's first breathless meeting with the love interest, David:

A boy of very much her own age was watching her curiously. He stood beside a great lamp and the light fell full on his face and his profusion of red-brown hair. Very pale he was with a dreaming exquisite face and a striking suggestion of confidence and Power in every feature. Juliet felt a great wave of colour spread over her face and neck. They stood staring into each other's eyes.[48]

Juliet learns that David is a gifted cellist, poised to voyage to Europe to further his career. She, too, is ready to leave her homeland to complete her education, lamenting:

*'I have heard so little music ... there are so few opportunities. And a 'cello – I
have never heard a 'cello'.*

*David's face was full of compassion and yet joy. 'Then I shall be the first to
show you what can be' he said.*[49]

Kathleen's experience of chamber music in turn-of-the-century
Wellington electrified her, triggering an emotional, even mildly sexual
awakening. Juliet expresses a powerfully physical undertow:

*[She] watched him with great pleasure and curiosity. A bright spot came into
her cheeks, her eyes opened – but when he drew his bow across the strings, her
whole soul woke and lived for the first time in her life.*[50]

℘

To win Tom's affections, Kathleen walked the three kilometres from
Thorndon to The Terrace to take cello lessons from his father. She'd
apparently even choose brown clothing to 'tone' with her instrument.[51]

Half a century on, Charlotte Beauchamp confirmed that her sister took
to the cello to such an extent that she even contemplated becoming a
professional musician. 'She had a lovely tone ... genuinely fond of playing
– practising and working at her cello.'[52] Vera, too, recalled family concerts
in the music room at Tinakori Road:

*Mr Trowell, the father of the two boys, used to direct us in chamber music.
I played the piano. My sister [Kathleen] played the cello, and my brother
intermittently played the violin. Father started his friendship with the Trowells
when he heard these twin boys play, and started a subscription amongst his
friends ...*[53]

Tom Trowell resisted Kathleen's crush, despite happily receiving a
stream of love letters after her move to London. His twin, Garnet, gifted
on the violin, would in time prove more accommodating. The boys'
travel to Europe (mentioned in 'Juliet') was made possible by a citywide campaign during 1902 which raised £885, or some $150,000, for a
full year's instruction for two at a top Frankfurt conservatorium. Harold
Beauchamp and his business partner Walter Nathan both chipped in £25

(about $4000 each); even the city council contributed. The *Graphic*, too, provided support, promoting a concert and stating of the boys: 'their taste and wonderful talent in music is so remarkable that it is proposed by a number of people interested in their welfare to send them Home to obtain the best tuition in Europe'.[54]

Like her character Juliet, 14-year-old Katherine Mansfield readied to pack her bags. Inspired by Trowell senior's example, Harold Beauchamp decided to send his children to London to complete their education.

He signed them on for a luxury cruise to England on board the SS *Niwaru*, a vessel of the Tyser line of which his company was the local agent. On 29 January 1903 they departed Wellington. The sense of ecstatic anticipation, of finally being aboard 'for this affair called life',[55] is conveyed in 'To the Last Moment', Katherine Mansfield's literary goodbye to Wellington, written in 1918:

> *For a moment, while he looked, it lay all bathed in brightness – so clear he could have counted the camellias on the trees – and then, without any warning, it was dark, quite dark, and lights began to appear, flowering in the soft hollows like sea anemones. His eyelids smarted. His throat ached; he could have wept. He could have flung out his arms and cried:– 'Oh my darling, darling little town!'*[56]

The Beauchamp parents and five children, plus Annie's siblings Belle and Sydney, sprawled across all the passenger accommodation: they had the boat to themselves. The 42-day voyage, during which the *Niwaru* stopped in the Canary Islands, Uruguay and Mexico, proved both glorious and strangely domesticated. Jeanne recalled 'a swing and a little yellow kitten'.[57] Vera made parallels with the Swiss Family Robinson: 'We had a clavichord to practise on, a canary in a cage, a sewing machine, and all the amenities that a ship of that kind could provide.'[58]

Kathleen wrote her first letter to Tom Trowell from Montevideo. His moody photograph lay deep in her luggage. The exchanges smouldered on by post for years, but nothing ever came of them. Her world, in any case,

Studio portrait of Tom Trowell, circa 1901, around the time Kathleen Beauchamp's infatuation began: 'Very pale he was with a dreaming exquisite face and a striking suggestion of confidence and Power in every feature.' ('Juliet')

Photographer unknown. Ref: PA1-q-984-03, ATL.

was now expanding by the day. A family portrait taken at a stopover at Las Palmas shows her lightly tanned in a straw boater, soft-eyed and radiant, hair up and wire glasses gone.

⸞

Henry Herron Beauchamp, the kindly relative who had in 1875 provoked the Beauchamp and Dyer dynasty, stood on the dock at Southampton when the family disembarked on 24 March 1903. Old Beauchamp sounds frail but hearty at 80, still recording daily life in his diary. A fortnight after the New Zealanders arrived, he scribbled: 'Today the Harold B family lunched and took teas with us – except poor Kassie (Kathleen) who was detained at home with a cold. Seven of them, including Belle Dyer: a very nice, well-behaved lot indeed, and we had a jolly day.'[59]

On 29 April, Kathleen, Vera and Charlotte enrolled as boarders at Queen's College, a progressive girls' school at 43 Harley Street, London, encircled by parks, galleries and museums. Aunt Belle lingered as a chaperone. On Kathleen's first day, she met a pale girl named Ida Baker who would become a life-long friend. It was a propitious beginning to what would be three heady years of lectures, debates, sporting activities and, above all, intellectual awakenings. In her room above bustling Harley Street, she embraced contemporary literature; but among her stories in the Queen's College magazine were the rough, affectionate outlines of Te Ropiha Moturoa's Pipitea ('A True Tale') and Karori's Chesney Wold ('It Was a Big Bare House').

At the same time, Kathleen's sense of coming 'Home' to England, of having reached familiar ground, appeared to deepen after her parents' return to Wellington. Besides, there was a rich family literary heritage to savour – from great-grandfather John Beauchamp, the 'Poet of Hornsey Lane', through to Henry Beauchamp's living daughter Mary, celebrity author of *Elizabeth and Her German Garden*. In September 1903, Kathleen joined her great-uncle on a pilgrimage to the old Beauchamp home in Hornsey Lane, Kentish Town.

Two diary entries allow us to eavesdrop on our subject farewelling her childhood as London claimed her. The first, dated 25 December

Las Palmas, 16 March 1903. Kathleen Beauchamp, lightly tanned in a straw boater, soft-eyed and radiant, hair up and wire glasses gone, is back row left.

Photographer unknown. Ref: PAColl-4131. ATL.

1903, is Henry Beauchamp's, written as Harold's daughters ('The Maori Girls') joined him for the Christmas vacation at his spacious Kent home. He describes a wildly assured, moderately tipsy 15-year-old Kathleen, declaiming verse in the midst of warm hilarity: 'a bottle of champagne … immediately developed the dear girls' young spirits and we became rather "royal" – with "Tol-de-rol" etc, with recitations afterwards by Vera and Kathleen, the latter's very good.'[60]

The second, by Kathleen herself, was scratched in a notebook days later at her great-uncle's, following a 'beautiful and solemn' midnight church service on New Year's Eve:

I mean this year to try and be a different person, and I want, at the end of this year to see how I have kept all the vows that I have made tonight … I am so tired. I think I must go to bed. Tomorrow will be the 1st of January. What a wonderful and what a lovely world this is.[61]

Epilogue: End of the beginning

I'm splashing about in a raincoat down Tinakori Road, navigating Katherine Mansfield footpaths: 'there were still puddles – broken stars – on the road'.[1] I'm up against yet another 'windstorm violent and terrible' that's battering a cityscape of 'narrow, sodden, mean draggled wooden houses, colourless save for the dull coarse red of the roof – and the long line of grey hills, impassable, spectral-like'.[2]

She wrote this after her return from intoxicating London, having crept back, reluctantly, to Thorndon at the end of 1906. Then, unexpectedly, on New Year's Eve, Margaret Dyer died before her granddaughter had bothered to call. She'd been back for weeks. The death appalled 18-year-old Kathleen: nothing would ever, could ever, be the same. Her family had meanwhile shifted to a mansion in the same long pine-shaded avenue as Miss Swainson's school. From there, she'd flee, climbing up into the thick mānuka with Edie Bendall, the Grant Road spring with its soft water far below.

Twenty interminable months passed there, an interlude other biographers have picked over in forensic detail and which we'll omit here. Katherine Mansfield had already styled herself a sophisticated European. Her brief expedition into the wilds of central North Island would be a rarity. Midway through 1908 she steamed out of Wellington, having written: 'this place – steals your Youth – that is just what it does – I feel years and years older and sadder'.[3]

From Europe, however, memories of her Wellington origins again consumed her. She'd begun recording them in Harley Street, and was soon re-imagining Karori and other resonant names on that well-trodden map. As a professional with a mercantile streak her father would value, she knew she had rare, exotic subject matter at hand.

But consciously breathing life into her childhood became an almost holy contract after the death of her brother Leslie in 1915. 'I feel I have a duty to perform to the lovely time when we were both alive. I want to write about it and he wanted me to.'[4]

Meanwhile, terrifyingly, she had contracted tuberculosis, one of the most feared infectious diseases, and had lethal complications linked to venereal disease. In 1923 she died, aged 34. In her final years, when she often wrote in bed and through the night in ill, fevered states, she confided to her friend Dorothy Brett that she felt *possessed*:

> *It is so strange to bring the dead to life again. There's my grandmother, back in her chair with her pink knitting, there stalks my uncle over the grass. I feel as I write 'you are not dead, my darlings. All is remembered. I bow down to you. I efface myself so that you may live again through me in your richness and beauty'.*[5]

Many of the dripping villas I'm passing on Tinakori Road contain old sad ghosts, pocket demons of my own – reminders of lost time and a life mostly spent in one city. Here, up the same long wooden staircase, slippery as ever, is the party house, gentrified now, where, beneath a red lightbulb, I first heard a Rolling Stones album that dazzled me, *Exile on Main Street.* There, on a wet, rose-entwined veranda on the corner of Tinakori Road and Upton Terrace, today decorated with a 'Historic House of Thorndon' decal, a hairy man sold us hashish oil in a jam jar.

But having padded these streets for many months with Katherine Mansfield, seeing them through her unblinking eyes, my own memories feel as if they're being overwritten. When I look across to 119 Hill Street, to the student flat where I scribbled verse in green felt pen decades ago, I now know this is also where Mrs Dyer lived and died half a century before me. I imagine her lying on her deathbed in a black silk frock beneath a feather eiderdown. And when I stand outside the dilapidated cottage at 170 Tinakori Road where I once waited for a dirty fingernail of heroin, I can now sense the mean cottages of Saunders Lane in the valley soaked and shadowed below.

After hunting for the traces, the signatures of the old Wellington that made Katherine Mansfield a writer, her grubby, haughty old town has materialised before me. I've tumbled, willy nilly, into the cracks of its history, the spaces between the paving stones, the perfumed lanes, the wind-crushed greenery, the shining mansions and low villas she observed, memorised, eternalised.

ℒ

To the west of Ahumairangi, a ridge runs for 12 kilometres between the Makara Saddle on the hills above Chesney Wold to the Old Coach Road by Johnsonville. The raw hills of the skyline walkway offer views down to the city and harbour below, and, on a good day, across to the same faraway Kaikoura Ranges Katherine Mansfield saw from Island Bay, 'shrouded in mist, like a fairy land – a dream country, the snow mountains of the South Island'.[6]

On long Sunday walks here I often drop down into the Otari Reserve, a forest sanctuary running over 100 hectares, home to such elderly residents as an 800-year-old rimu tree. Previously rare and unseen native birds dwell here: voluble, half-drunken tūī, thick-thighed kākā and chestnut-breasted saddleback among them. Thanks to Zealandia, a predator-free bird haven near Karori's entrance, the birds are returning. And because of Katherine Mansfield and her love of parrots, I've become fixated on the parakeets with the red topknot, the native kākāriki that soared over these hills in bright clouds. I've even seen a pair or two flashing by the edge of Karori Cemetery, but they vanish so quickly that I'm convinced I hallucinated them.

One afternoon, walking and thinking once again of Katherine Mansfield, I notice a young woman standing on a wooden picnic table above Otari. She's wearing headphones and is waving what looks like a blue television aerial. I'm intrigued. When I enquire what she's doing, she answers, politely, 'Tracking kākāriki.' This is Ellen Irwin, an American Master's student. The parakeets are coming back, she says. Zealandia banded its 500th kākāriki chick in 2015. She's helped attach tail-mounted radio transmitters to 20 juveniles and is tracking them. They remain vulnerable to predators, however. A cat recently killed one. But the teenage birds are forming gangs and flourishing. I am exhilarated by the news.

Do the birds nest in crevices of steep banks like they did in the hills at Pakuao, above Tinakori Road? Ellen shrugs. 'These guys will nest anywhere.' They've even hunkered down in suburban Karori. She tells of pairs nesting in 'someone's garage roof' in a thickly bushed lane off Campbell Street. She forwards a photograph of a resident dad feeding the chicks; his waltz along the guttering.

A quartet of kākāriki, one merrily upended, murmur together on a branch above the Otari canopy as I descend from the hills six months later. I'm struck by how quietly they huddle – unlike the raucous, screamy kākā that tell the whole valley they're about. These insurgents are keeping their heads low.

I set the wheeling kākāriki aside and return to Karori School to revisit the grounds, slipping past the bright staffroom where teachers share an after-work drink. It's a little over a year since I stood here by the broken-down macrocarpa that shielded Katherine Mansfield's court. The tree has long departed, sliced up, carted away. New classrooms stand above the clay bank once honeycombed with its swollen roots. The birdbath floats on the basketball court. I swear it has moved since I last came, inching its way towards the gate, out onto Karori Road. It abides, a decayed, mossy pile of black and white stones, forever washed up by the wire fence. I notice fresh rainbows of graffiti on its nether regions.

So can these murky old river stones tell us anything? Above all, they mark the point at which Katherine Mansfield's repute was such that the pain she'd caused by mining the human terrain of her childhood had begun to ease. She knew she'd poked a spider's web in her hometown, as a 1913 letter, postmarked London, to her sister showed:

I wrote a story called 'Old Tar' the other day about Makra Hill, and sent it to the Westminister [Gazette] who accepted it … Don't leave the paper on the Karori Road or I shall be taken up for libel. They have asked for some more New Zealand work so I am going to write one on the Karori School.[7]

Mayor Tarr was long dead at Karori Cemetery by the time he became the butt of her story. But when American librarian and biographer Ruth Mantz interviewed living classmates, teachers, friends and family during a 1931 research trip to Wellington, she encountered what could only be described as polite fury: 'Particularly interesting have been the meetings with some of the originals of characters portrayed in the short stories, though some of those depicted have not been very sympathetic in their attitude towards the writer.'[8]

I depart, sad to abandon Katherine Mansfield's birdbath looking like this. I head for my car, parked in Donald Street, where an aloe flowered in 1889. Then, above the wind, I hear the soft, warm plunk coming from a bus stop over the road. I look across to see a figure, hooded in scarves and shadows, bent over a blue ukulele. I stand there for minutes, taking in a tuneless ruffle. The Karori Park bus, shiny wet, arrives like glow worms in an empty tin. Still shielded from sight, the strummer boards, flops back into a seat. The trolley lurches on upwards, past the whitewashed church with the bell tower, deep into the night.

Notes

Prologue: Down by the birdbath

1. Vincent O'Sullivan and Margaret Scott (eds), *The Collected Letters of Katherine Mansfield, vol. 4: 1920–1921* (Oxford: Oxford University Press, 1996), p. 106.
2. 'The Doll's House', in Gerri Kimber and Vincent O'Sullivan (eds), *The Edinburgh Edition of the Collected Works of Katherine Mansfield, vol. 2: The collected fiction of Katherine Mansfield, 1916–1922* (Edinburgh: Edinburgh University Press, 2012), p. 416.
3. 'The Garden Party', in Kimber and O'Sullivan (eds), *The Edinburgh Edition, vol. 2*, p. 408.
4. Margaret Scott (ed.), *The Katherine Mansfield Notebooks, vol. 1* (Canterbury: Lincoln University Press and Daphne Brasell Associates, 1997), p. 111.
5. Vincent O'Sullivan (ed.), *Poems of Katherine Mansfield* (Auckland: Oxford University Press, 1988), p. 10.
6. 'A True Tale', in Gerri Kimber and Vincent O'Sullivan (eds), *The Edinburgh Edition of the Collected Works of Katherine Mansfield, vol. 1: The collected fiction of Katherine Mansfield, 1898–1915* (Edinburgh: Edinburgh University Press, 2012), p. 15.
7. Vincent O'Sullivan and Margaret Scott (eds), *The Collected Letters, vol. 1: 1903–1917* (Oxford: Oxford University Press, 1984), p. 252.
8. Gerri Kimber and Claire Davison (eds), *The Edinburgh Edition of the Collected Works of Katherine Mansfield, vol. 4: The diaries of Katherine Mansfield including miscellaneous works* (Edinburgh: Edinburgh University Press, 2016), p. 241.
9. Beverley Randell Price, 'Memories of Karori School 1937–1943', unpublished MS, p. 15.
10. Scott (ed.), *The Katherine Mansfield Notebooks, vol. 2*, p. 297.
11. 'The Garden Party', in Kimber and O'Sullivan (eds), *The Edinburgh Edition, vol. 2*, p. 408.
12. *New Zealand Truth*, 8 April 1953.

One: Parakeets of Pa-kuao

1. *Evening Post*, 14 July 1905.
2. *New Zealand Herald*, 13 January 1973.
3. 'Ole Underwood', in Gerri Kimber and Vincent O'Sullivan (eds), *The Edinburgh Edition of the Collected Works of Katherine Mansfield, vol. 1: The collected fiction of Katherine Mansfield, 1898–1915* (Edinburgh: Edinburgh University Press, 2012), p. 319.
4. *Evening Post*, 20 December 1926.
5. 'At the Bay', in Kimber and O'Sullivan (eds), *The Edinburgh Edition of the Collected Works of Katherine Mansfield, vol. 2: The collected fiction of Katherine Mansfield, 1916–1922* (Edinburgh: Edinburgh University Press), p. 344.
6. Elsdon Best, 'Te Whanga-nui-a-Tara: Wellington in pre-Pakeha days', *Journal of the Polynesian Society*, vol. 10, no. 3, 1901, p. 153.
7. Elsdon Best, *The Land of Tara and They Who Settled It* (New Plymouth: Polynesian Society, 1919), p. 21: www.wcl.govt.nz/maori/wellington/landoftara.html
8. Geoff Park, *Nga Uruora: The groves of life* (Wellington: Victoria University Press, 1995), p. 81.
9. J. Middleton Murry (ed.), *Scrapbook of Katherine Mansfield* (London: Constable, 1937), p. 95.
10. Park, *Nga Uruora*, p. 79.
11. *Evening Post*, 6 August 1912.
12. Friedrich August Krull, *An Indescribable Beauty: Letters home to Germany from Wellington, New Zealand, 1859 & 1862*

13   (Wellington: Awa Press, 2012), p. 31.
13   *Evening Post*, 28 July 1928.
14   Park, *Nga Uruora*, p. 86.
15   *Evening Post,* 4 May 1912.
16   'A True Tale', in Kimber and O'Sullivan (eds), *The Edinburgh Edition, vol. 1*, p. 15.
17   Edward Jerningham Wakefield, *Adventure in New Zealand* (Auckland: Golden Press, 1975), p. 198.
18   *Independent*, 9 December 1848.
19   Mary Taylor to Ellen Nussey, 9 February 1849, WS no. 422, Berg Collection, New York Public Library.
20   Henry Herron Beauchamp, unpublished Journals, vol. 4, 2 November 1875, Beauchamp family.
21   Winsome Shepherd, *Wellington's Heritage: Plants, gardens and landscapes*, (Wellington, Te Papa Press, 2000), p. 9.
22   Ibid., p. 198.
23   *Thorndon Primary: 125th Jubilee Publication, 1852–1981* (Wellington: Thorndon Primary School, 1981), p. 17.
24   Baron C.E. von Alzdorf to Colonial Secretary, *Enclosing an account in making Molesworth Street and Tinakori Road*, 8 January 1852, Archives New Zealand.
25   Louis Ward, *Early Wellington* (Auckland: Whitcombe & Tombs, 1928), p. 308.
26   Redmer Yska, *Wellington: Biography of a city* (Auckland: Reed, 2006), p. 36.
27   Jessica Rankin, unpublished diary 1867–69, Pharazyn family.
28   Raewyn Dalziel, *Julius Vogel: Business politician* (Auckland: Auckland University Press, 1986), p. 159.
29   *Evening Post*, 29 August 1870.
30   Wellington City Council Minute Books, Wellington City Archives, vol. 7, 28 January 1886, p. 183.
31   *Evening Post*, 29 January 1886.
32   'A Birthday', in Kimber and O'Sullivan (eds), *The Edinburgh Edition, vol. 1*, p. 206.

Chapter 2: Mr Beauchamp's doll's house

1   'A Birthday', in Gerri Kimber and Vincent O'Sullivan (eds), *The Edinburgh*

Edition of the Collected Works of Katherine Mansfield, vol. 1: The collected fiction of Katherine Mansfield, 1898–1915 (Edinburgh: Edinburgh University Press, 2012), p. 210.
2   'Sea Song', in Vincent O'Sullivan (ed.), *Poems of Katherine Mansfield* (Auckland: Oxford University Press, 1988).
3   'Revelations', in Gerri Kimber and Vincent O'Sullivan (eds), *The Edinburgh Edition of the Collected Works of Katherine Mansfield, vol. 2: The collected fiction of Katherine Mansfield, 1916–1922* (Edinburgh: Edinburgh University Press, 2012), p. 213.
4   'The Aloe', in Kimber and O'Sullivan (eds), *The Edinburgh Edition, vol. 1*, p. 473
5   'Daphne', in Kimber and O'Sullivan (eds), *The Edinburgh Edition, vol. 2*, p. 430.
6   'The Aloe', in Kimber and O'Sullivan (eds), *The Edinburgh Edition, vol. 1*, p. 474.
7   'The Wind Blows', in Kimber and O'Sullivan (eds), *The Edinburgh Edition, vol. 2*, p. 229.
8   *Evening Post*, 8 October 1986.
9   Kevin L. Jones, 'Archaeology of the Katherine Mansfield Birthplace, Wellington, New Zealand: "It's all memories now …"' *New Zealand Journal of Archaeology*, vol. 14, 1992, pp. 109–41.
10   Ibid.
11   Harold Beauchamp, *Reminiscences and Reflections* (New Plymouth: 1937), p. 82.
12   Ibid., p. 83
13   Jones, 'Archaeology of the Katherine Mansfield Birthplace', p. 137.
14   'The Aloe', in Kimber and O'Sullivan (eds), *The Edinburgh Edition, vol. 1*, p. 472–73.
15   Margaret Scott (ed.), *The Katherine Mansfield Notebooks, vol. 2* (Canterbury: Lincoln University Press and Daphne Brasell Associates, 1997), p. 89.
16   Ibid.
17   Katherine Mansfield Birthplace House files, 8/13/142, Heritage New Zealand.
18   'The Aloe', in Kimber and O'Sullivan (eds), *The Edinburgh Edition, vol. 1*, p. 470.

19 'Prelude', in Kimber and O'Sullivan (eds), *The Edinburgh Edition, vol. 2*, p. 57.
20 *Sydney Bulletin*, 8 October 1903.
21 Ibid.
22 'The Aloe', in Kimber and O'Sullivan (eds), *The Edinburgh Edition, vol. 1*, p. 469.
23 'At the Bay', in Kimber and O'Sullivan (eds), *The Edinburgh Edition, vol. 2*, p. 566.
24 Simon Nathan, comment to author, 2 December 2016.
25 *New Zealand Listener*, 29 March 1963.
26 Ruth Elvish Mantz and J. Middleton Murry, *The Life of Katherine Mansfield* (London: Constable & Co., 1933), p. 78.
27 'Prelude', in Kimber and O'Sullivan (eds), *The Edinburgh Edition, vol. 2*, p. 58.
28 'The Aloe', in Kimber and O'Sullivan (eds), *The Edinburgh Edition, vol. 1*, p. 470.
29 *Dominion*, 8 March 1963.
30 'Prelude', in Kimber and O'Sullivan (eds), *The Edinburgh Edition, vol. 2*, p. 57.
31 Ibid., p. 58.
32 Robin Hyde, *Journalese* (Auckland: National Printing Co., 1934), p. 23.
33 Ibid.
34 Pat Lawlor, *Old Wellington Days* (Wellington: Whitcombe & Tombs, 1959), p. 172.
35 Ronald Burt, *The Last of Unscarred Thorndon* (Wellington: Ryder-Cheshire Foundation, 1967).
36 *Evening Post*, 2 July 1965.
37 Hyde, *Journalese*, p. 23.
38 *New Zealand Listener*, 31 October 1987.

Three: The little girl in the picture

1 Memorial to Governor Grey, 1848, G 7, p. 86, Archives New Zealand.
2 *Evening Post*, 20 February 1922.
3 Margaret H. Alington, *Unquiet Earth: A history of the Bolton Street Cemetery* (Wellington: Wellington City Council and Ministry of Works and Development, 1978), p. 125.
4 *Evening Post*, 3 July 1882.
5 Interpretation board at Bolton Street Cemetery Chapel, Wellington City.
6 Margaret Scott (ed.), *The Katherine Mansfield Notebooks, vol. 2* (Canterbury: Lincoln University Press and Daphne Brasell Associates, 1997), p. 95.
7 Ibid., p. 96.
8 Ibid.
9 A.N. Wilson, *The Victorians* (London: Hutchinson, 2002), p. 34.
10 F.S. Maclean, *Challenge for Health: A history of public health in New Zealand*, (Wellington: Government Printer, 1964), p. 142.
11 Lawrence Wright, *Clean and Decent, the Fascinating History of the Bathroom and the Water Closet* (London: Penguin 1960), p. 149.
12 *Evening Post*, 5 September 1892.
13 'Cholera and Mode of Treating It', *Appendices to the Journals of the House of Representatives*, 1892, H-46.
14 'She', in Gerri Kimber and Vincent O'Sullivan (eds), *The Edinburgh Edition of the Collected Works of Katherine Mansfield, vol. 1: The collected fiction of Katherine Mansfield, 1898–1915* (Edinburgh: Edinburgh University Press, 2012), pp. 13–14.
15 Scott (ed.), *The Katherine Mansfield Notebooks, vol. 2*, p. 96.
16 'Weak Heart', in Gerri Kimber and Vincent O'Sullivan (eds), *The Edinburgh Edition, vol. 2: The collected fiction of Katherine Mansfield, 1916–1922* (Edinburgh: Edinburgh University Press, 2012), p. 428.
17 Scott (ed.), *The Katherine Mansfield Notebooks, vol. 2*, p. 97.

Four: Something rotten

1 Miriam Frankland – Notebook, 1886, Frankland, Miriam, 1857–1945, MS-0805, Alexander Turnbull Library.
2 Ibid.
3 Ibid.
4 Ibid.
5 'A Birthday', in Gerri Kimber and Vincent O'Sullivan (eds), *The Edinburgh Edition of the Collected Works of Katherine Mansfield, vol 1: The collected fiction*

of *Katherine Mansfield, 1898–1915* (Edinburgh: Edinburgh University Press, 2012), p. 208.

6   Ibid., p. 68.

7   *New Zealand Times*, 16 September 1892.

8   'A Birthday', in Kimber and O'Sullivan (eds), *The Edinburgh Edition, vol. 2: The collected fiction of Katherine Mansfield, 1916–1922* (Edinburgh: Edinburgh University Press, 2012), p. 208.

9   *Evening Post*, 4 March 1867.

10   'A Birthday', in Kimber and O'Sullivan (eds), *The Edinburgh Edition, vol. 2*, p. 208.

11   City of Wellington: Reports and Proceedings of the City Council on a Water Supply to the City, 00030:1:1, Wellington City Archives (WCA).

12   *Evening Post*, 31 January 1879.

13   Simon Nathan, *James Hector: Explorer, scientist, leader* (Lower Hutt: Geoscience Society of New Zealand, 2015), p. 129.

14   *New Zealand Times*, 11 July 1879.

15   *New Zealand Times*, 14 July 1879.

16   Tristram Hunt, *Building Jerusalem: The rise and fall of the Victorian city* (London: Weidenfeld & Nicolson, 2004), p. 219.

17   *Evening Post*, 20 October 1876.

18   *New Zealand Parliamentary Debates*, vol. 101, 1898, pp. 219–21.

19   Wellington City Council Minutes Books, WCA, vol. 8, 21 March 1889, p. 272.

20   Ibid.

21   *Evening Post*, 18 December 1889.

22   WCA, 00233:25:1889/1510, 25 July 1889.

23   *Wairarapa Daily Times*, 2 January 1892.

24   WCA, 00233:34:1892/737, 26 May 1892.

25   *Evening Post*, 25 July 1892.

26   *New Zealand Times*, 16 September 1892.

27   Dr Chapple, 'Prevention of Typhoid Fever', WCA, 00233:34:1892/740, 1892.

28   Ibid.

29   Ibid.

30   *New Zealand Times*, 12 April 1892.

31   *Evening Post*, 28 March 1892.

32   Chapple, 'Prevention of Typhoid Fever'.

33   *New Zealand Times*, 23 March 1893.

34   *Auckland Star*, 21 March 1893.

35   *Evening Post*, 13 November 1882.

36   Judith Burch and Jan Heynes (eds), *Karori and its People* (Wellington: Karori Historical Society and Steele Roberts, 2011), p. 33.

37   Much of the substance of this and the previous chapter is touched on in Gerri Kimber's *Katherine Mansfield: The early years* (Edinburgh University Press, 2016), without attribution to published accounts of the author's research relating to public health issues: 'Mansfield's writings hint at sewage secret', *Dominion Post*, 3 August 2013; 'Historian probes deadly Mansfield undertones', 18 December 2014. In early 2017 Edinburgh University Press undertook to 'remedy the situation with appropriate citations in all future editions of the work (in print and digitally)'.

38   Harold Beauchamp, *Reminiscences and Reflections* (New Plymouth: 1937), p. 85.

39   Ruth Elvish Mantz and J. Middleton Murry, *The Life of Katherine Mansfield* (London: Constable & Co., 1933), p. 97.

40   Antony Alpers, *The Life of Katherine Mansfield* (New York: Viking, 1980), p. 10.

41   Jeffrey Meyers, *Katherine Mansfield: A biography* (London: Hamish Hamilton, 1978), p. 6.

42   Claire Tomalin, *Katherine Mansfield: A secret life* (London: Viking, 1987), p. 11.

43   'Prelude', in Kimber and O'Sullivan (eds), *The Edinburgh Edition, vol. 2*, p. 71.

44   Ibid., p. 75.

45   'The Doll's House', in Kimber and O'Sullivan (eds), *The Edinburgh Edition, vol. 2*, p. 418.

46   'The Garden Party', in Kimber and O'Sullivan (eds), *The Edinburgh Edition, vol. 2*, p. 408.

Five: The wind! The wind!

1   Robin Hyde, *Journalese* (Auckland: National Printing Co., 1934), p. 22.

2   *New Zealand Herald*, 19 January 1888.

3   *New Zealand Colonist and Port Nicholson Advertiser*, 7 March 1843.

4   William Wordsworth, *The Prelude: The Four Texts* (London: Penguin, 2004).

5   J. Middleton Murry (ed.), *Journal of Katherine Mansfield* (London: Constable, 1954), p. 290.

6   'The Wind Blows', in Gerri Kimber and Vincent O'Sullivan (eds), *The Edinburgh Edition of the Collected Works of Katherine Mansfield, vol. 2: The collected fiction of Katherine Mansfield, 1916–1922* (Edinburgh: Edinburgh University Press, 2012), p. 228.

7   'Psychology', in Kimber and O'Sullivan (eds), *The Edinburgh Edition, vol. 2*, p. 197.

8   'Revelations', in Kimber and O'Sullivan (eds), *The Edinburgh Edition, vol. 2*, p. 215.

9   'The New Baby', in Kimber and O'Sullivan (eds), *The Edinburgh Edition, vol. 2*, p. 481.

10 'A Birthday', in Gerri Kimber and Vincent O'Sullivan (eds), *The Edinburgh Edition of the Collected Works of Katherine Mansfield, vol. 1: The collected fiction of Katherine Mansfield, 1898–1915* (Edinburgh: Edinburgh University Press, 2012), p. 211.

11 Murry (ed.), *Journal of Katherine Mansfield*, p. 289.

12 'The Wrong House', in Kimber and O'Sullivan (eds), *The Edinburgh Edition, vol. 2*, p. 210.

13 'Juliet', in Kimber and O'Sullivan (eds), *The Edinburgh Edition, vol. 1*, pp. 41–42.

14 'A Birthday', in Kimber and O'Sullivan (eds), *The Edinburgh Edition, vol. 1*, p. 211.

15 'The Wind Blows', in Kimber and O'Sullivan (eds), *The Edinburgh Edition, vol. 2*, p. 229.

16 'The Tale of the Three', in Kimber and O'Sullivan (eds), *The Edinburgh Edition, vol. 1*, p. 65.

17 Maurice Gee, *Going West* (Auckland: Penguin, 1996), p. 156.

18 Ibid.

19 'Prelude', in Kimber and O'Sullivan (eds), *The Edinburgh Edition, vol. 2*, p. 59.

20 Ibid., p. 61.

21 'It was a big bare house', in Kimber and O'Sullivan (eds), *The Edinburgh Edition, vol. 1*, p. 16.

22 Nancy M. Taylor (ed.), *The Journal of Ensign Best 1837–1843* (Wellington: Government Printer, 1966), p. 152.

23 *Evening Post*, 3 April 1888.

24 Dante, *The Divine Comedy: Cantica 1: Hell*, translated by Dorothy Sayers (London: Penguin, 1979), p. 98.

25 'Bank Holiday', in Kimber and O'Sullivan (eds), *The Edinburgh Edition, vol. 2*, p. 224.

26 *New Zealand Graphic and Ladies' Journal*, 9 December 1897.

27 *New Zealand Graphic and Ladies' Journal*, 16 October 1897.

28 James Belich, *Making Peoples: A history of the New Zealanders from Polynesian settlement to the end of the nineteenth century* (Auckland: Penguin, 1996), p. 281.

29 John Wood, *Twelve Months in Wellington, Port Nicholson* (London: Pelham Richardson, 1843), p. 9.

30 Alexander Marjoribanks, *Travels in New Zealand* (London: Smith Elder, 1845), p. 11.

31 W.C. Cotton, *Journals*, vol. 6, 7 December 1843, pp. 28–29, Alexander Turnbull Library.

32 Gavin McLean, *Wellington: The first years of European settlement, 1840–1850*, (Auckland: Penguin, 2000), p. 26.

33 Taylor (ed.), *The Journal of Ensign Best*, p. 152.

34 'A Birthday', in Kimber and O'Sullivan (eds), *The Edinburgh Edition, vol. 1*, p. 210.

35 N.L McLeod and B.H. Farland (eds), *Wellington Prospect, Survey of a City 1840–1970* (Wellington: Hicks Smith & Sons, 1970), p. 49.

36 *Guardian*, 15 October 2015.

37 *Press*, 25 January 1888.

38 *Evening Post*, 29 March 1888.

39 Ibid.

40 *Evening Post*, 13 October 1888.

41 *Evening Post*, 3 January 1891.

42 'Ole Underwood', in Kimber and O'Sullivan (eds), *The Edinburgh Edition, vol. 1*, p. 319.

43 'The Escape', in Kimber and O'Sullivan (eds), *The Edinburgh Edition, vol. 2*, p. 219.

44 'The Wind Blows', in Kimber and O'Sullivan (eds), *The Edinburgh Edition, vol. 2*, p. 227.

45 'Late at Night', in Kimber and O'Sullivan (eds), *The Edinburgh Edition, vol. 2*, p. 26.

Six: The inventor

1 Henry Herron Beauchamp, unpublished journal, vol. 7, 15 April 1894, p. 56, Beauchamp family.

2 Henry Herron Beauchamp, unpublished journal, vol. 8, 26 December 1905, p. 172.

3 See Antony Alpers, *The Life of Katherine Mansfield* (New York: Viking, 1980) and Gerri Kimber, *Katherine Mansfield: The early years* (Edinburgh: Edinburgh University Press, 2016).

4 Henry Herron Beauchamp, unpublished journal, vol. 4, 1 December 1875, p. 123.

5 Ruth Elvish Mantz and J. Middleton Murry, *The Life of Katherine Mansfield* (London: Constable & Co., 1933), p. 57.

6 'The Aloe', in Gerri Kimber and Vincent O'Sullivan (eds), *The Edinburgh Edition of the Collected Works of Katherine Mansfield, vol. 1: The collected fiction of Katherine Mansfield, 1898–1915* (Edinburgh: Edinburgh University Press, 2012), p. 486.

7 Ibid.

8 *Sydney Morning Herald*, 5 March 1857.

9 *Wanganui Herald*, 10 May 1875.

10 *Wairarapa Times Age*, 8 March 1890.

11 *Sydney Morning Herald*, 27 September 1869.

12 Henry Herron Beauchamp, unpublished journal, vol. 7, 15 April 1894.

13 'The Aloe', in Kimber and O'Sullivan (eds), *The Edinburgh Edition, vol. 1*, p. 486.

14 Ibid.

15 *Evening Post*, 6 March 1872.

16 'The Aloe', in Kimber and O'Sullivan (eds), *The Edinburgh Edition, vol. 1*, p. 486.

17 Ibid.

18 *Evening Post*, 3 November 1874.

19 'The Aloe', in Kimber and O'Sullivan (eds), *The Edinburgh Edition, vol. 1*, p. 487.

20 *Evening Post*, 22 June 1876.

21 Ibid.

22 Jeffrey Meyers, *Katherine Mansfield: A biography* (London: Hamish Hamilton, 1978), p. 6.

23 'The Aloe', in Kimber and O'Sullivan (eds), *The Edinburgh Edition, vol. 1*, p. 487.

24 *Evening Post*, 15 May 1877.

25 Ibid.

26 Vincent O'Sullivan (ed.), *The Aloe with Prelude* (Wellington: Port Nicholson Press, 1982), p. 131.

Seven: Labour of Sorrow

1 Henry Godsiff and Arthur Beauchamp: Declaration of Insolvency, Blenheim Court, 1879, ABYB, Series 23224, W55732, Box 45/48, Archives New Zealand (ANZ).

2 Harold Beauchamp, *Reminiscences and Reflections* (New Plymouth: 1937), p. 16.

3 Sylvia Berkman, *Katherine Mansfield: A critical study* (New Haven: Yale University Press, 1951), p. 208.

4 Antony Alpers, *The Life of Katherine Mansfield* (New York: Viking, 1980), p. 5.

5 Beauchamp, *Reminiscences and Reflections*, p. 22.

6 Ethel Beauchamp Hazelwood, *Life at Anakiwa: The first 100 years 1863–1963* (Nelson: Lucas Print, 1974), p. 6.

7 Ruth Elvish Mantz and J. Middleton Murry, *The Life of Katherine Mansfield* (London: Constable & Co., 1933), p. 36.

8 'The Voyage', in Gerri Kimber and Vincent O'Sullivan (eds), *The Edinburgh Edition of the Collected Works of Katherine Mansfield, vol. 2: The collected fiction of Katherine Mansfield, 1916–1922* (Edinburgh: Edinburgh University Press, 2012), p. 374.

9 Henry Herron Beauchamp, unpublished journal, vol. 4, 11 November 1875, p. 116.

10 Beauchamp, *Reminiscences and Reflections*, p. 42.

11 Mantz and Murry, *The Life of Katherine Mansfield*, p. 44.

12 Beauchamp, *Reminiscences and Reflections*, p. 16.

13 Mantz and Murry, *The Life of Katherine Mansfield*, p. 49.
14 Ibid., p. 52.
15 *Nelson Examiner and New Zealand Chronicle*, 24 October 1867.
16 Ibid.
17 *West Coast Times*, 6 January 1868.
18 Beauchamp, *Reminiscences and Reflections*, p. 29.
19 *Evening Post*, 1 August 1868.
20 Beauchamp, *Reminiscences and Reflections*, p. 30.
21 Ibid., p. 32.
22 *Wanganui Herald*, 14 March 1873.
23 Beauchamp, *Reminiscences and Reflections*, p. 70.
24 Official Assignee's Bankruptcy Files: Christchurch, Beauchamp Arthur, 1884, CAMO, CH214, Box 97/129, ANZ.
25 Gerri Kimber and Claire Davison (eds), *The Edinburgh Edition of the Collected Works of Katherine Mansfield, vol. 4: The diaries of Katherine Mansfield including miscellaneous works* (Edinburgh: Edinburgh University Press, 2016), p. 407.
26 'The Voyage', in Kimber and O'Sullivan (eds), *The Edinburgh Edition, vol. 2*, p. 376.
27 Henry Herron Beauchamp, unpublished journal, vol. 8, 4 May 1902.
28 Ibid.
29 R.J. Seddon to Harold Beauchamp, 11 July 1902, PM9 4/26, ANZ.
30 Letter to Richard Murry, 3 February 1921, in Vincent O'Sullivan and Margaret Scott (eds), *The Collected Letters of Katherine Mansfield: vol. 4: 1920–1921* (Oxford: Clarendon Press, 1996), p. 178.

Eight: Little brown owl

1 Letter to Anne Drey, January 1921, in Vincent O'Sullivan and Margaret Scott (eds), *The Collected Letters of Katherine Mansfield: vol. 4: 1920–1921* (Oxford: Clarendon Press, 1996), p. 168.
2 'About Pat', in Gerri Kimber and Vincent O'Sullivan (eds), *The Edinburgh Edition of the Collected Works of Katherine Mansfield, vol.1: The collected fiction of Katherine Mansfield, 1898–1915* (Edinburgh: Edinburgh University Press, 2012), p. 29.
3 'Old Tar', in Kimber and Vincent O'Sullivan (eds), *The Edinburgh Collection, vol. 1*, p. 340.
4 'Prelude', in Gerri Kimber and Vincent O'Sullivan (eds), *The Edinburgh Edition of the Collected Works of Katherine Mansfield, vol. 2: The collected fiction of Katherine Mansfield, 1916–1922* (Edinburgh: Edinburgh University Press, 2012), p. 62.
5 'The Aloe', in Kimber and O'Sullivan (eds), *The Edinburgh Edition, vol. 1*, p. 509.
6 Margaret H. Alington, *High Point: St Mary's Church, Karori, Wellington 1866–1991* (Wellington: Parish of St Mary's, Karori, and Karori Historical Society, 1998), p. 18.
7 Louis Ward, *Early Wellington* (Auckland: Whitcombe & Tombs, 1928), p. 391.
8 Mary Swainson, letter to her grandparents in England, 25 September 1842, Unpublished MS, Alexander Turnbull Library (ATL).
9 Mary Taylor to Ellen Nussey, 14 October 1850, WS no. 610, Brontë Parsonage Museum, Haworth, UK.
10 Charles Dickens, *Bleak House* (London: Penguin Classics, 2003).
11 Jenifer Roberts, *Fitz: The colonial adventures of James Edward FitzGerald* (Dunedin: Otago University Press, 2014), p. 273.
12 Ibid., p. 276.
13 Ibid., p. 281.
14 *Evening Post*, 6 July 1877.
15 Ibid.
16 'The Aloe', in Kimber and O'Sullivan (eds), *The Edinburgh Edition, vol. 1*, p. 492.
17 'Prelude', in Kimber and O'Sullivan (eds), *The Edinburgh Edition, vol. 2*, p. 61.
18 Ibid., p. 62.
19 Ibid., p. 86.
20 Letter from Jeanne (Beauchamp) Renshaw to Karori Historical Society, 23 February 1977, ATL.

21 *Evening Post*, 18 December 1889.
22 'It was a big bare house', in Kimber and O'Sullivan (eds), *The Edinburgh Edition, vol. 1*, p. 16.
23 'About Pat', in Kimber and O'Sullivan (eds), *The Edinburgh Edition, vol. 1*, p. 29.
24 'My Potplants', in Kimber and O'Sullivan (eds), *The Edinburgh Edition, vol. 1*, p. 32.
25 'Prelude', in Kimber and O'Sullivan (eds), *The Edinburgh Edition, vol. 2*, pp. 71–72.
26 'About Pat', in Kimber and O'Sullivan (eds), *The Edinburgh Edition, vol. 1*, p. 30.
27 Ibid.
28 *Dominion*, 11 March 1963.
29 Margaret Scott (ed.), *The Katherine Mansfield Notebooks, vol. 2* (Canterbury: Lincoln University Press and Daphne Brasell Associates, 1997), p. 87.
30 Alington, *High Point*, p. 161.
31 Ibid., p. 162.
32 *Evening Post*, 21 October 1893.
33 Ibid., 30 October 1893.
34 'Prelude', in Kimber and O'Sullivan (eds), *The Edinburgh Edition, vol. 2*, p. 79.
35 Antony Alpers, *The Life of Katherine Mansfield* (New York: Viking, 1980), p. 13.
36 'The Little Girl', in Kimber and O'Sullivan (eds), *The Edinburgh Edition, vol. 1*, p. 302.
37 Ibid., p. 301.
38 Letter to Charlotte Beauchamp Perkins and Jeanne Beauchamp Renshaw, 21 August 1921, in Vincent O'Sullivan and Margaret Scott (eds), *The Collected Letters of Katherine Mansfield, vol. 4: 1920–1921* (Oxford: Clarendon Press, 1996), p. 266.
39 'Maata', in Kimber and O'Sullivan (eds), *The Edinburgh Edition, vol. 1*, pp. 346–47.
40 T.E.Y. Seddon, *The Seddons: An autobiography* (Auckland and London: Collins, 1968), p. 54.
41 'Her First Ball', in Kimber and O'Sullivan (eds), *The Edinburgh Edition, vol. 2*, p. 326.
42 City Engineers Department, Premises, 372 Karori Road, 1936–1988, 00009:1747:45/276/3, Wellington City Archives.
43 Pat Lawlor, *Old Wellington Days* (Wellington: Whitcombe & Tombs, 1959), pp. 175–75.
44 Ibid.
45 Ibid.
46 https://sites.google.com/site/bestofpropertyrenovationideas/feature--chesney-wold

Nine: The washerwoman's children

1 Ruth Elvish Mantz and J. Middleton Murry, *The Life of Katherine Mansfield* (London: Constable & Co., 1933), p. 123.
2 'The Doll's House', in Gerri Kimber and Vincent O'Sullivan (eds), *The Edinburgh Edition of the Collected Works of Katherine Mansfield, vol. 2: The collected fiction of Katherine Mansfield, 1916–1922* (Edinburgh: Edinburgh University Press, 2012), p. 417.
3 Ibid.
4 Ibid., p. 416.
5 'Autumns I', in Gerri Kimber and Vincent O'Sullivan (eds), *The Edinburgh Edition of the Collected Works of Katherine Mansfield, vol. 1: The collected fiction of Katherine Mansfield, 1898–1915* (Edinburgh: Edinburgh University Press, 2012), p. 451.
6 Mantz and Murry, *The Life of Katherine Mansfield*, p. 114.
7 www.familytreecircles.com/looking-for-annie-howe-in-england-before-1887-31855.html
8 Erik Olssen and Marcia Stenson, *A Century of Change: New Zealand 1800–1900* (Auckland: Longman Paul, 1989), p. 383.
9 Ibid.
10 Brent Parker, *Karori School: Frontier classroom to city school, 1857–2007* (Wellington: Karori Normal School, 2007), p. 23.
11 Logbook of Karori School, National Library of New Zealand.
12 Gerri Kimber, *Katherine Mansfield: The early years* (Edinburgh: Edinburgh University Press, 2016), p. 46.

13 'Mary', in Kimber and O'Sullivan (eds), *The Edinburgh Edition, vol. 1*, p. 168.

14 Letter from Ray Willis, MS-Papers-11326-051, Alexander Turnbull Library.

15 Helen May, *School Beginnings: A nineteenth century colonial story* (Wellington: NZCER Press, 2005), p. 194

16 Ibid., p. 177.

17 'The Doll's House', in Kimber and O'Sullivan (eds), *The Edinburgh Edition, vol. 2*, p. 418.

18 Brent Parker, comment to author, April 2016.

19 'A Married Man's Story', in Kimber and O'Sullivan (eds), *The Edinburgh Edition, vol. 2*, p. 387.

20 'The Dolls House', in Kimber and O'Sullivan (eds), *The Edinburgh Edition, vol. 2*, p. 416.

21 Judith Burch and Beryl Hughes, 'Karori Lunatic Asylum, 1854–1873', *The Stockade*, no. 31, 1998, p. 4.

22 Judith Burch and Jan Heynes (eds), *Karori and its People* (Wellington: Karori Historical Society and Steele Roberts, 2011), p. 114.

23 Ibid., p. 25.

24 Logbook of Karori School.

25 *Press*, 8 January 1868.

26 Parker, *Karori School*, p. 23.

27 Ibid.

28 *Evening Post*, 19 December 1896.

29 Ruth Elvish Mantz Collection, undated interview with Mrs A.J. Norie née Lockett, Harry Ransom Centre, University of Texas at Austin, USA.

30 Sylvia Berkman, *Katherine Mansfield: A critical study* (New Haven: Yale University Press, 1951), p. 19.

31 Mantz and Murry, *The Life of Katherine Mansfield*, p. 121.

32 Ibid.

33 See Antony Alpers, *The Life of Katherine Mansfield* (New York: Viking, 1980); Gillian Boddy, *Katherine Mansfield: The woman and the writer* (Auckland: Penguin, 1988); and Gerri Kimber,

Katherine Mansfield: The early years (Edinburgh: Edinburgh University Press, 2016).

34 'The Great Examination', in Kimber and O'Sullivan (eds), *The Edinburgh Edition, vol. 1*, p. 8.

35 'Mary', in Kimber and O'Sullivan (eds), *The Edinburgh Edition, vol. 1*, pp. 168–71.

36 Letter to John Middleton Murry, 11 April 1920, in Vincent O'Sullivan and Margaret Scott (eds), *The Collected Letters of Katherine Mansfield, vol. 3* (Oxford: Clarendon Press, 1996).

37 *Evening Post*, 16 December 1897.

38 Peter Ackroyd, *Dickens* (London: Sinclair Stevenson, 1990), p. 86.

39 Descendants of William McKelvey: http://homepages.ihug.co.nz/~Smckelvey/NZMcKelvey/william_mckelvey/d1.htm

40 Ibid.

41 *Evening Post*, 17 December 1898.

42 *Church Chronicle and Official Gazette for the Wellington Diocese*, February 1899, p. 25, ATL.

43 Descendants of William McKelvey: http://homepages.ihug.co.nz/~Smckelvey/NZMcKelvey/william_mckelvey/d1.htm

44 Ibid.

45 *High School Reporter* (Wellington Girls' High School), Second Term, 1898, National Library of New Zealand.

46 *Evening Post*, 26 October 1898.

Ten: Their heads in the buttercups

1 Vincent O'Sullivan (ed.), *Poems of Katherine Mansfield* (Auckland: Oxford University Press, 1988), p. 2.

2 Karori Borough Council Minute Book (KBCMB), Wellington City Archives (WCA), vol. 1, 16 July 1896, p. 151.

3 KBCMB, WCA, vol. 1, 18 April 1893, p. 50.

4 Charles Heaphy, *Narrative of a Residence in Various Parts of New Zealand* (London: Smith Elder, 1842).

5 Brent Parker, *Karori School: Frontier classroom to city school, 1857–2007*

(Wellington: Karori Normal School, 2007), p. 23.

6   *Evening Post*, 26 October 1904.

7   'The Dolls House', in Gerri Kimber and Vincent O'Sullivan (eds), *The Edinburgh Edition of the Collected Works of Katherine Mansfield, vol. 2: The collected fiction of Katherine Mansfield, 1916–1922* (Edinburgh: Edinburgh University Press, 2012), p. 416.

8   KBCMB, WCA, vol. 1, 17 December 1896, p. 172.

9   'The Dolls House', in Kimber and O'Sullivan (eds), *The Edinburgh Edition, vol. 2*, p. 420.

10 'Prelude', in Kimber and O'Sullivan (eds), *The Edinburgh Edition, vol. 2*, p. 66.

11 Alfred Kilmister, unpublished MS, Alexander Turnbull Library.

12 Maxwell Gage, 'The Makara and Karori Valleys and Their Bearing Upon the Physiographic History of Wellington', *Transactions and Proceedings of the Royal Society of New Zealand 1868–1961*, vol. 69, 1940, pp. 401–08.

13 'My Potplants', in Gerri Kimber and Vincent O'Sullivan (eds), *The Edinburgh Edition of the Collected Works of Katherine Mansfield, vol. 1: The collected fiction of Katherine Mansfield, 1898–1915* (Edinburgh: Edinburgh University Press, 2012), p. 32.

14 *Evening Post*, 6 February 1877.

15 'Prelude', in Kimber and O'Sullivan (eds), *The Edinburgh Edition, vol. 2*, p. 66.

16 KBCMB, WCA, vol. 1, 15 September 1896, p. 161

17 Cherry A. Hankin (ed.), *Letters of John Middleton Murry to Katherine Mansfield* (London: Constable, 1983), p. 207.

18 'Juliet', in Kimber and O'Sullivan (eds), *The Edinburgh Edition, vol. 2*, p. 42.

19 Beryl Smedley, *Homewood and its Families: A story of Wellington* (Wellington: Mallinson Rendel, 1980), p. 16.

20 'Rewa', in Kimber and O'Sullivan (eds), *The Edinburgh Edition, vol. 1*, p. 131.

21 'Prelude', in Kimber and O'Sullivan (eds), *The Edinburgh Edition, vol. 2*, p. 66.

22 Vincent O'Sullivan (ed.), *Poems of Katherine Mansfield* (Auckland: Oxford University Press, 1988), p. 54.

23 'The Child-Who-Was-Tired', in Kimber and O'Sullivan (eds), *The Edinburgh Edition, vol. 1*, p. 161.

24 Margaret H. Alington, *High Point: St Mary's Church, Karori, Wellington 1866–1991* (Wellington: Parish of St Mary's, Karori, and Karori Historical Society, 1998), p. 227.

25 Ibid., p. 117.

26 Ibid., p. 100.

27 'Prelude', in Kimber and O'Sullivan (eds), *The Edinburgh Edition, vol. 2*, p. 61.

28 Judith Burch and Jan Heynes (eds), *Karori and its People* (Wellington: Karori Historical Society and Steele Roberts, 2011), p. 115.

29 'Carnation', in Kimber and O'Sullivan (eds), *The Edinburgh Edition, vol. 2*, p. 162.

30 *Auckland Star*, 25 July 1889.

31 Ibid.

32 *Thames Star*, 11 April 1894.

33 Claire Nicoll, *Tarr Family Biography*, unpublished MS, Tarr Family.

34 'Prelude', in Kimber and O'Sullivan (eds), *The Edinburgh Edition, vol. 2*, p. 75.

35 *Evening Post*, 17 April 1970.

36 'A Married Man's Story', in Kimber and O'Sullivan (eds), *The Edinburgh Edition, vol. 2*, p. 387.

37 George Barton, personal letter to author, 26 January 2007.

38 Parker, *Karori School*, p. 23.

39 'The Doll's House', in Kimber and O'Sullivan (eds), *The Edinburgh Edition, vol. 2*, p. 416.

Eleven: The bride wore black

1   'The Aloe', in Gerri Kimber and Vincent O'Sullivan (eds), *The Edinburgh Edition of the Collected Works of Katherine Mansfield, vol. 1: The collected fiction of Katherine Mansfield, 1898–1915* (Edinburgh: Edinburgh University Press, 2012), p. 505–06.

2 Ibid., p. 506.
3 'A Man and His Dog', in Kimber and
O'Sullivan (eds), *The Edinburgh Edition*,
vol. 2, p. 487.
4 Ibid.
5 *Evening Post*, 14 October 1882.
6 *Clutha Leader*, 20 October 1882.
7 *Thames Star*, 18 October 1882.
8 Ibid.
9 Antony Alpers, *The Life of Katherine
Mansfield* (New York: Viking, 1980), p. 11.
10 Wellington City Archives (WCA),
00233:14:1886/783, 10 June 1886.
11 Ibid.
12 'A Man and his Dog', in Kimber and
O'Sullivan (eds), *The Edinburgh Edition*,
vol. 2, p. 488.
13 Ruth Elvish Mantz and J. Middleton
Murry, *The Life of Katherine Mansfield*
(London: Constable and Co., 1933), pp.
99–100.
14 'The Little Girl', in Kimber and
O'Sullivan (eds), *The Edinburgh Edition*,
vol. 1, p. 303.
15 'Prelude', in Kimber and O'Sullivan
(eds), *The Edinburgh Edition*, vol. 2, p. 78.
16 'At the Bay', in Kimber and O'Sullivan
(eds), *The Edinburgh Edition*, vol. 2, p. 345.
17 Ibid., p. 365.
18 Letter to Dorothy Brett, 12 September
1921, in Vincent O'Sullivan and Margaret
Scott (eds), *The Collected Letters of
Katherine Mansfield, vol. 4: 1920–1921*
(Oxford: Clarendon Press, 1996), p. 278.
19 'At the Bay', in Kimber and O'Sullivan
(eds), *The Edinburgh Edition*, vol. 2, p. 364.
20 Mantz and Murry, *The Life of Katherine
Mansfield*, p. 101.
21 F.V. Waters to Police Commissioner,
9 September 1898, ACIS 17627 P1/261,
1898/1577, Archives New Zealand (ANZ).
22 WCA, 00233:143:1907/11557, 5 July 1907.
23 WCA, 00233:141:1907/803, 10 August
1907.
24 WCA, 00233:211:1911/2134, 14 October
1911.
25 F.V. Waters to Colonial Secretary, 29
October 1907, AGGO 8333, 1A1/1020/[7],
1907/2223, ANZ.

26 Mantz and Murry, *The Life of Katherine
Mansfield*, p. 98.
27 *Evening Post*, 28 November 1918.
28 Judith Burch and Jan Heynes (eds),
Karori and its People (Wellington: Karori
Historical Society and Steele Roberts,
2011), p. 115.

Twelve: Moon at the top of the stairs

1 Karori Historical Society: Interview with
Edith Miller and Robert Caldwell, 1973,
OHInt-0068/2, National Library of New
Zealand.
2 F.L. Irvine-Smith, *Streets of My City,
Wellington, New Zealand* (Wellington:
A. H. & A.W. Reed, 1974), p. 156.
3 *Evening Post*, 10 April 1899.
4 J. Middleton Murry (ed.), *Journal of
Katherine Mansfield* (London: Constable,
1954), p. 106.
5 'The Sisters', in Gerri Kimber and
Vincent O'Sullivan (eds), *The Edinburgh
Edition of the Collected Works of Katherine
Mansfield, vol. 2: The collected fiction
of Katherine Mansfield, 1916–1922*
(Edinburgh: Edinburgh University
Press, 2012), p. 442.
6 Margaret Scott (ed.), *The Katherine
Mansfield Notebooks*, vol. 2 (Canterbury:
Lincoln University Press and Daphne
Brasell Associates, 1997), p. 24.
7 'That Woman', in Kimber and O'Sullivan
(eds), *The Edinburgh Edition*, vol. 2, p. 3.
8 *Dominion*, 8 March 1963.
9 Scott (ed.), *The Katherine Mansfield
Notebooks*, vol. 2, p. 32.
10 Gerri Kimber and Claire Davison (eds),
*The Edinburgh Edition of the Collected
Works of Katherine Mansfield, vol. 4: The
diaries of Katherine Mansfield including
miscellaneous works* (Edinburgh:
Edinburgh University Press, 2016),
p. 170.
11 Letter to Jeanne Renshaw, 14 October
1921, in Vincent O'Sullivan (ed.),
Katherine Mansfield: Selected Letters
(Oxford: Clarendon Press, 1990), p. 229.
12 'By Moonlight', in Kimber and

O'Sullivan (eds), *The Edinburgh Edition,* vol. 2, p. 400.

13 Ruth Elvish Mantz and J. Middleton Murry, *The Life of Katherine Mansfield* (London: Constable & Co., 1933), p. 126.

14 Ibid., p. 127.

15 *Dominion*, 11 March 1963.

16 Scott (ed.), *The Katherine Mansfield Notebooks, vol. 2*, p. 24

17 'The Garden Party', in Kimber and O'Sullivan (eds), *The Edinburgh Edition,* vol. 2, p. 411.

18 Ibid., p. 408.

19 *Evening Post*, 6 August 1887.

20 *Evening Post*, 15 March 1893.

21 Ibid.

22 Harold Beauchamp to Inspector Pender, Alleged Larrikinism on Tinakori Road, 5 January 1900, ACIS 17627 P1/273, 1898/1989, Archives New Zealand.

23 Ibid.

24 Ibid

25 Ibid.

26 Ibid.

27 'A Happy Christmas Eve', in Kimber and O'Sullivan (eds), *The Edinburgh Edition,* vol. 1, p. 5.

28 Harold Beauchamp to Town Clerk, 9/12/04, 00233:110:1904/2312, Wellington City Archives (WCA).

29 Ibid.

30 *Evening Post*, 28 May 1906.

31 Scott, *The Katherine Mansfield Notebooks,* vol. 2, p. 24.

32 Harold Beauchamp to Town Clerk, 4/3/07, 00233:138:1907/350, WCA.

33 Pat Lawlor, *Old Wellington Days* (Wellington: Whitcombe & Tombs, 1959), p. 180.

34 Ibid.

35 Ibid.

36 *Evening Post*, 2 July 1965.

Thirteen: Fly on the wall

1 Marion C. Ruddick, 'Incidents in the Childhood of Katherine Mansfield', unpublished typescript, MS-Papers 1339,

194–?, National Library of New Zealand, p. 7.

2 *Evening Post*, 17 June 1898.

3 Sandra Coney, *Standing in the Sunshine: A history of New Zealand women since they won the vote* (Auckland; Viking, 1993), p. 204.

4 Olga Harding, *One Hundred Years: A history of Wellington Girls' College* (Upper Hutt: Wright & Carman, 1982), p. 26.

5 Gerri Kimber, *Katherine Mansfield: The early years* (Edinburgh: Edinburgh University Press, 2016), p. 62.

6 Ian Gordon (ed.), *Victorian Voyage: The shipboard diary of Katherine Mansfield's mother, March to May 1898* (Auckland: Wilson & Horton, 2000), p. 64.

7 Ibid., p. 73.

8 Ibid.

9 Ruddick, 'Incidents in the Childhood', p. 7.

10 Ibid., p. 11.

11 Ruth Elvish Mantz Collection, Box 3, Harry Ransom Centre, University of Texas at Austin, USA, quoted in Kimber, *Katherine Mansfield: The early years*, p. 50.

12 Ruddick, 'Incidents in the Childhood', p. 3.

13 Ibid., p. 11.

14 Ibid., p. 8

15 Ibid., p. 12.

16 Ibid., p. 4.

17 Ibid., p. 16.

18 Ibid., p. 17.

19 Celia Manson, *Widow of Thorndon Quay* (Wellington: Pigeon Press, 1981), p. 243.

20 Ruddick, 'Incidents in the Childhood', p. 5.

21 Ibid., p. 8.

22 Ibid., p. 25.

23 Ibid., p. 6.

24 'Taking the Veil', in Gerri Kimber and Vincent O'Sullivan (eds), *The Edinburgh Edition of the Collected Works of Katherine Mansfield, vol. 2: The collected fiction of Katherine Mansfield, 1916–1922* (Edinburgh: Edinburgh University Press, 2012), p. 469.

25 Ruddick, 'Incidents in the Childhood', p. 10.
26 Harding, *One Hundred Years*, p. 30.
27 Ruth Elvish Mantz Collection, Harry Ransom Centre, University of Texas at Austin, USA.
28 Ruth Elvish Mantz and J. Middleton Murry, *The Life of Katherine Mansfield* (London: Constable & Co., 1933), p. 146.
29 Ibid., p. 6.

Fourteen: A place in the sun

1 'The Voyage', in Gerri Kimber and Vincent O'Sullivan (eds), *The Edinburgh Edition of the Collected Works of Katherine Mansfield, vol. 2: The collected fiction of Katherine Mansfield, 1916–1922* (Edinburgh: Edinburgh University Press, 2012), p. 373.
2 Letter to John Murry, 8 April 1920, in Vincent O'Sullivan and Margaret Scott (eds), *The Collected Letters of Katherine Mansfield, vol. 4: 1920–1921* (Oxford: Oxford University Press, 1996).
3 *Marlborough Express*, 20 November 1888.
4 *Evening Post*, 19 December 1888.
5 Ruth Elvish Mantz and J. Middleton Murry, *The Life of Katherine Mansfield* (London: Constable & Co., 1933), p. 64.
6 'Six Years After', in Kimber and O'Sullivan (eds), *The Edinburgh Edition, vol. 2*, p. 422.
7 Pat Lawlor, *Old Wellington Days* (Wellington: Whitcombe & Tombs, 1959), p. 180.
8 'The Voyage', in Kimber and O'Sullivan (eds), *The Edinburgh Edition, vol. 2*, p. 378.
9 J. Middleton Murry (ed.), *Scrapbook of Katherine Mansfield* (London: Constable, 1937), p. 207.
10 Mantz and Murry, *The Life of Katherine Mansfield*, p. 84.
11 Ibid., p. 77.
12 Ibid.
13 Henry Herron Beauchamp, unpublished journal, vol. 4, p. 126.
14 Ibid.
15 Ethel Beauchamp Hazelwood, *Life at Anakiwa: The first 100 years 1863–1963* (Nelson: Lucas Print, 1974), p. 6.
16 Letter to Harold Beauchamp, 6 March 1916, in Vincent O'Sullivan and Margaret Scott (eds), *The Collected Letters of Katherine Mansfield, vol. 1, 1903–1917* (Oxford: Clarendon Press, 1984), p. 251.
17 *Marlborough Express*, 11 May 1962.
18 Bruce E. Collins, *The Wreck of the Penguin* (Wellington: Steele Roberts, 2000), p. 28.
19 T.E.Y. Seddon, *The Seddons: An autobiography* (Auckland and London: Collins, 1968), p. 54.
20 David Johnson, *Wellington Harbour* (Wellington: Wellington Maritime Museum Trust, 1996), p. 217.
21 Robin Hyde, *The Godwits Fly* (Auckland: Auckland University Press, 2001), p. 114.
22 *Evening Post*, 14 April 1897.
23 *Evening Post*, 7 January 1913.
24 'At the Bay', in Kimber and O'Sullivan (eds), *The Edinburgh Edition, vol. 2*, p. 356.
25 Hyde, *The Godwits Fly*, p. 117.
26 *New Zealand Listener*, 5 April 1963.
27 Jock Phillips, 'Beach culture – Travellers on the beach', Te Ara – the Encyclopedia of New Zealand: www.TeAra.govt.nz/en/beach-culture/page-1
28 *New Zealand Graphic*, 6 February 1897.
29 'At the Bay', in Kimber and O'Sullivan (eds), *The Edinburgh Edition, vol. 2*, p. 344.
30 Ibid., p. 363.
31 'Katherine Mansfield's At the Bay', *Turnbull Record*, November 1968.
32 *Evening Post*, 3 December 1902.
33 'At the Bay', in Kimber and O'Sullivan (eds), *The Edinburgh Edition, vol. 2*, p. 363.
34 Scott (ed.), *The Katherine Mansfield Notebooks, vol. 1*, p. 99.
35 Darryl Coburn, interview with author, 15 December 2015.
36 *Dominion Post*, 25 June 2013.
37 Ibid.
38 Chris Stevenson, interview with author, 27 May 2016.

Fifteen: Ablutions: Thorndon trail

1   Margaret Scott (ed.), *The Katherine Mansfield Notebooks, vol. 2* (Canterbury: Lincoln University Press and Daphne Brasell Associates, 1997), p. 290.
2   J. Middleton Murry (ed.), *Journal of Katherine Mansfield* (London: Constable, 1954), p. 214.
3   Ibid., p. 325.
4   'A Birthday', in Gerri Kimber and Vincent O'Sullivan (eds), *The Edinburgh Edition of the Collected Works of Katherine Mansfield, vol. 1: The collected fiction of Katherine Mansfield, 1898–1915* (Edinburgh: Edinburgh University Press, 2012), p. 209.
5   Ibid., p. 208.
6   Marion C. Ruddick, 'Incidents in the Childhood of Katherine Mansfield', unpublished typescript, MS-Papers 1339, 194–?, National Library of New Zealand, p. 33.
7   Ibid., p. 34.
8   'Weak Heart', in Gerri Kimber and Vincent O'Sullivan (eds), *The Edinburgh Edition of the Collected Works of Katherine Mansfield, vol. 2: The collected fiction of Katherine Mansfield, 1916–1922* (Edinburgh: Edinburgh University Press, 2012), p. 426.
9   Ibid., p. 428.
10 Ibid.
11 Ruddick, 'Incidents in the Childhood', p. 34.
12 Pat Lawlor, *Old Wellington Hotels* (Wellington: Millwood Press, 1974), p. 80.
13 Terence Hodgson, *Colonial Capital: Wellington 1865–1910* (Auckland: Random Century, 1990), p. 46.
14 *Evening Post*, 24 February 1885.
15 Lawlor, *Old Wellington Hotels*, p. 44.
16 John E. Martin, *The House: New Zealand's House of Representatives 1854–2004* (Palmerston North: Dunmore Press, 2004), p. 114.
17 'A Married Man's Story', in Kimber and O'Sullivan (eds), *The Edinburgh Edition, vol. 2*, p. 386.
18 Margaret H. Alington, *Unquiet Earth: A history of the Bolton Street Cemetery* (Wellington: Wellington City Council and Ministry of Works and Development, 1978), p. 171.
19 W.A. Chapple, *Physical Education in Our State Schools* (Wellington, 1894), p. 8.
20 Tosti Murray, *Marsden: The history of a New Zealand school for girls* (Christchurch: Marsden Old Girls' Association, 1967), p. 140.
21 Ruddick, 'Incidents in the Childhood', p. 20.
22 Ibid.
23 Caroline Daley, *Leisure and Pleasure: Reshaping and revealing the New Zealand body, 1900–1960* (Auckland: Auckland University Press, 2003), p. 200.
24 'Prelude', in Kimber and O'Sullivan (eds), *The Edinburgh Edition, vol. 2*, p. 66–67.
25 'I am afraid I must be very old-fashioned', in Kimber and O'Sullivan (eds), *The Edinburgh Edition, vol. 1*, p. 17.
26 Wellington City Council Minute book, Book 12, Wellington City Archives, p. 431.
27 *Sydney Morning Herald*, 11 March 1904.
28 Gerri Kimber and Claire Davison (eds), *The Edinburgh Edition of the Collected Works of Katherine Mansfield, vol. 4: The diaries of Katherine Mansfield including miscellaneous works* (Edinburgh: Edinburgh University Press, 2016), p. 324.
29 'A Cup of Tea', in Kimber and O'Sullivan (eds), *The Edinburgh Edition, vol. 2*, p. 463.
30 'A Married Man's Story', in Kimber and O'Sullivan (eds), *The Edinburgh Edition, vol. 2*, p. 388.
31 Ruddick, 'Incidents in the Childhood', p. 22.
32 'The Wind Blows', in Kimber and O'Sullivan (eds), *The Edinburgh Edition, vol. 2*, p. 229.
33 Pat Lawlor, *Pat Lawlor's Wellington* (Wellington: Millwood Press, 1976), p. 79.
34 Ibid.

35 Ruddick, 'Incidents in the Childhood', p. 35.
36 Lawlor, *Pat Lawlor's Wellington*, p. 80.
37 *Evening Post*, 22 December 1899.
38 'Ole Underwood', in Kimber and O'Sullivan (eds), *The Edinburgh Edition, vol. 1*, p. 319.
39 *Colonist*, 16 November 1893.
40 *Otago Witness*, 16 November 1893.
41 *Evening Star*, 16 November 1893.
42 Lawlor, *Pat Lawlor's Wellington*, p. 80.

Sixteen: Picked out in primroses

1   *New Zealand Graphic and Ladies' Journal*, 8 June 1901.
2   *Evening Post*, 3 April 1900.
3   Wellington City Council Minutes Books (WCCMB), vol. 14, 22 March 1900, Wellington City Archives (WCA), p. 48.
4   *Free Lance*, 7 December 1901.
5   Margaret Scott (ed.), *The Katherine Mansfield Notebooks, vol. 2* (Canterbury: Lincoln University Press and Daphne Brasell Associates, 1997), p. 26.
6   'Maata', in Gerri Kimber and Vincent O'Sullivan (eds), *The Edinburgh Edition of the Collected Works of Katherine Mansfield, vol. 1: The collected fiction of Katherine Mansfield, 1916–1922* (Edinburgh: Edinburgh University Press, 2012), p. 364.
7   'Kezia and Tui', in Ian Gordon (ed.), *Undiscovered Country: The New Zealand stories of Katherine Mansfield* (London: Longman, 1974), p. 169.
8   Ibid., p. 170.
9   Antony Alpers, *The Life of Katherine Mansfield* (New York: Viking, 1980), p. 19.
10 Tosti Murray, *Marsden: The history of a New Zealand school for girls* (Christchurch: Marsden Old Girls' Association, 1967), p. 66.
11 Scott (ed.), *The Katherine Mansfield Notebooks, vol. 1*, p. 49.
12 *Evening Post*, 2 April 1900.
13 Ibid.
14 'The Garden Party', in Gerry Kimber and Vincent O'Sullivan (eds), *The*

Edinburgh Edition of the Collected Works of Katherine Mansfield, vol. 2: The collected fiction of Katherine Mansfield, 1916–1922 (Edinburgh: Edinburgh University Press, 2012), p. 407.
15 *New Zealand Graphic and Ladies' Journal*, 23 January 1897.
16 *New Zealand Graphic and Ladies' Journal*, 6 June 1901.
17 *New Zealand Graphic and Ladies' Journal*, 7 June 1902.
18 *New Zealand Graphic and Ladies' Journal*, 10 August 1901.
19 David Hamer and Roberta Nicholls (eds), *The Making of Wellington, 1800–1914* (Wellington: Victoria University Press, 1990), p. 196
20 Ibid., p. 210.
21 *New Zealand Graphic and Ladies' Journal*, 18 October 1902.
22 *New Zealand Graphic and Ladies' Journal*, 9 August 1902.
23 Ibid.
24 *New Zealand Graphic and Ladies' Journal*, 8 July 1899.
25 *New Zealand Graphic and Ladies' Journal*, 13 April 1901.
26 Ibid.
27 C.K. Stead (ed.), *The Letters and Journals of Katherine Mansfield, A Selection* (London, Allen Lane, 1977), p. 16.
28 *New Zealand Graphic and Ladies' Journal*, 8 June 1901.
29 Vincent O'Sullivan, communication to author, May 2016.
30 'Misunderstood', in Gerri Kimber and Vincent O'Sullivan (eds), *The Edinburgh Edition of the Collected Works of Katherine Mansfield, vol. 1: The collected fiction of Katherine Mansfield, 1898–1915* (Edinburgh: Edinburgh University Press, 2012), p. 12.
31 'Two Ideas and One Moral', in Kimber and O'Sullivan (eds), *The Edinburgh Edition, vol. 1*, p. 19.
32 *New Zealand Graphic and Ladies' Journal*, 17 November 1900.
33 *New Zealand Graphic and Ladies' Journal*, 24 August 1901.

34 *New Zealand Graphic and Ladies' Journal*, 21 September 1901.
35 Alpers, *The Life of Katherine Mansfield*, p. 401.
36 'The Great Examination', in Kimber and O'Sullivan (eds), *The Edinburgh Edition, vol. 1*, pp. 7–9.
37 Ibid.
38 Letter to John Murry, 21 March 1918, in Vincent O'Sullivan and Margaret Scott (eds), *The Collected Letters of Katherine Mansfield, vol. 2: 1918–1919* (Oxford: Clarendon Press, 1987), p. 133.
39 Alpers, *The Life of Katherine Mansfield*, p. 401.
40 Erik Olssen and Marcia Stenson, *A Century of Change: New Zealand 1800–1900* (Auckland: Longman Paul, 1989), p. 386.
41 *New Zealand Graphic and Ladies' Journal*, 24 August 1901.
42 Murray, *Marsden*, p. 51.
43 Ibid.
44 'The Singing Lesson', in Kimber and O'Sullivan (eds), *The Edinburgh Edition, vol. 2*, pp. 235–36.
45 'The Wind Blows', in Kimber and O'Sullivan (eds), *The Edinburgh Edition, vol. 2*, p. 227.
46 Jeffrey Meyers, *Katherine Mansfield: A biography* (London: Hamish Hamilton, 1978), p. 10.
47 Pat Lawlor, *Old Wellington Days* (Wellington: Whitcombe & Tombs, 1959), p. 184.
48 'Juliet', in Kimber and O'Sullivan (eds), *The Edinburgh Edition, vol. 1*, p. 40.
49 Ibid., p. 41.
50 Ibid., p. 42.
51 Meyers, *Katherine Mansfield*, p. 11.
52 *New Zealand Listener*, 5 April 1963.
53 Ibid.
54 *New Zealand Graphic and Ladies' Journal*, 8 November 1902.
55 'To the Last Moment', in Kimber and O'Sullivan (eds), *The Edinburgh Edition, vol. 2*, p. 159.
56 Ibid., p. 157.

57 *New Zealand Listener*, 5 April 1963.
58 Ibid.
59 Henry Herron Beauchamp, unpublished journal, vol. 8, 5 April 1904, p. 148.
60 Ibid., 25 December 1904, p. 163.
61 Gerri Kimber and Claire Davison (eds), *The Edinburgh Edition of the Collected Works of Katherine Mansfield, vol. 4: The diaries of Katherine Mansfield including miscellaneous works* (Edinburgh: Edinburgh University Press, 2016), p. 14.

Epilogue: End of the beginning

1 'Our Hilda', in Gerri Kimber and Vincent O'Sullivan (eds), *The Edinburgh Edition of the Collected Works of Katherine Mansfield, vol. 2: The collected fiction of Katherine Mansfield, 1916–1922* (Edinburgh: Edinburgh University Press, 2012), p. 505.
2 J. Middleton Murry (ed.), *Journal of Katherine Mansfield* (London: Constable, 1954), p. 8.
3 Letter to Sylvia Payne, 8 January 1907, in Vincent O'Sullivan and Margaret Scott (eds), *The Collected Letters of Katherine Mansfield, vol. 1: 1903–1917* (Oxford: Oxford University Press, 1984), p. 21.
4 Gerri Kimber and Claire Davison (eds), *The Edinburgh Edition of the Collected Works of Katherine Mansfield, vol. 4: The diaries of Katherine Mansfield including miscellaneous works* (Edinburgh: Edinburgh University Press, 2016), p. 172.
5 Letter to Dorothy Brett, 12 September 1921, in Vincent O'Sullivan and Margaret Scott (eds), *The Collected Letters of Katherine Mansfield, vol. 4: 1920–1921* (Oxford: Clarendon Press, 1996), p. 278.
6 Murry (ed.), *Journal of Katherine Mansfield*, p. 9.
7 Letter to Jeanne Beauchamp, 11 October 1913, in O'Sullivan and Scott (eds), *The Collected Letters of Katherine Mansfield, vol. 1*, p. 132.
8 *Auckland Star*, 2 October 1931.

Select Bibliography

Manuscripts and archives

Archives New Zealand, Head Office, Wellington (ANZ)

ABYB, Series 23224, W55732, Box 45/48: Henry Godsiff and Arthur Beauchamp, Declaration of Insolvency, Blenheim Court, 1879.

ACIS 17627 P1/273, 1898/1889: Harold Beauchamp to Inspector Pender, Alleged Larrikinism on Tinakori Road, 5 January 1900.

ACIS 17627 P1/261, 1898/1577: Larrikinism in Karori, F.V. Waters to Police Commissioner, 9 September 1898.

AGGO 8333, 1A1/1020/[7], 1907/2223: Opossum Permits, F.V. Waters to Colonial Secretary, 29 October 1907.

CAMO, CH214, Box 97/129: Official Assignee's Bankruptcy Files: Christchurch, Beauchamp Arthur, 1884.

G 7, p. 86: Memorial to Governor Grey, 1848.

Alexander Turnbull Library, Wellington (ATL)

Cotton, W.C., *Journals*, vol. 6, pp. 28–29, 7 December 1843.

Karori Historical Society: Interview with Edith Miller and Robert Caldwell, 1973, OHInt-0068/2.

Letter from Jeanne (Beauchamp) Renshaw to Karori Historical Society, 23 February 1977, donated to ATL 2003.

Letter from Ray Willis, MS-Papers-11326-051.

Logbook of Karori School, 1875–1900, MSX-5973.

Marion C. Ruddick, 'Incidents in the Childhood of Katherine Mansfield', unpublished typescript, MS-Papers-1339, 194–?.

Mary Swainson, letter to her grandparents in England, 25 September 1842, unpublished MS.

Miriam Frankland – Notebook, 1886, Frankland, Miriam, 1857–1945, MS-0805.

Wellington City Archives (WCA)

Minutes

00166:0:1, vols 3–127: Minutes of meetings of Wellington City Council (WCC), 1870–1997.

00112, vols 1–3: Minutes of Karori Borough Council (KBC), 1891–1920.

Files

00030:1:1: Reports and Proceedings of the City Council on a Water Supply to the City, 1870.

00233:34:1892/740: Prevention of Typhoid Fever, Dr Chapple, 1892.

00233:34:1892/737: Information on Liernur System (Pneumatic Drainage), supplied by Harold Beauchamp.

00009:1747:45/276/3: Premises, 372 Karori Road, 1936–1988.

00233:14:1886/783: F.V. Waters, Overcharge of nightsoil contractors, 1886.

00233:143:1907/11557: F.V. Waters, Fowl House Nuisance, 1907.

00233:141:1907/803: F.V. Waters, Spitting on Karori Tram, 1907.

00233:211:1911/2134: F.V. Waters, Sanitation of city, 1911.

00233:110:1904/2312: Harold Beauchamp to Town Clerk, 1904.

00233:138:1907/350: Harold Beauchamp to Town Clerk, 1907.

Heritage New Zealand

Katherine Mansfield Birthplace House files, 8/13/142, Heritage New Zealand.

Miscellaneous

Beverley Randell Price, 'Memories of Karori School 1937–1943', unpublished MS.

Claire Nicoll, Tarr Family Biography, unpublished MS, Tarr family.

Henry Herron Beauchamp, unpublished journals, vols 1–8, 1870–1907, Beauchamp family.

Jessica Rankin, unpublished diary, 1867–1869, Pharazyn family.
Mary Taylor Correspondence, WS no. 422, Berg Collection, New York Public Library, USA.
Mary Taylor to Ellen Nussey, 14 October 1850, WS no. 610, Brontë Parsonage Museum, Haworth, UK.
Ruth Elvish Mantz Collection, Harry Ransom Centre, University of Texas at Austin, USA.

Books

Peter Ackroyd, *Dickens* (London: Sinclair Stevenson, 1990).
Margaret H. Alington, *High Point: St Mary's Church, Karori, Wellington 1866–1991* (Wellington: Parish of St Mary's, Karori, and Karori Historical Society, 1998).
Margaret H. Alington, *Unquiet Earth: A history of the Bolton Street Cemetery* (Wellington: Wellington City Council and Ministry of Works and Development, 1978).
Antony Alpers, *The Life of Katherine Mansfield* (New York: Viking, 1980).
Harold Beauchamp, *Reminiscences and Reflections* (New Plymouth: 1937).
James Belich, *Making Peoples: A history of the New Zealanders from Polynesian settlement to the end of the nineteenth century* (Auckland: Penguin, 1996).
Sylvia Berkman, *Katherine Mansfield: A critical study* (New Haven: Yale University Press, 1951).
Gillian Boddy, *Katherine Mansfield: The woman and the writer* (Auckland: Penguin, 1988).
Judith Burch and Jan Heynes (eds), *Karori and its People* (Wellington: Karori Historical Society and Steele Roberts, 2011).
Bruce E. Collins, *Wreck of the* Penguin (Wellington: Steele Roberts, 2000).
Sandra Coney, *Standing in the Sunshine: A history of New Zealand women since they won the vote* (Auckland: Viking, 1993).

Raewyn Dalziel, *Julius Vogel: Business politician* (Auckland: Auckland University Press, 1986).
Caroline Daley, *Leisure and Pleasure: Reshaping and revealing the New Zealand body, 1900–1960* (Auckland: Auckland University Press, 2003).
Charles Dickens, *Bleak House* (London: Penguin Classics, 2003).
Ian Gordon (ed.), *Victorian Voyage: The shipboard diary of Katherine Mansfield's mother, March to May 1898* (Auckland: Wilson & Horton, 2000).
Ian Gordon (ed.), *Undiscovered Country: The New Zealand stories of Katherine Mansfield* (London: Longman, 1974).
David Hamer and Roberta Nicholls (eds), *The Making of Wellington, 1800–1914* (Wellington: Victoria University Press, 1990).
Cherry A. Hankin (ed.), *Letters of John Middleton Murry to Katherine Mansfield* (London: Constable, 1983).
Olga Harding, *One Hundred Years: A history of Wellington Girls' College* (Upper Hutt: Wright & Carman, 1982).
Ethel Beauchamp Hazelwood, *Life at Anakiwa: The first 100 years 1863–1963* (Nelson: Lucas Print, 1974).
Charles Heaphy, *Narrative of a Residence in Various Parts of New Zealand* (London: Smith Elder, 1842).
Tristram Hunt, *Building Jerusalem: The rise and fall of the Victorian city* (London: Weidenfeld & Nicolson, 2004).
Robin Hyde, *Journalese* (Auckland: National Printing Co., 1934).
Robin Hyde, *The Godwits Fly* (Auckland, Auckland University Press, 2001).
F.L. Irvine-Smith, *Streets of My City, Wellington, New Zealand* (Wellington: A.H. & A.W. Reed, 1974).
David Johnson, *Wellington Harbour* (Wellington: Wellington Maritime Museum Trust, 1996).
Gerri Kimber, *Katherine Mansfield: The early years* (Edinburgh: Edinburgh University Press, 2016).

Gerri Kimber and Claire Davison (eds), *The Edinburgh Edition of the Collected Works of Katherine Mansfield, vol. 4: The diaries of Katherine Mansfield including miscellaneous works* (Edinburgh: Edinburgh University Press, 2016).

Gerri Kimber and Vincent O'Sullivan (eds), *The Edinburgh Edition of the Collected Works of Katherine Mansfield, vol. 1: The collected fiction of Katherine Mansfield, 1898–1915* (Edinburgh: Edinburgh University Press, 2012).

Gerri Kimber and Vincent O'Sullivan (eds), *The Edinburgh Edition of the Collected Works of Katherine Mansfield, vol. 2: The collected fiction of Katherine Mansfield, 1916–1922* (Edinburgh: Edinburgh University Press, 2012).

Friedrich August Krull, *An Indescribable Beauty: Letters home to Germany from Wellington, New Zealand, 1859 & 1862* (Wellington: Awa Press, 2012).

Pat Lawlor, *The Mystery of Maata: A Katherine Mansfield novel* (Wellington: Beltane Book Bureau, 1946).

Pat Lawlor, *Old Wellington Days* (Wellington: Whitcombe & Tombs, 1959).

Pat Lawlor, *Old Wellington Hotels* (Wellington: Millwood Press, 1974).

Pat Lawlor, *Pat Lawlor's Wellington* (Wellington: Millwood Press, 1976).

F.S. Maclean, *Challenge for Health: A history of public health in New Zealand* (Wellington: Government Printer, 1964).

Gavin McLean, *Wellington: The first years of European settlement, 1840–1850,* (Auckland: Penguin, 2000).

N.L McLeod and B.H. Farland (eds), *Wellington Prospect, Survey of a City 1840–1970* (Wellington: Hicks Smith & Sons, 1970).

Celia Manson, *Widow of Thorndon Quay* (Wellington: Pigeon Press, 1981).

Ruth Elvish Mantz and J. Middleton Murry, *The Life of Katherine Mansfield* (London: Constable & Co., 1933).

Alexander Marjoribanks, *Travels in New Zealand* (London: Smith Elder, 1845).

John E. Martin, *The House: New Zealand's House of Representatives 1854–2004* (Palmerston North: Dunmore Press, 2004).

Helen May, *School Beginnings: A nineteenth century colonial story* (Wellington: NZCER Press, 2005).

Jeffrey Meyers, *Katherine Mansfield: A biography* (London: Hamish Hamilton, 1978).

Tosti Murray, *Marsden: The history of a New Zealand school for girls* (Christchurch: Marsden Old Girls' Association, 1967).

J. Middleton Murry (ed.), *Scrapbook of Katherine Mansfield* (London: Constable, 1937).

Simon Nathan, *James Hector: Explorer, scientist, leader* (Lower Hutt: Geoscience Society of New Zealand, 2015).

Erik Olssen and Marcia Stenson, *A Century of Change: New Zealand 1800–1900* (Auckland: Longman Paul, 1989).

Vincent O'Sullivan (ed.), *The Aloe with Prelude* (Wellington: Port Nicholson Press), 1982.

Vincent O'Sullivan (ed.), *Katherine Mansfield: Selected letters* (Oxford: Clarendon Press, 1990).

Vincent O'Sullivan (ed.), *Poems of Katherine Mansfield* (Auckland: Oxford University Press, 1988).

Vincent O'Sullivan and Margaret Scott (eds), *The Collected Letters of Katherine Mansfield, vol. 1: 1903–1917* (Oxford: Clarendon Press, 1984).

Vincent O'Sullivan and Margaret Scott (eds), *The Collected Letters of Katherine Mansfield, vol. 4: 1920–1921* (Oxford: Oxford University Press, 1996).

Geoff Park, *Nga Uruora: The groves of life* (Wellington: Victoria University Press, 1995).

Brent Parker, *Karori School: Frontier classroom to city school, 1857–2007* (Wellington: Karori Normal School, 2007).

Jenifer Roberts, *Fitz: The colonial adventures of James Edward FitzGerald* (Dunedin: Otago University Press, 2014).

Margaret Scott (ed.), *The Katherine Mansfield Notebooks, vols 1 & 2*, (Canterbury: Lincoln University Press and Daphne Brasell Associates, 1997).

T.E.Y. Seddon. *The Seddons: An autobiography* (Auckland and London: Collins, 1968).

Winsome Shepherd, *Wellington's Heritage: Plants, gardens and landscapes* (Wellington: Te Papa Press, 2000).

Beryl Smedley, *Homewood and its Families: A story of Wellington* (Wellington: Mallinson Rendel, 1980).

C.K. Stead (ed.), *The Letters and Journals of Katherine Mansfield, A Selection* (London, Allen Lane, 1977).

Nancy M. Taylor (ed.), *The Journal of Ensign Best 1837–1843* (Wellington: Government Printer, 1966).

Claire Tomalin, *Katherine Mansfield: A secret life* (London: Viking, 1987).

Edward Jerningham Wakefield, *Adventure in New Zealand* (Auckland: Golden Press, 1975).

Louis Ward, *Early Wellington* (Auckland: Whitcombe & Tombs, 1928).

A.N. Wilson, *The Victorians* (London: Hutchinson, 2002).

Charles Wilson, *New Zealand Cities*, (Auckland: Whitcombe and Tombs, 1919).

John Wood, *Twelve Months in Wellington, Port Nicholson* (London: Pelham Richardson, 1843).

Lawrence Wright, *Clean and Decent, the Fascinating History of the Bathroom and the Water Closet* (London: Penguin, 1960).

Redmer Yska, *Wellington: Biography of a city* (Auckland: Reed, 2006).

Articles and papers

Elsdon Best, 'Te Whanga-nui-a-Tara: Wellington in Pre-Pakeha Days', *Journal of the Polynesian Society*, vol. 10, no. 3, 1917.

Judith Burch and Beryl Hughes, 'Karori Lunatic Asylum, 1854–1873', *Stockade: Magazine of the Karori Historical Society*, no. 31, 1998.

Phillip Cleaver, 'The Pakeha Treatment of Death in Nineteenth and Early Twentieth Century Wellington', *Wellington Historical and Early Settlers' Association Inc*, 1996.

Maxwell Gage, 'The Makara and Karori Valleys and Their Bearing Upon the Physiographic History of Wellington', *Transactions and Proceedings of the Royal Society of New Zealand 1868–1961*, vol. 69, 1940.

Helena Hawke, 'Katherine Mansfield and Karori', *Stockade: Magazine of the Karori Historical Society*, vol. 3, no. 2, 1975.

Kevin L. Jones, 'Archaeology of the Katherine Mansfield Birthplace, Wellington, New Zealand: "It's all memories now …"' *New Zealand Journal of Archaeology*, vol. 14, 1992.

Morris Love, 'Te Āti Awa of Wellington – Migrations of the 1820s', Te Ara – the Encyclopedia of New Zealand: www.TeAra.govt.nz/en/te-ati-awa-of-wellington/page-2

Jock Phillips, 'Beach culture – Travellers on the beach', Te Ara – the Encyclopedia of New Zealand: www.TeAra.govt.nz/en/beach-culture/page-1

Redmer Yska, 'Katherine Mansfield's family in the time of cholera', Public Lecture, Katherine Mansfield Birthplace (2012).

—— 'Flight to South Karori: How Katherine Mansfield's family coped with life and death in the time of cholera (1890-93)', Public Seminar, Wellington Central Library (August, 2013).

—— 'Death Stalks the Doll's House: How a season of epidemics shaped Katherine Mansfield and her world', Seminar, School of Public Health, University of Otago, Wellington (December, 2013).

Acknowledgements

My first thanks go to Gabor Toth, stalwart of this project, and to other Wellington Central Library staff, especially the endlessly kind and helpful Ann Rewiti.

The other linchpin has been Vincent O'Sullivan, who first gave me the confidence to eye up the KM mountain, and whose great scholarship, humour and kindness helped pave the way.

I'm indebted, too, to Malcolm McKinnon. His decision in 2012 to duck a talk to the Katherine Mansfield Birthplace Society about 1890s Wellington led Helena Hawke to approach me. The research for that paper became the kernel of this book. Malcolm later read the MS and, as always, made vital input.

I also want to acknowledge Dr Charles Ferrall, distinguished scholar and dear friend, for his support and wisdom over many years.

I particularly want to thank Emily Perkins, co-ordinator of the MA Creative Writing Programme at Victoria University's International Institute of Modern Letters. The 2015 year, with Emily as my supervisor, was indelible. She was a generous, patient, hugely attentive reader, helping crystalise ideas over multiple drafts.

I want to shout out to my dear classmates: Libby Farris, Jackson Nieuwland, Justine Jungerson-Smith, Catherine Robertson, Alisha Tyson, Johnny McCaughan, Meryl Richards, Whitney Cox and Helen Crampton. An unforgettable year.

Special thanks are also due to Adrian Humphris and always-helpful staff at Wellington City Archives. Thanks, too, to Peter Atwood, Nick Bollinger, Nick Buck, Judith Burch, Chris Bourke, Daryl Coburn, Cliff Fell, Mary Ann Gillies, Isabel Grubi, Katie Hardwick-Smith, Sue Jamieson, Kathleen Jones, Fiona Kidman, James Kinnon, Vincent O'Malley, John Martin, Simon Nathan, John Newton, Suzanne Pollard, Nina Powles, Dinah Priestley, John Quilter, Roger Steele, Bruce Stirling, Nick Wilson, Ben Schrader, Kevin Stent, Jane Tolerton and Damien Wilkins.

Rachel Scott from Otago University Press has been an attentive and encouraging publisher. Huge thanks to the New Zealand History Research Trust Fund for providing the substantial funding that made this project possible. I owe a debt to the redoubtable Jane Parkin, editor extraordinary and fellow Karori School alumni from another lifetime. Her input made a huge difference. And many thanks to Allan Kynaston for the beautiful maps.

The book is dedicated with love to Ruth Laugesen, and to our children Daniel and Rosa.

Index

Bold page numbers refer to photographs, captions and maps.

11/25 Tinakori Road 21, 26, 33, 35–38, **39**, 59; after the Beauchamps 41–43; archaeology of 36–37, 43
23 Fitzherbert Terrace 22, 237
75 Tinakori Road 159–64, **161**, **169**, **172**, 176–77, 198; after the Beauchamps 171; in KM's writing 162–64
372 Karori Road *see* Chesney Wold

'About Pat' 108, 109–10
Ahumairangi Hill 21
Allan, William 29
Allen, Frank 170
'The Aloe' 38, 83, 85–88, 103, 106, 147–48
Alpers, Antony 66, 92
Alzdorf, Charles Ernest von 29–30
Anakiwa **90**, 94, 185–89, 190
Anderson, Farquhar Campbell ('Farkey') 110
Arnim, Elizabeth von *see* Beauchamp, Mary
'At the Bay' 22–23, 40, 83, 152–53; setting at Muritai 190–93
'Autumns I' 119

Bagnall family (in Karori) 106
Baker, Ida 234
'Bank Holiday' 74
Bank of New Zealand 160
Bannatyne and Company 82, 88, 159
Barraud, Sydney 190
Barraud's chemist and druggist 203
Beauchamp, Annie 111, 112, **113**, **153**; as mother 16, 48, 52, 133, 175–76, 185, 198; as society hostess 216; voyage to England 174–76; *see also* Dyer, Annie Burnell
Beauchamp, Arthur 26, 81–82, **90**, 91–99, 186
Beauchamp, Charles 65
Beauchamp, Charlotte (Chaddie) 36–37, 109, **113**, 133, **139**, **153**, **172**, 173, 177–78, 182, 198, 234; recollections 40–41, 110, 162, 231

Beauchamp, Cradock 26, 81, **90**, 93, 94, 185–88
Beauchamp, Ethel (Harold's cousin) 176
Beauchamp, Ethel (Herbert's daughter) 188
Beauchamp, Gwendoline 38, **44**, 45–53
Beauchamp, Harold 15, 36–40, 174–75, 193, 211, 227, 231–33; in business and society 97–98, 111, 141, 159–60, 216; complaints about sanitation and urchins 63, 166–70; courtship and marriage 82–83, 86–88; early years 93, 96–97, 185; as father 16, 129, **153**, 176; in father Arthur's bankruptcy 91, 97
Beauchamp, Harriet **90**, 185, 187–88
Beauchamp, Henry Herron 81–82, 93, 96–97, 98, 187–88, 234, 235
Beauchamp, Herbert 188
Beauchamp, Jane (great-great aunt) 26
Beauchamp, Jeanne 87, 107, **113**, **139**, **153**, 163, **172**, 215, 232; letters in *Graphic* 227–28
Beauchamp, John (Highgate, London) 81, 234
Beauchamp, Kathleen: character and physique 127–28, 175–76, 187, 207; stout, with 'a penetrating gaze' 112–13, **113**, 145; physical agility grows 178–80, 206; 'sombre brown eyes' 188; teachers' recollections 128, 213; teenage exuberance 235
Beauchamp, Kathleen: early childhood 35, 37–41, 185
Beauchamp, Kathleen: Karori School years 16–17, 120–31, **139**, **153**; holidays at Anakiwa 186–88; ill-health 121–22; prizes go to others 128–29
Beauchamp, Kathleen: Thorndon school years **172**, 173–82, 206, 212–14; first love interest 230–32; as performer 182, 212
Beauchamp, Kathleen: voyage to England in 1903: 232–36, **235**; return to Wellington 1906–08: 237

Beauchamp, Kathleen: writing 108, 128;
published in *Graphic* in 1900: 217–28;
teacher's criticism 213; in Thorndon
school years 27, 108, 131, 162, 167–68,
174, 176, 182, 214, 228
Beauchamp, Leslie Heron (Chummie) 15,
73, 82, 109, 111, **113, 153**, 163, **172**, 212, 238
Beauchamp, Mary (Elizabeth von Arnim)
176, 234
Beauchamp, Mary Stanley 92–93, 94, 97–99,
186
Beauchamp, Vera 36, 109, 112, **113**, 128, 131,
133, **139**, 155, 173, 177, 187, 198, 234, 235;
recollections 40, 192, 231, 232; role in
Ruddick's memoir 183
Beauchamp family **90, 113, 153, 161, 172,
235**; funerals 65; 'keen on the right
word' 189; voyage to England in 1903:
232–35, **235**
Beauchamp homes 36–38; *see also* 11/25
Tinakori Road; 23 Fitzherbert Terrace;
75 Tinakori Road; Chesney Wold
Beauchamp Street 141
Bell, Francis Dillon 57–58, 62, 63–64, 178
Bendall, Edie 21–22, 237
Best, Elsdon 23
'Binzer, Andreas' 197
birdbath memorial **12**, 14–17, 240–41
birdlife **20**, 22–23, 25, 29, 110, 138, 239–40; at
Anakiwa 187; in KM's writing 22, 103,
136, 144, 227
'A Birthday' 33, 56–57, 58, 72–73, 77, 197–98,
202
birthplace in Thorndon *see* 11/25 Tinakori
Road
Birthplace Society 43
Bolton Street Cemetery 45–48, **47**, 52–53, 65,
88–89, **89**, 204
Bradnock (roadman) 136, 137
Brett, Dorothy 238
brewery in Thorndon 203–04
Brogan, Emmie 123
Brown, Denzil 145
Brown, Eliza Balcombe 164
Brown family (in Karori) 105
Buck, Nick and Jenny 81
'Burnell, Isabel' 13, 123

'Burnell, Kezia' 40–41, 67, 103, 106–07, 109,
112, 136, 142, 212–13
'Burnell, Linda' 67, 107
'Burnell, Lottie' 41
'Burnell, Stanley' 67, 152
Burnell Avenue 22, 160
'Burnell' family 15–17, 67, 106–07, 122–23, 226
Burrows Hill 137–40, 139–40
'By Moonlight' 163

Caledonian (grog shop) 27, 29
'The Candle' 38
'Carnation' 142
Cathie, Jessie 123, 127
Chapple, William 64–66, 205
Chesney Wold **102**, 103–15, 120, 127, **132**, 136;
in KM's writing 73, 103, 106–10, 113–14,
119, 136–37, 234; move to 41, 66–67,
106–07
'The Child-Who-Was-Tired' 140
cholera 49–51
church attendance *see* religious observance
Clark, Annie 209
class differences 212, 228; in KM's writing
117–18, 228
Cliff Pa 27
Clifford, Charles 36
Coburn, Darryl 194
'Cole, Emmie' 123
Cookson, Frank 170
Cottel, Mary 71–72, 75
Couper, William 27, 29–30
Cranley, Lord 62
Crescent Bay *see* Muritai
'A Cup of Tea' 207

Dasent, Alexander 111
'David' (in 'Juliet') 230–31
Day, Oroya 43
Days Bay ('Daylight Cove') 190, 193–95
'Dead Man's Bread' 139
death and sickness (in KM's fiction) 16, 51,
52, 56–57, 58, 213–14, 223, 226
Dickens, Charles 104, 123, 128–29, 212, 226
'The Doll's House' 13, 16, 57, 67, 117, 122–24,
136, 182, 228
Donald, Robert 108
Downes Point 193–95

Dyer, Agnes *see* Waters, Agnes Mansfield (née Dyer)
Dyer, Annie Burnell 15, 21, 85; courtship and marriage 82–83, 86–88; *see also* Beauchamp, Annie
Dyer, Belle 37, 88, 111, 112–13, **172**, 173, 189, 232, 234
Dyer, Frank 21–22, 82, 160, 189, 215
Dyer, Henry 65, 88, 89
Dyer, Henry (headmaster) 121, 125
Dyer, Joseph 31, **80**, 82–89, 97
Dyer, Kitty 37, 189
Dyer, Lulu 15
Dyer, Margaret Isabella **80**, 83, 87–89, **113**, 204, 237, 238–39; as grandmother 37–38, **44**, 48–49, 53, 176–77
Dyer, Sydney 232
Dyer family tomb and gravestones 88–89, **89**

earthquakes 26, 28, 30
Eastbourne 189
Ecclesfield, Isabel 180
Eccleston Hill 178
Egmont Street 61
Elizabeth and Her German Garden 176, 234
'Enna Blake' 174, 177
'The Escape' 79
Estall, Charles 165
Evans, George 177–78
Evening Post 46, 50–51, 59, 62, 63–64, 78, 85, 87, 137, 190, 211

'Fairfield, Beryl' 88
'Fairfield, Linda' 83, 86–88
'Fairfield, Mr' 83, 85, 87
'Fairfield, Mrs' 107
Featherston, Isaac 30
FitzGerald, James and Fanny 108
Fitzherbert Terrace 22, 41, 208
Fitzherbert Terrace School 182, 212–13, 216, 226, 229
Frankland, Frederick, Miriam and Ava 55–56, 61
Frasers Lane 202–03

'The Garden Party' 14, 16, 57, 67, **158**, 162, 165; seeds in 1900 story 213–14, 228

gardens 38, 43, 162–63, **172**, 178, 181; in KM's writing 85, 103, 106, 108, 109, 181, 200, 218, 220
Gee, Maurice 73
General Assembly building 30
George Street 212
The Glen (bungalow) **191**, 191–92
Glensor, Bruce 139–40, 144–45
The Godwits Fly 190, 192
gold mining 93–94
Golders Hill 177–78, 181
gorse 138
Graphic see *New Zealand Graphic and Ladies' Journal*
'The Great Examination' 128, 228
Grey, George 200

Hamilton, Martha 174, 178–80
'A Happy Christmas Eve' 167–68, 182
Hatton Street, Karori 150
Hawkestone Street 36
Hazelwood, Ethel Beauchamp 188–89
Hector, James and Georgiana 59
'Her First Ball' 113–14
Hill Street 36, 78, 204, 238
'His Little Friend' 220–26, 228
Historic Places Trust 43, 114
Hobson Street 207–09
holidays: in Marlborough Sounds **184**, 185–95; across Wellington Harbour 189–94
Holland Street 64
Hyde, Robin 41–43, 71, 190, 192

In a German Pension 56–57
infectious diseases 46, 49–52, 55–67, 121, 149, 155, **210**, 211–14
Irwin, Ellen 240
Island Bay 189
'It was a big bare house' 73, 108, 234

Jacks, William 209
Jensen, Peter 170
Johnson, Alfred 61
Jones, Edwin 193
Joseph, Jacob 40
'Josephs' family 40–41
'Juliet' 72, 213, 230–31

kākāriki **20**, 25, 29, 136, 138, 239–40
Karori **65**, 104–05, 107, **134**; departure from 159; in KM's writing 73, 136–38, 142, 144, 241; parish hall activities **139**, 140–41, 159; road to Wellington **65**, 135, 137, 173; *see also* Chesney Wold
Karori General Store and Bakery 142, **143**
Karori Historical Society 159
Karori Lunatic Asylum 123–24
Karori Road: Beauchamp girls' walk to school 133–45
Karori School 13–17, 120–31, 240–41; in KM's writing 117–18, 124, 140
Karori Stream 13, 135–36, 137
Katherine Mansfield Birthplace Society 43
Katherine Street 22
'Kelvey, Else' 16, 117, 136
'Kelvey, Lil' 16, 117, 136
'Kelvey, Mrs' 119
'Kelvey' girls 67, 123
'Kezia and Tui' 212–13
King, Truby 41
Kirkby, Temperance 203
Krull, Friedrich August 25

Lamb, Minnie 194
Lancaster, Stephen 104, 107, 109, 114, **132**
'Late at Night' 79
Lawlor, Pat 41–43, 114–15, 171, 186, 208, 209, 230
Lee, Robert 125–27, **126**
Lester, Justin 77–78
Lewis, William 147–49
Liberal Party 98, 111, 216–17
'The Little Girl' 112, 152
Little Pipitea Street 203
Lockett, Annie 124, 127–28
'Logan, Lena' 123
Lorne Street 61

'Maata' 112
Macdonald, Thomas 46
Macintosh-Bell, Mrs J. *see* Beauchamp, Vera
Mahupuku, Maata 212–13
'A Man and his Dog' 148, 150–52
'The Man With the Wooden Leg' 110
Mandel, Joseph 171
Mansfield, Katherine: 'baby' stories 226;

return to Wellington 1906–08: 194, 237; death 15, 238; memories of childhood 136–37, 160, 162–64, 229, 238; memories of people 51, 53, 98, 99, 109, 141, 170, 188; memories of Wellington 13, 14–15, 35–36, 197–98, 207; thoughts on New Zealand 21; *see also* Beauchamp, Kathleen
Mansfield, Margaret Isabella *see* Dyer, Margaret Isabella
Mantz, Ruth 40, 66, 83, 118, 120, 187, 241
Māori: in early Wellington 22–28, 74; school friendship 212–13; in young Kathleen's writing 27
Marlborough Sounds **184**, 185–87
'A Married Man's Story' 124, 144, 203, 207
Martin, Dr 51, 229
Martin, Herbert 193
'Mary' 121–22, 128
'May, Jessie' 123
May Street 197, 200
McCarthy, Mrs T.G. 216
McHugh, Philomena 203
McKelvey, Annie **116**, 118–20, **119**
McKelvey, Elsie Ada **116**, 118, 120, 129
McKelvey, Lily Maud 118, 120–27, 129–31, **130**
McKelvey, Samuel **119**
McKelvey, Thomas **116**, 118, 120
McKelvey, Zoe **116**, 118, 120
McLean, William 202
Meade, L.T. 227
Melbourne 84, 93
Memorial Trail 45
memorials: Anakiwa 189; birdbath, Karori **12**, 14–17, 240–41; Fitzherbert Terrace, Thorndon 15, 41, **42**
Merz, Rosaly 200
Metropolitan Hotel 203
Meyers, Jeffrey 66
Miller, Edith 159
Ministry of Works 171
'Misunderstood' 226
Mojo coffee bar 198, 200
Molesworth Street 29, 200–203
Monaghan, Lena 123, 141
Monaghan, William 141
Monkey Tree Cottage 150
motorway 21, 26, 43, 88, 159, 197, 204
Moturoa, Te Rohipa 27, 234

Moturoa Street 27, **179**, 204
Munt and Cottrel 168, 198
Muritai 190–93, **191**
Murry, John Middleton 137
museum 21
music 216, 229–32; at school 122, 174
'My Potplants' 109, 136–37

Nathan, Amelia (Amy) **34**, 40
Nathan, Sybil 40
Nathan, Walter 40, 231–33
Nathan, Zaidee 40
Nathan family 38–40
Naverne, Charles Cosmo de 180
neighbours in Thorndon **34**, 38–40, 166–70
'The New Baby' 72
New Zealand Company 26–27, 71, 75, 135–36, 177–78, 216
New Zealand Forest Service 22
New Zealand Graphic and Ladies' Journal **210**, 211, 213, 214–28, 229, 232; Kathleen's letters and story 217–28
New Zealand Times 64, 66
Ngāi Tara 24–25
Ngāti Awa 74
Ngāti Ira 25
Ngāti Tama 25, 135
Niwaru, SS 232

'Old Tar' 142, 241
Olds, Miss (teacher) 122
'Ole Underwood' 79, 209
'One Day' 227
Onslow, Lady Florence 62, 142
Onslow, Lord 62–63
O'Rorke, Maurice 203
Outward Bound Trust 189

Pannell, Joseph 205–07, **206**
Park Street 21–22
Parker, Robert 229
Parkvale Road 142–44
Parnell, Samuel 45
Parsons and Clark 52–53
Partridge, Emily J. 177
Pearce, Edward 41
Penguin, SS (the 'Picton boat') **184**, 185–86, 189

Picton 93–94, 96, 99, 185–86
Picton, Florence 66
Pipitea 234
Pipitea Point 204
Plimmer, John 59–60, 63
politics (Beauchamp family's) 98, 111, 160
pollution in Wellington 21, 31–33, **32**, 49–50, **54**, 56–67, 168
Poplar Grove 31, 85
Porter, Thomas 106
'Potts, Mr' 150–52
'Potts, Mrs' 148
'Prelude' 73, 115, 136–37, 139, 206–07; characters in 40–41, 152; homes in 103, 106–09; places in 41, 50, 57, 67, 144
Princess Hotel 197–98, 200, **201**
prizegivings 128, 129–31, 182, 228
'Psychology' 72

Queen's College, London 234
Queen's Park, Thorndon 21, 24

Rainbow, Gladys 15
Randell, Beverley 15
Rankin, Jessica 30
religious observance 110–11, 164, 176, 235
Revans, Samuel 75–77, **76**
'Revelations' 72
'Rewa' 138
Rewiti, Ann 24
Ridler, Rose 112, 150, 154, 155
'Roddie' (in 'Weak Heart') 52, **89**
Rogers, Sean 103
Rowling, Julia 103, 115
Ruddick, Marion (Molly) 162, **172**, 173, 175–83, 198, 203, 205–06

Sacred Heart Cathedral 178
Sandow, Eugen 206
sanitation *see* infectious diseases
Saunders, Joseph 164–66, 168–70
Saunders Lane ('mean little dwellings') **158**, 164–66, 168–70, 198, 211–12, 214, 226, 239
Scott, Henry Samuel 213–14, 226
'A Sea Voyage' 128
Seddon, Phoebe 160, 189, 215
Seddon, Richard 61, 62, 98–99, 111, 160, 178, 182, 202, 211, 216–17, 220

Seddon, Tom 112–13, 189
Selwyn, George 77
Shamrock Hotel 202
'She' 51
Sheehan, Pat 73, 106, 108, 109–10, 133
Shepherd's Arms 160
'Sheridan' family 67, 165, 213–14, 226
Sims family 195
'The Singing Lesson' 229
'Six Years After' 186
slums 16, 61, 164–66, 198, 203, 211–12, 214
Smith, Mrs Henry 213, 226
Somes Island 50
Spiers, Joe 125
spring in Thorndon 21–22, 24, 26, 33
St Mark's Church 147, 150
St Mary's Church, Karori 111, 150, 155
St Mary's College 178
St Paul's Church and Sunday school 164
Stevenson, Chris 195
Stewart-Savile, Robert 62
'Stubbs, Mrs' 193
Sutherland, Nathaniel and Marion 46
Swainson, Mary 212
swimming 186, 190, 192–93, 205–07, **206**

'Taking the Veil' 181
'Tarana Street/Road' 83, 200
Tarr, James 142–43, 241
Taylor, Mary and Waring 104
Te Aro 60–61
Te Āti Awa 24–25, 27, 187
'That Woman' 162
Thompson, Sidney **130**
Thorndon **32**, 164, 197–209, **199**; exodus in
    1890s 65–66; history of land 23–31; in
    KM's writing 56–57, 59, 77, 197–98, 200,
    203, 207–08; ravages in 20th century
    171
Thorndon Esplanade 35, **196**, 207–08, 209,
    229; baths 204–07
Tinakori Road 21, 29–30, 31, 197–200, 209,
    237–39
'To the Last Moment' 232
Tomalin, Claire 67
'Trout, Doady' 147–48, 154
'Trout, Jonathan' 152–53
'Trout, Pip' 112, 152

'Trout, Rags' 112, 152, **153**
Trowell, Garnet 230–32
Trowell, Thomas 230–31
Trowell, Tom (Arnold) 230–32, **233**
'A True Tale' 27, 234
'Two Ideas with One Moral' 226
typhoid 50, 57–58, 59, 61–66, 97, 176, 211
'Tyrrell Street' 200

Underwood, 'Jess' 208–09
'Underwood, Ole' 209
United States Embassy, Thorndon 22

'Virginia' (in 'Late at Night') 79
Vogel, Julius 31
von Alzdorf, Charles Ernest 29–30
von Arnim, Elizabeth *see* Beauchamp, Mary
'The Voyage' 92, 98, 186

Wadestown 37, 74
Wainuiomata 189
Wakefield, Jerningham 28
Wallace, Mary 170
Walrond, Rivendell 62
Waters, Agnes Mansfield (née Dyer) 66, 111,
    146, 147–50, **153**, 154–55
Waters, Barrington (Barrie) 111–12, 149, 155
Waters, Eric 111–12, 149, **153**
Waters, Frederick 66, 111, 147, 149–55, **151**,
    153
'Weak Heart' 52, **89**, 200
Wellington: boom periods 60–61, 211; capi-
    tal city status 30–31; in early settlement
    23–33, 75–77; in KM's childhood 14–15,
    23, 35–36; in KM's writing 23, 33, 35–36,
    56–59, 67, 75, 232, 237; *see also* winds of
    Wellington
Wellington Girls' College 171
Wellington Girls' High School 27, 131,
    173–74, 176, 178–80, **179**, 200, 203,
    206–07, 213
Wellington Harbour 23, 35–36, **54**, 61, 74
Westport 94–96
Whanganui 96–97
Wilkinson, Iris *see* Hyde, Robin
Williams, J.H. 190
'The Wind Blows' 24, 36, 72–73, 79, **196**,
    207–08, 229–30

winds of Wellington 24–25, 37–38, **70**,
    71–79; in KM's writing 72–75, 79,
    207–09, 209, 237
Wrights Hill 138
'The Wrong House' 72

Young, Isaac 170